Tout Sweet

Hanging up my High Heels for a New Life in France

KAREN WHEELER

NEW LIFE

LOVE?

summers

D0191400

TOUT SWEET

Copyright © Karen Wheeler 2009

All rights reserved.

No part of this book may be reproduced by any means, nor transmitted, nor translated into a machine language, without the written permission of the publishers.

The right of Karen Wheeler to be identified as the author of this work has been asserted in accordance with sections 77 and 78 of the Copyright, Designs and Patents Act 1988.

Condition of Sale
This book is sold subject to the condition that it shall not, by way of trade or otherwise, be lent, resold, hired out or otherwise circulated in any form of binding or cover other than that in which it is published and without a similar condition including this condition being imposed on the subsequent publisher.

Summersdale Publishers Ltd
46 West Street
Chichester
West Sussex
PO19 1RP
UK

www.summersdale.com

Printed and bound in Great Britain

ISBN: 978-1-84024-761-9

Substantial discounts on bulk quantities of Summersdale books are available to corporations, professional associations and other organisations. For details telephone Summersdale Publishers on (+44-1243-771107), fax (+44-1243-786300) or email (nicky@summersdale.com).

Contents

Note From the Author

There are several villages called Villiers in France, but my village in the Poitou-Charentes is not one of them. I have changed names and details throughout the book in order to protect the innocent (and the not so innocent) and have occasionally embellished facts for the same reason.

Chapter 1

Which Way to Portsmouth?

OH DEAR GOD, what have I done? Somewhere on the lumbering ferry between Portsmouth and Caen, my feet are not so much turning cold as sprouting icicles in their jade-encrusted Miu Miu flip-flops. Three hours ago I closed the door on my west London life, leaving behind a broadband connection, bathtub, a fully functioning kitchen (complete with floor) and a building full of attractive neighbours who I counted as friends.

I am now a few hours away from 'a new life' in France. Earlier, sitting in the on-board cafe surrounded by so-called 'emi-greys', it occurred to me that I might be moving three decades too early. After all, most people go to France to retire. But my friends have been telling me for months how envious they are and how lucky I am. They seemed so genuinely thrilled when I told them I was moving abroad that I started to feel a little paranoid. 'It's going to be wonderful – you won't want to come back,' they said. So no pressure then.

But what if it's not wonderful? What if I hate it and want to come back immediately? A year ago, I was planning my wedding. Now I am planning to live *alone* in a remote village, where I will be half an hour's drive from the nearest decent supermarket, several hours by train from the nearest Prada store and a five-hour journey (and Channel-crossing) from the nearest M&S food hall.

My new home has no indoor loo, no bathtub, no kitchen sink and no hot water. It has flowery brown wallpaper in almost every room, damp climbing up the crumbly walls and a gaping hole looking down into a dank cellar instead of a kitchen floor. Then there's the pile of rubbish the size of the Pyrenees in the rear courtyard. I don't even have the clothes for this kind of life. After a decade and a half of working in fashion, most of my wardrobe is designed for going to cocktail parties – or, at the very least, breakfast at Claridges – and my shoes are so high that I need a Sherpa and an oxygen tank to wear them.

Downstairs, on deck 3B, my ancient Golf is laden with the remnants of eighteen years in London. My furniture and twenty-four huge brown boxes of possessions were dispatched to the Poitou-Charentes in an enormous lorry earlier in the week. This morning – with the help of my neighbour Jerome – I packed up what remained after the removal lorry had gone. Unfortunately, what remained could easily have filled another van.

Between 9.00 a.m. and noon, we stuffed my remaining clothes and possessions into bin bags and plastic carriers and ferried them down four flights of stairs. 'Darling, this really is *very* last-minute,' said Jerome, lips pursed disapprovingly. 'Even by your standards. Most people would at least have dismantled the bookshelves and packed everything in boxes weeks ago.'

'But I did,' I protested. 'And this is what was left over.'

The last three hours of my London life seemed to slip by in minutes. Finally, I ran the vacuum cleaner around the bedroom, left a bottle of champagne and some chocolates in the fridge for the new occupants and locked the door for the last time. Downstairs, I surveyed the colourful pile of miscellanea on the pavement with dismay. In addition to the bin bags stuffed with clothes, there were work files, my laptop, table lamps, rugs, plants, dusters, random coat hangers, a pair of zebra-print stilettos stuffed inside a wastepaper bin and a big black hat trimmed with roses that I kept specifically for weddings. The car boot was already filled with duvets, pillows and fifteen bags of dried fruit, the rear seats with bin bags, boxes of china and my stockpile of Farrow & Ball paint, along with the handbags and shoes that I put into storage… and then rescued again. It can't all be mud and waxed green jackets, I told myself.

'You'll have to get in the car,' said Jerome, a window dresser by profession. 'And I'll somehow stuff the rest of it around you.' When he had finished cramming in shoes, clothes and magazines at random, I couldn't see out of the rear window and my nose was almost touching the windscreen thanks to the giant potted palm wedged behind the driver's seat.

'Good luck,' said Jerome as I pulled away. 'Don't forget to email me when you arrive.'

'Bon voyage!' yelled Daisy, my neighbour. 'Hopefully see you in France next summer.'

As the car limped to the end of the road, its suspension several inches closer to the ground than usual, I realised I had forgotten something. Panicking, I reversed at speed, the sound of china rattling ominously as we hit the traffic bumps.

Fortunately, Daisy and Jerome were still standing by the gate.

'How do I get to Portsmouth?' I yelled

'The A3,' Daisy shouted back. 'Follow the signs from Hammersmith.'

'I give it a month,' said Jerome, shaking his head, 'before you're back.'

So my exit was not an orderly one. But as I drove through the familiar streets of west London – sunny but empty on an August Bank Holiday Monday – it felt liberating to leave behind the playground of over a decade, which, in truth, had started to feel like a prison over the past year. Even my flat had become a place of sad memories, filled like the streets of my neighbourhood with the ghosts of my last relationship. I couldn't walk past certain restaurants in Notting Hill, sit in the French cafe behind Kensington High Street or stroll through Holland Park without feeling sad at the thought of what I had lost. But as I whipped past Olympia that August morning and flew around the Hammersmith roundabout – both normally choked with traffic – it seemed that London was releasing me without a fight.

In addition to the flat, I also gave up a career that many would kill for, as fashion and beauty director of a glossy magazine. Although I had loved working in fashion in my twenties and early thirties, I had reached the stage where I could no longer deal with fashion designers and their ridiculous egos. It had taken me fifteen years to come to the conclusion that I couldn't bear fashion people. I was tired of conspiring in key fashion myths: that it's necessary to spend £600-plus on a new designer handbag every six months, or that a grown-up woman could look good in a ra-ra skirt, micro-shorts or whatever unseemly trend designers were pushing that season. I also felt guilty about persuading readers to rush out and buy 'must-have' items that

I knew were 'must-nots' and that would end up on a fast track to landfill within six months.

In truth, I had been persuaded to take the magazine job by a friend, the then features editor. After the cut and thrust of a newspaper, I figured it would be a cushy number. And it was: decisions that took me five minutes to make on a newspaper were discussed and mulled over for days by at least half a dozen people. We spent hours sitting around in the editor's office drinking coffee and eating cake. The only problem (and it was a big one) was that I ended up having to work with an unedifying procession of photographers chosen by the bookings editor, many of whom were his personal friends or the baggage of his love life. And so I travelled to Miami with a photographer who had an ego the size of Africa, to New York with a borderline psychopath and to Australia with a photographer who had never done a professional fashion shoot before, where I stood for hours on an unsheltered beach, slowly being barbecued while he fiddled around with his exposure. I could have painted a watercolour of the scene in the time it took him to focus his lens.

And invariably, they would do the exact opposite of the brief. Floral and pretty? The photographer would instruct the make-up artist to kohl up the eyes and do something 'edgy' with the hair, 'edgy' being the photographer's favourite word – no matter that they had been hired to work for a magazine that was very unedgy, commercial and safe. If I had a euro for every photographer who thought he was pushing the envelope by making a model look ugly, I would be moving to a villa in St Tropez now rather than a small cottage in the Poitou-Charentes.

The final straw, or as the French would say, 'the drop of water that caused the vase to overflow', however, came in the form of Larry Malibu, a fashion photographer who nearly every magazine editor in London refused to work with because of his unpredictable behaviour and inability to stick to a brief. One of my editors, however, had once enjoyed a passionate fling with him, and so it was that I found myself en route to California with him to shoot summer covers. This might sound wonderful in theory – being paid to spend a week in California – but let me tell you: it *so* wasn't. On the flight over, Larry Malibu became drunk and abusive, insulted the gay hairdresser and reduced the make-up artist to tears; on the first day, he told us all to 'fuck off', since he needed to be left alone to 'bond' with the model and 'create some chemistry'. He then disappeared into the sand dunes with her for several hours. The resultant shots – which showed a model lying supine in the sand, emerging topless from the sea, and ecstatically clutching her breasts while straddling a sand dune – were more suitable for *Loaded* than a fashion and beauty magazine, and totally unusable. On the second day, he refused point blank to shoot the visuals for a 'Get That Summer Glow' feature, saying that the shots were 'effing boring', and on days three and four, he refused to shoot anything at all. On day five, he threatened to kill the make-up artist, who then asked to be flown home. I didn't bother arguing. I just came back to London and resigned.

'Ladies and gentlemen, we are now approaching Caen…'

It is time to ditch the cabin where I have been holed up with a mound of magazines for the past six hours. As I am closing the door in the narrow corridor, I overhear a couple in their mid-thirties emerging from a nearby cabin. 'DON'T. EVEN. TALK. TO. ME,' the guy is saying, the palm of his hand raised towards her as if to keep her out of his face – and they are not even in the car yet. It seems like a sign of encouragement. Better to travel alone, I tell myself, than with an angry companion.

I make my way to the outside deck and, with a sea breeze whipping my hair across my face, watch Caen draw closer in the fading summer light. The lights of the port twinkle like Harry Winston diamonds in the semi-darkness, but all I can think about is the five-hour drive through the night to Poitiers that awaits me on landing. Suddenly exhausted from all the packing and dismantling of the previous two weeks, I make a snap decision: I will spend the night in one of the little hotels around the ferry port and set out early tomorrow morning. That way I can start the first day of my new life in sunshine rather than darkness. And there is a more pressing reason: while waiting to disembark, I notice the petrol tank is almost empty. And since the self-service petrol station near the port does not take credit cards – as I discovered to my detriment on a previous visit – I wouldn't get much further than passport control this evening, even if I wanted to.

An hour or so later I am standing in the dingy reception of La Baleine, which, like most of the bars and brasseries in the centre of the town, has a few modest hotel rooms attached. The restaurant stopped serving *moules frites*, the standard dish around the port, an hour ago and the bar is deserted. I seem to be the only person checking in. Most of the passengers on my ferry – if not stoically pushing down to the south during the night – will at least get as far as Caen to stay in the Novotel there.

The receptionist is in a hurry to leave for the evening and does not ask for a credit card, passport or any of the usual checking-in details. 'Second floor,' she says, without looking up. She hands me a key and points to a narrow wooden staircase.

A surprise awaits me on the second-floor landing, where a man is slumped on the steps. At first I think he must be drunk, but he looks me in the eye and nods, as if it were quite normal to be lying on a hotel staircase late in the evening. He is dressed in black jeans and a bomber jacket, and has a small rucksack. I assume that he has missed the ferry and has somehow sneaked up the stairs of the La Baleine to spend the night somewhere warm. 'Good luck to him,' I think, though it seems a little strange – not to mention audacious – to camp out on a hotel staircase rather than in the ferry terminal.

I open the door to a small room with nicotine-yellow walls and an ointment-pink bathroom suite. Claridges it isn't. There is no hot water in the bathroom and, despite the fact that it is late August, the room is very cold. After fiddling around with the radiators for a while and failing to get a reaction, I call down to reception. There is no reply. Freezing, I climb fully clothed under the blue and yellow flowery bedcover. After a few minutes of shivering under the thin cover and single sheet, I get out of bed and search the white melamine wardrobe for blankets, but there aren't any. I think longingly of the duvet in my car, but to get to it would involve burrowing through a mountain of possessions in the dark. There must be *somebody* from the hotel around, I think. I creep out of the room and along the narrow landing, noticing that the man on the staircase has fallen asleep, using his rucksack as a pillow.

Downstairs, the reception is in darkness and the doors are locked. There is no night porter and no one from the hotel is on the premises. It occurs to me that I could be alone in the building with the man in black on the stairs. I rush back up the semi-lit staircase and creep along the landing, not wanting to wake him. But he stirs as I pass him. Heart pumping faster than the engine of a TGV, I unlock the door to my room – half-expecting him to appear behind me and force his way in – spring inside and turn the key as quickly as I can. The thought of the spare keys hung up on the board behind reception flashes into my mind just as I realise that there is no way of bolting my room from the inside. This is not an auspicious start to My New Life in France. Finding myself alone in a deserted hotel in Caen with a stranger on the other side of the door was never part of the script. I think of what I have given up: the cosy flat where I could go to bed without fear of being murdered and where I lived a life cosseted by every material comfort, from 400-thread-count cotton sheets to a limestone bathroom with a state-of-the-art power shower. I didn't need to do this. I could have carried on living my easy life for decades.

I sit on the bed wondering who I can call, but the answer, I realise, is no one – at least not without great loss of face. Having been waved off to France by enthusiastic friends, this would represent a huge failure, a fall at the first fence, to call in a panic from a hotel room on my first night. I can't even phone my mother, as I haven't told her I'm going to live abroad and she will probably say something typically Northern and unsympathetic such as 'Serves you right. What do you want to go moving to France for anyway?' As I look around the cold, desolate room, it seems like a metaphor for what my life has become.

Now, stuck in this hotel room, and with a sudden sound of movement in the corridor, even a week in California with Larry Malibu seems preferable. The man on the staircase, I realise to my horror, is pacing up and down outside my door. What am I going to do? No one knows I am here. I don't even know the French equivalent of 999. I rush to the window and can see some kind of small courtyard garden two storeys below. But the window is very high and it is locked. I can hear the stranger directly outside my door – which looks like it would cave in at the slightest shove – and I brace myself for a knock or a sudden crash as he tries to force it. In a panic, I place my bag – which is the size of a small cupboard and stuffed with magazines – directly behind the door. At least this will trip him up if he breaks in, giving me a few extra seconds to run for it. Who knew that last season's 'must-have' bag could transform so neatly into a weapon of self-defence?

I sit down next to the phone and spot the number for the gendarmes, or police: 17, which I gratefully dial. A gruff male voice answers: *'Oui?'*

'I am in a hotel in Caen, La Baleine, and I am scared because there is a strange man outside my room.'

'Outside your room?'

'Yes, he is walking up and down in the corridor.'

'Is your room locked?'

'Yes. But he could break in.'

'Has he tried to break in?'

'No. But he is walking up and down all the time. It is very strange.'

'Madame, if your room is locked, there is no problem.'

'But please could you come to the hotel and find out what this man is doing here?'

The voice of emergency services wishes me a good evening and hangs up – just as I hear a sudden bang outside in the corridor. Someone is knocking loudly on a door – not my door, but nonetheless it is terrifying. Then I hear the footsteps heading towards my room once more, and then away again. What is this man doing? He is clearly psychologically unbalanced. I phone 17 again. 'It's me again. At La Baleine hotel. I already phoned.'

'Yes, Madame,' says a weary voice.

'The man is now standing outside my room and he is making a strange noise in the corridor.'

The voice on the other end of the phone asks again if my door is locked and when I reply in the affirmative, repeats that there is no problem. He remains unmoved by my pleas to dispatch a gendarme to investigate. Instead, he wishes me goodnight and hangs up. Outside in the corridor, Staircase Man continues, terrifyingly, to pace up and down outside my room.

I phone the gendarmes four more times over the next couple of hours but fail to convince them that I am in mortal danger. And still, the pacing in the corridor continues. At one point I can even hear him talking to himself – in a low, gruff voice. I sit bolt upright in my bed, terrified. The first night of My New Life in France is turning into a scene from a Hitchcock movie. Not since the night I spent on a fashion shoot in a Kenyan safari park with food poisoning and a large, heavy-footed beast snorting and pacing around outside my tent have I been so desperate for morning to come. This wasn't what I had in mind for my first night in France. I was planning to expand my horizons, seek happiness and harmony in nature, and find a new sense of 'belongingness'. (In London, the place where I had come to feel I most belonged was the shoe department of Selfridges.) And, if all that failed, I told myself, I could always seek happiness in an excellent supply of red wine.

To be honest, my life in London had started to seem very empty. I had wardrobes crammed with 'It' bags and 'must-have' shoes, most of them gifts from designers to thank me for articles I'd written, and I had cupboards full of free beauty products. I had spent most of my life so far focused on work and chasing material possessions. Now I had them in abundance and yet, at thirty-five, I was unhappy. There had to be more to life, I decided, than a stockpile of sought-after accessories.

And if I am being truthful, there was another reason for moving to France. Finding myself unexpectedly single again at thirty-five, I could not cope with the competition. In the four years I had been living in blissful complacency with my French boyfriend, Eric, the competition had been in training. They had put in the hours at the gym and with the Botox specialist, the hair colourist and the cosmetic dentist. They had also developed some very aggressive tactics. Wherever I went out in London – whether to a friend's dinner party or the local wine bar – I noticed with alarm a new breed of very predatory female, taking an alarmingly proactive approach to the hunt for a man. In her twenties or early thirties, she had permanently radiant skin (despite a copious intake of alcohol) and a very flat abdomen. All the designer shoes in the world, I realised, could not compete against a determined twenty-something with a low BMI, Agent Provocateur underwear and an ability to down ten units of Sauvignon Blanc without blinking. Better to make a graceful exit, I told myself, to slink off to rural France where, as a single Englishwoman, I would at least have novelty value.

But France, it seemed, was not exactly waiting with welcoming arms. I have always had an ambivalent attitude to the land of the long lunch and epic dinner. My first visit was a school trip and, unimpressed by the bread and cheese we were given for breakfast and the pigeon that targeted my eleven-year-old head from high above Galeries Lafayette, I couldn't wait to get back on the ferry home. Nor, I imagine, could Mr

Pugh, our beleaguered French teacher. As he marshalled us around the sights of Paris, we were invariably followed by a pack of hormonal French teenagers, mesmerised by one of the sixth-formers among us who had long blonde hair. In Notre Dame, I recall, certain members of our group (from a strict Catholic school in the north of England) stuffed their pockets with rosary beads and mini prayer books lifted from the gift shop. The only bright spot in that school trip was the Palace of Versailles, where, intoxicated by all the gilt, I felt that France was offering me something mesmerising and beautiful.

Later, as a student, I went back and endured several penurious and far-from-perfect weekends in Paris. Even as a fledgling fashion writer for a trade fashion magazine, things did not improve. Dispatched by my boss to a dismal two-star hotel on Rue Bonaparte to cover the ready-to-wear shows, I was assured that the tickets from various designers would be waiting at reception. But – *quelle surprise* – there wasn't a single ticket when I arrived. I spent a stressful twenty-four hours phoning and eventually doorstepping snooty French PRs, who remained impervious to my smattering of A-level French and desperate pleas. As yet another well-dressed piece of asparagus delivered a disdainful and very final *'non, ce n'est pas possible'*, I hated Paris and its inhabitants almost as much as I hate taupe trousers.

Later, when I was the fashion editor of a very successful British newspaper, tickets were not a problem. They were waiting in my hotel room, alongside a swag pile of gifts, tasteful arrangements of white flowers and 'Bienvenue à Paris' notes from well-known designers. But my biannual secondment to the City of Light was never going to show the city off to its best advantage. Each day was comprised of a 9.00 a.m. until midnight obstacle course, trying to get to the various shows on time fuelled only by black coffee and (if really lucky) a croque-monsieur. It was hard to love Paris when locked in total darkness in a dilapidated church with a scrum of well-dressed people and no fire exits, waiting for a fashion show to start, or shivering in a disused Métro station as a hot young 'deconstructionist' designer unveiled his latest shredded offerings. The glossy magazine editors had chauffeur-driven cars at their disposal; newspaper journalists were forced to endure endless slow shuffles to the front of a taxi queue. Invariably, there would be a (very welcome) champagne interlude at some point in the evening, but then it was back to your hotel room to write copy until 2.00 a.m. The strange diet, punctuated by frequent *coups de champagne* and combined with a lack of sleep, does strange things to your blood sugar levels and mood. No wonder fashion people are so unlovable.

The turning point came when I met Eric, my French boyfriend. Only then did I really learn to love France. With him, I saw Paris through different eyes. I have a particular soft spot for the Hôtel Costes, where, dressed in shabby jeans and summer flip-flops but always given a warm welcome by the staff, we would go for early evening drinks. Usually, I would be there for work (the magazine that I worked for at the time insisted on sending me to Paris to do cover shoots) and Eric would meet me there, before the two of us travelled on to his father's place on the Île de Ré. Engulfed in the Costes' moody, sexy, rose-scented atmosphere, we would drink aperitifs and then head to a dimly lit dinner in the Marais. I almost feel more affection for the Hôtel Costes than I do for the city itself. My future, as I had often smugly reflected, seemed assured: a sexy French husband, a second home in France and bilingual *enfants* dressed in Bonpoint clothing.

I consider the day spent crab fishing with Eric on the Île de Ré to be possibly the happiest of my life. The summer evenings spent cycling through the island's narrow village streets lined with hollyhocks or fields of sunflowers on our way to the little port of St Martin had a bitter-sweet resonance now. But with Eric in my life, France opened up from a tight flower bud into a big, voluptuous bloom.

He had asked me many times to marry him, from the earliest days of the relationship, but then, just as I was ready to sign up to the deal and had started to plan a glamorous wedding on the Île de Ré, he returned from a trip to France, where he had been escorting rich American tourists around 'Van Gogh's Provence', and told me that he was leaving. I still don't know where he went – it could have been round the corner for all I knew – but such was his haste that he left behind his wine rack, coffee machine and the skyscraper-sized speakers of his sound system. I gave the speakers to my friend Brigid and left the other stuff on the street, so that all that remained of him was a twisted metal hanger in an empty cupboard and some very painful memories.

Now here I am, holed up in a cold hotel with a scary stranger prowling around outside my door. For a moment I dabble with the idea of booking myself a passage right back to Portsmouth on the 8.00 a.m. ferry tomorrow, but there's just the small question of where I am going to live if I do that. At least in France there is a decaying old house waiting for me. Miraculously, at some point before dawn, I fall asleep. When I wake up it is 10.00 a.m. and the door is still intact. No one has broken in and it feels like I have survived the first major test of My New Life in France. And with a huge surge of relief, I am grateful for the simple fact that it is morning and I am still alive.

There is no sign of Staircase Man as I leave and I am beginning to think I might have imagined him. Downstairs, I ask the receptionist if it is possible to get a coffee and a croissant.

'No,' is the reply. 'You are too late. Breakfast finished at ten o'clock.'

'But I got up late because I did not sleep very well.'

'Ah, no? How do you wish to pay?'

'It was very cold in the room.'

'Ah, no, it wasn't cold,' she says.

'Yes it was. The radiators weren't working.'

'Yes, they were working.'

'No, they were not.'

'Yes, but of course, they are,' she grimaces at me as if she has just bitten into a sour *citron*.

'And there was no hot water.'

'No hot water? But of course there was hot water,' she insists and in my fatigued state, I want to slap her or at least drag her back upstairs to prove the point.

'And more, there was a strange man asleep on the stairs,' I say. She arches an overly plucked eyebrow as if I'd just told her that the sun is croissant-shaped.

'A man asleep on the stairs? No, it's not possible,' she says.

'Yes, I am telling you. There was, for sure, a strange man asleep on the stairs.'

'What was he wearing, this strange man?' she asks, looking sceptical.

I tell her.

'Aah,' she says. 'That was not a strange man. That was a gendarme.'

'No, I don't think so. He wasn't wearing the clothes of a gendarme.'

'Yes, he was a gendarme,' she says, pointing behind me, 'but he was in normal clothes. Look! There are some more gendarmes – his colleagues.'

I turn around, just in time to see five uniformed policemen climbing out of a dark van and coming our way. It starts to feel like the denouement of George Orwell's *1984*, where the Thought Police come storming in through a window. Finally, I think, the gendarmes are reacting to the emergency calls that I made last night. But now that Staircase Man has gone, they are probably going to arrest me instead for wasting their time.

But the gendarmes head straight up the narrow staircase without stopping.

'Who are they looking for?' I ask, feeling nervous.

'A *clandestin*,' she replies.

'A *clandestin*? That means what?'

She explains that it is someone who is in the country illegally.

'So the man on the staircase was a *clandestin*?'

'No, Madame,' she says, losing patience. 'He was *guarding* the *clandestin*. Those are the other gendarmes who have come to make sure that the *clandestin* leaves. He is going to your country, I think, as he has family there.'

'But if he was a gendarme, why wasn't he wearing a uniform?'

'Because he was performing exceptional duties and staying in a hotel; we did not want to frighten the other guests.' Suddenly, in my fatigued state, I understand what she is telling me and my cheeks turn pink with embarrassment.

Feeling like the village idiot, I pay the bill and get out of that hotel as quickly as possible, skulking shamefacedly past the three gendarmes who are guarding the van outside. The exquisite irony of it all is not lost on me: I spent the entire night worrying that I was about to be murdered and desperately looking for a policeman and there was one outside my door the whole time. There is a lesson in there somewhere. Safely inside my car, I see the funny side – well, almost. And then I head off, uncaffeinated – and with a stack of shoeboxes obscuring my rear window – to negotiate the terrifying, multiple merging lanes of the Caen *périphérique*.

Chapter 2

The House That Found Me

IT IS LATE afternoon when I finally arrive in the square at Villiers. The little cluster of French flags fluttering outside the *mairie* always causes my heart to flip, as does the sight of the *boulangerie* and the Café du Commerce, with its tables and chairs arranged outside in the late August sunshine. I turn into the narrow cobbled street that leads to Maison Coquelicot. As usual, with its charmless grey pebble-dash exterior and its shutters closed, it looks daunting – and this time, without the benefit of a return ticket in my bag, doubly so. I think back to the Saturday morning and the strange quirk of fate that led me to the house just over a year ago.

After I split up with Eric, I lost two stone in weight. Unfortunately, I also lost my mind – or almost. Gratifying though it was to catch sight of my jeans sliding down my skinny hips thanks to a diet of coffee and dark chocolate, it was a poor substitute for the emotional devastation of finding myself alone at thirty-five, just as my few remaining single friends were suddenly announcing that they had met 'someone'. It was several months before I could stop spontaneously bursting into tears in public. Night after night I woke up at almost exactly 3.20 a.m. wondering what to do with the rest of my life and the endless, lonely weekends ahead of me. At no point, in those bleak days, did the answer 'move to France and renovate a house' pop into my mind.

But at some point I stopped crying long enough to take my future into my own hands. I enrolled on a creative writing course in Yorkshire (courses being my antidote to misery back then) and on the first night I made friends with an advertising director called Dave. He was unpacking his car and I was reversing mine into a stone wall. It broke the ice as well as my rear light. Later, over the introductory drinks on the terrace, we got talking further. Dave worked for a well-known advertising agency in London, acting as the link between clients and 'creatives'. He didn't like the job very much. I could tell this because he referred to the creative directors at his agency as 'pretentious prats' and the clients as 'a pain in the arse'. He was looking for an exit strategy before his new boss pushed him out, and was hoping to write an exposé of the advertising industry, loosely disguised as fiction, which is why he had enrolled on the course. Then he told me about the house in France that he and his wife had just bought, and his plans to convert his barn into a writing retreat. I was a captive audience. 'Come and stay,' he offered before the evening was out. 'That's if you don't mind roughing it with a few pilots.'

'Pilots?'

'Yes, one of my mates owns an airfield nearby, where he teaches people to fly microlights. The pilots rent rooms from me – it's a bit like a B&B, only more relaxed.'

I didn't even know what a microlight was, but the invitation sounded appealing. I imagined myself sitting at a wooden trestle table, sharing a bottle of wine with a posse of flirtatious men in flying jackets. Dave was a very affable character who spent most of his time socialising and taking advantage of the retreat's generous wine supplies and 'honesty box' system. One evening, word had it that he had forsaken the communal meal to drive over forty miles for a curry. As for me, I spent most of my time holed up in my monastic white room grimly determined to complete the writing exercises we had been set.

A few months later, I was surprised to receive an email from Dave:

Hi Karen, how's it all going? It was great meeting you in Yorkshire. I'm going down to the house in France next week and was hoping to do some writing there. I was wondering if you would like to come? We could do some writing and give each other a bit of moral support. Interested?
Let me know,
All best, Dave. :)

By coincidence, I was going be in Paris that week for a perfume launch. And I did really want to see Dave's house which had sounded idyllic (and possibly full of pilots). So I typed back:

I'm in Paris for work anyway that week. Could take the TGV down on Friday afternoon. Would love to see your house. Best, Karen.

The reply came back immediately:

Great. Let me know what time your TGV gets in (Poitiers is the nearest station) and I'll pick you up. Best, Dave.

PS: Does this mean you are now flying short haul?

I was thrown by his cryptic sign-off. Flying short haul? It sounded like secret code for something naughty. And then, slowly, the embarrassing truth dawned. I typed back:

Dear Dave,
I am not flying short haul – or long haul. Sadly, I am stationary in London, writing about the comeback of the bob. I think you might be mixing me up with another Karen, the blonde BA stewardess!
Best, Karen W.

How embarrassing to have responded so eagerly to an offer that was not intended for me but the flamboyant blonde lesbian from BA. I heard nothing for a few days and then a sheepish reply:

Hi Karen,
Oops!! Yes, the email was intended for the other Karen. But why don't you come down anyway? Bring your laptop and maybe we can do some writing. I have also got another (prize-winning) writer friend staying. Maybe he can give us some advice. Look forward to seeing you, Dave.

I know I should have been too embarrassed to accept. But he had invited me that first night in Yorkshire, I was going to be in France and I did want to see his house. Shamelessly, I looked up the train timetable on the Internet and typed back the time of my TGV's arrival.

I came out of Poitiers station to find a town in the full bloom of summer – rosy golden light bouncing off the surrounding buildings and every available surface, people hugging and kissing, the cries of 'Ça va?' or 'Comment vas tu?' and the sounds of car boots and doors slamming shut. Everything was full of the promise of the weekend to come. But, in truth, I was a little nervous. I was about to spend forty-eight hours with a semi-stranger. It was three months since the course and I was worried I might not even recognise Dave.

Fortunately, he was waiting for me outside the station. 'Hi Karen, so how's it going?' he asked, taking my bag and leading me to his car. He looked very suntanned and attractive. 'What were you doing in Paris?' I told him about the perfume launch I had been attending as we left the town behind and drove into the French countryside. I looked out of the open window at a vivid yellow and blue landscape, at the fields bursting with sunflowers and blond haystacks against the vibrant turquoise evening sky. As I felt the warm evening breeze on my arm, resting on an open window, and watched the long-armed irrigators send arcs of water soaring over the fields, I felt a surge of excitement for the first time in ages.

'Bloody hell, that sounds glamorous!' said Dave, turning to me with a smile.

'I can't wait to see your house,' I said. 'Did you say you had a friend staying with you?'

'Yeah, that's right, Gerard Wilton. He recently won a major literary award.'

The name rang no bells.

'What kind of stuff does he write?'

'Well, he likes historical stuff and is very interested in aviation.'

'So where is... er, Gerard?' I imagined an old buffer in a navy blazer poring over books of historical facts and aviation history.

'I left him in the garden with a jug of sangria.'

Forty-five minutes later and we were all sitting in Dave's garden drinking sangria with a view of his neighbours' allotments sloping down towards the old chateau of Villiers. Now in ruins, it still looked impressive against the blue July sky. Gerard (or Gerry as he preferred to be called) was not an old buffer in grey flannel but a cool dude in combat trousers with long blond hair. He looked like he was on day release from a rock band or surf school. He was also very charming and modest – particularly since it transpired that he *had* won a major literary prize. He had become a writer, he said, because he wasn't good at anything else and, apart from casual work in bars, he had never really had a proper job. But rather than talk about himself or his novels, he seemed very interested in *my* job – although some of his questions struck me as a little deep for a first meeting.

'So would you say you were happy?' he asked me suddenly.

'Well, who wouldn't be?' I said. 'Sitting in a garden in France on a warm summer evening with a view of a medieval chateau?'

Gerry looked thoughtful.

'He seems really nice. How do you two know each other?' I asked Dave when Gerry went back into the house to make another jug of sangria. Dave looked suddenly embarrassed and evaded the question.

'So, what do you think of the house then?' he asked.

'It's fantastic. I'm very jealous,' I replied.

I asked him how he'd found it and why he'd chosen this village. Dave launched into a story about how he had checked weather charts and motorway maps and websites of house prices in France and had decided that this was the best area in terms of affordability, location and weather.

'So you didn't just stick a pin in a map then?' I said.

'I looked at dozens of villages and loads of houses,' he replied, 'before I found this. It's by far the best village in the region.'

'What about your wife? Does she come out a lot?'

'Not really. Linda runs a beauty salon and is always busy. And she's not really that keen on France anyway.' This struck me as a little odd – that Dave should choose to buy a house and spend large amounts of time alone in a country that his wife was not very keen on – but he seemed happy enough with the situation, so who was I to question his marital arrangements?

An hour later and we were all sitting in the garden of the local crêperie, with Amy Winehouse's 'Rehab' playing in the background, drinking sweet white wine – the only kind of wine Dave liked, it transpired. It was nearly 10.00 p.m. but still warm. As the scent of jasmine drifted over from the stone flowerbed, I couldn't believe my luck to have landed here – albeit by default. This is the life, I thought.

'So Dave told me about the mix up with the email,' said Gerry, as our starters arrived.

'Yeah, bloody hell!' said Dave. 'How weird was that?'

'Very. It was so nice of you to invite me anyway, even if the email wasn't meant for me!'

'Yes it was,' said Gerry, suddenly.

'What do you mean?'

'That email was *meant* to go to you. Some things are just meant to be.'

It was an attractive idea and Gerry followed it up with another: 'Shall we get a bottle of Bordeaux? I can't drink any more of this wine – it's far too sweet,' he said, wrinkling his nose and reaching for the wine list.

'I'm really glad things worked out the way they did,' said Dave, leaning back with a benevolent smile. 'Talking to you, I've realised that we've got a lot in common.'

I couldn't really see that we had that much in common. His job was to liaise between the creative people at his agency who came up with the ads and the 'tosser' clients; I wrote about handbags and wrinkle prevention. But then Gerry and Dave didn't seem to have that much in common either. Dave had worked his way up through the ranks of a big advertising agency; apart from writing, Gerry, by his own admission, had never had a full-time job. I could not see how their paths had crossed. 'So how do you both know each other?' I asked, again.

There was an awkward pause.

'A-ha,' said Gerry. 'That's a story for another day.'

After the short stroll back to the house, Dave suggested a *digestif* – pronouncing it 'digestive', as in the biscuit – and the three of us sat in the candlelit *salon* until the early hours while he talked about how he hated his job, his plans to turn his barn into a writing retreat and how great it would be to live in France full-time. Later that night, I lay in one of Dave's guest bedrooms, cocooned in floral wallpaper – even the ceiling and door were papered in it – with Gerry asleep in the room next door. And, for the first time in ages, I fell asleep easily and did not wake until morning.

It was well after 10.00 a.m. before Dave or Gerry stirred. I read for a while and then walked up the cobblestone street to the bakery and bought croissants and a loaf of bread. Just walking across the square – already busy with people heading to the market with straw shopping baskets or pull-along trolleys – seemed more exciting than anything I had done in London for years. When I got back, Gerry was up and making coffee in the kitchen. Wearing wire-rimmed glasses, unshaven and with his long blond hair falling in his eyes, he looked sort of vulnerable and even more attractive.

'What a star you are!' he said, as I put the croissants on the table.

'Is Dave up yet?' I asked.

'No,' said Gerry. 'He's still snoring away up there. I'll go and give him a shout.'

Dave finally emerged – looking very much like a man who'd drunk two bottles of sweet white wine the night before – and the three of us had breakfast at the long wooden table in the kitchen. After jolting himself awake with viscous black coffee, Dave suggested going to the market. Gerry, disappointingly, wanted to work, so we left him with his laptop and walked up to the square in the sunshine.

The fashion possibilities in Villiers, I noted, were limited. Arranged around the square were a hunting shop (useful should the military look ever come back into fashion), a funeral parlour, a florist (specialising in funeral arrangements) and two women's clothes shops, both selling an eye-poppingly awful selection of clothes in sludgy colours. Polyester *partout*. At least my credit cards could take a well-earned break if I lived here. But the small town also boasted two beauty salons, two pharmacies, two *boulangeries*, two cafes and a wine shop

– all clues to the villagers' priorities. The market, which was housed in a modern concrete hall in the centre of the square, was much smaller than I expected. There was one fishmonger, one long table laden with fruit and veg and one cheerful, round-faced teenager selling goats cheese. I was expecting piles of glistening purple-black olives, mouth-watering displays of plump *saucissons*, oozing French cheeses and other delicious delicacies, but, if I'm being honest, the market seemed to have far less to offer than the organic section of my local M&S. However, bivalve-lovers were extremely well catered for with no less than three different oyster sellers. One of them, I noted from his van, came from the Île de Ré.

Dave must have sensed my disappointment. 'The Thursday morning fair is much better. It spreads right across the town,' he said. 'But the fishmonger is excellent.'

It was true. The fishmonger, a man with compelling blue eyes and a big nose, had a great deal to offer, with more varieties of sea-life and crustacea than I had ever seen before.

'So is Gerry with someone?' I asked Dave, as he examined a large pink salmon. He shook his head.

'He and his girlfriend split up over a year ago. It was all a bit messy.'

'Oh, really?'

'Yeah. He's actually a very complicated person.'

'Oh. I thought he seemed pretty straightforward.'

'Trust me,' said Dave, as if reading my thoughts. 'You wouldn't want to get into a relationship with him.'

We were interrupted by a cry of 'Ah, Dav-eed, *comment vas-tu?*' and an elderly woman grasped Dave's face and planted numerous kisses on it. As the only *Anglais* in the village, Dave, I soon realised, enjoyed something close to celebrity status.

Several people (male and female) greeted him ecstatically, flinging their arms in the air with delight when they saw him. Dave spoke only patchy French and clearly could not understand what they were saying but he nodded and smiled a lot and invited at least two of them around for a drink. 'Possi-bili-tay. *Vous* [pointing at the other person]. *Aperi-teef* [here he would mime lifting a glass to his mouth] *Shozz mwuh*,' he would say, pointing in the direction of his house. This was invariably met by a delighted nodding of heads.

Our progress around the small market was slow, since when he wasn't being greeted like a homecoming hero by the locals, Dave liked to examine everything very closely. Eventually, he bought the large pink salmon and suggested that we go to the cafe on the square for a coffee. As we sat in the sunshine outside the Café du Commerce, drinking black espressos, he was accosted again, this time by a thin, wiry man with a big, bushy moustache.

'Ah Daveed! *Ça va?*'

'This is Victor, the estate agent who found me the house,' said Dave, inviting him by expansive hand movements to sit down and join us. Victor did so without a moment's hesitation. He lit a cigarette and asked Dave who I was. Dave didn't understand, so I answered on his behalf.

'I'm a friend of Dave's. I'm here for the weekend,' I said.

'So what do you think of his house?' asked Victor.

'It's fantastic. I'm very jealous. I'd love to have a house in France.'

'You'd like a house in France? Really?' Victor suddenly became very animated. 'Because I have one, also in the centre of the village. It has only just become available. It is very rare for a house to come up for sale in the centre of the village.'

'Blimey, your French is good,' said Dave. 'What's he saying?'

I translated. Dave looked very interested. He turned to Victor: 'Possi-bili-tay... regard-ay?' Nearly all of Dave's attempts to speak French, I realised, began with the word 'possi-bili-tay'.

'But of course,' Victor replied. 'When?'

'Possi-bili-tay *main-tenant*?' asked Dave.

'*Bien sûr*,' said Victor.

'Bloody hell,' said Dave, as Victor went off to get the keys from the agency. 'There's another coincidence for you. You said you were thinking of buying a house in France and here's one that's just dropped into your lap.' The three of us walked over to Rue St Benoit, a narrow, cobbled street just off the main square. The house, a two-up, two-down with a garage attached, was shuttered up and uninviting. It had an ugly grey exterior and the shutters were painted sludgy brown, rather than the pale blue-grey of the textbook *style français*. The front door, made from etched yellow glass and wrought iron, was also a long way from anyone's idea of the charming French house. But, even before Victor opened the front door, I knew that I was looking at my future.

Victor opened the door and we stepped into a narrow stone passageway. To the left was *le petit salon*. Victor switched on the light to reveal a dour-looking square room that looked like it hadn't been touched in decades. The walls were papered in a dense brown floral pattern, while all other available surfaces – doors, dado rail, skirting boards and window frames – were painted mid-tone brown. Below the dado rail, the wallpaper had peeled away to reveal damp and crumbling plaster underneath. The house smelled old. (In beauty world parlance, you would say that it had 'top notes of wet paper and floor polish and a base of damp, mossy earth'.) It felt like a woman neglected and abandoned – a thing of faded beauty, the paint peeling like cracked make-up on an old face. Her personality was sombre and inward looking, while the fireplace, once the heart of this little house, was boarded up and empty and had not been lit for a long time. Despite this, I could see that the house had once been very pretty and had the potential to be so again. So I ignored the peeling wallpaper and crumbling plaster, focusing instead on the beautiful old narrow floorboards and original features such as the glass panelled doors.

I had a strong sense that something sad had happened here. The house had not been shown any love for a long time. And yet it was far from depressing. As I watched Victor struggling to open the shutters and let in light and air, I experienced a huge wave of optimism.

'Christ, look at this,' I could hear Dave saying in the room beyond the salon. I followed him into a room that was visibly falling apart, with an ugly mass of pipes, tanks and strange tubular appendages on the wall. There was an antique oil boiler with the front panel hanging off, and a sink unit sagging towards the floor. This was covered in ancient linoleum that curled up at the corners like stale bread. The pale green wallpaper was hanging off the wall in large strips.

'Who lived here before?' I asked, as Victor followed us into the kitchen.

'A very old lady,' he replied. 'In her eighties. She was renting it until she moved into an old people's home.'

I wondered how on earth an eighty-year-old woman had managed to live here. The boiler didn't work, the kitchen was unusable and there was no indoor loo. But then I noticed what Dave was looking at, and suddenly all the faults paled into insignificance. Beyond the kitchen there was an enclosed courtyard, with high stone walls, a stone flowerbed full of weeds and a shed in one corner with a tiled roof that housed the outdoor loo. I did not need to see any more. I had already made up my mind.

'You see. It's completely private,' said Victor. 'You can run around naked here if you want.'

'Fantastic!' said Dave with an enthusiasm that scared me – though not as much as his next sentence. 'I'm wondering if I should buy it myself,' he said. 'Just look at that courtyard. And you've got a garage, which is really unusual for the centre of the village.'

'But Dave, you've already got a house,' I said.

'Yeah, I know. Don't worry,' he said. 'I've already got enough on my hands. But this would be a brilliant project for you.'

Victor led the way up the narrow staircase (dark brown with an ox-blood-coloured ceiling) that led from the kitchen to a small landing on the first floor. The large main bedroom was decorated (you've guessed it) entirely in brown: brown carpet, brown skirting boards and walls covered in what looked like brown parcel paper. I lifted up the edge of the brown carpet – releasing decades of dust as I did so – to find near-perfect wooden floorboards underneath.

'They're in good nick, the floorboards,' said Dave, bending over to pull up another corner. 'You'd just have to rip up all this crappy carpet.'

We followed Victor into the rear bedroom, which looked out onto the church spire and a sweep of green and golden countryside. 'Bloody hell,' said Dave, as I readjusted my vision. The spare room, in contrast to the relentless brownness of the rest of the house, was papered in vibrant, hot pink 1970s swirls. It was hard to imagine anyone getting any sleep in there.

But the psychedelic swirls offered a glimpse of a happier, more vibrant personality. The house hadn't always been this sad and downtrodden. 'That wallpaper will have to go,' said Dave.

'I quite like it,' I said. Ironically, the wallpaper, like the jumpsuit and the kaftan, had been out of fashion for so long that it had come back in again. My friends in London, I thought to myself, would pay a fortune for wallpaper like this.

Reluctantly, I tore myself away from the hot pink flowers and followed Dave and Victor up a rickety staircase to an enormous attic. It had stone walls, wooden beams and two windows with a fantastic view over the village and surrounding fields. Dave gasped. 'Just think what you could do with this. You've got another three bedrooms here, if you wanted.'

I imagined the grey stone walls painted white, the grey beams sanded back and tinted chestnut brown and the attic converted into an enormous study.

'So the house costs how much?' I asked Victor. He handed me a piece of paper with the details: €49,000. I thought I had misread it at first, but no, that really was the price.

'Christ,' said Dave, looking over my shoulder. 'Where in the UK can you find a house for thirty-five thousand pounds?'

'The price might seem a little high,' said Victor, misinterpreting the look of amazement on my face. 'But I am certain I can get the owners to reduce it.'

'Possi-bili-tay doon reduction?' asked Dave.

Victor nodded. *'Pas de problème.'*

'Bloody hell,' said Dave. 'You've lucked out there. I'd jump at it if I were you.'

I didn't need to be convinced. I wasn't sure if I would be able to borrow the money, but it was one of the easiest decisions I have ever made. 'Yes,' I said, turning to Victor. 'I want it.' We agreed that I would return that afternoon with my passport, so that he could prepare the preliminary documents. And as we walked back up to the square in the hot sunshine, I even thought of a name for it. For some reason *'coquelicot'* sprang to mind. It sounded like 'coquette', had a nice ring to it and suggested bright colour. And so, even though there were only weeds growing in the stone flowerbed for the moment, I named the house Maison Coquelicot – or 'house of the wild poppy'.

Chapter 3

Miranda

LATER THAT AFTERNOON, Dave, Gerry and I walked across the square to Victor's office. The village was now completely deserted: no old men in flat caps playing boules and not a single soul sitting under the parasols outside the Café du Commerce. Everyone, it seemed, was sheltering from the potent Poitevin sun behind closed shutters. But Victor was waiting for us, with the paperwork ready. I signed the *compromis de vente*, which meant that, just a couple of hours after seeing the house for the first time, I had committed to the purchase. Then Victor lent us the keys and we went back over to Maison Coquelicot. Gerry's reaction was very gratifying, especially when I showed him the attic.

'I can see why you have jumped at this,' he said. 'This space is amazing. You could have a huge office up here with views of the church and the surrounding countryside.'

'Exactly what I thought,' I said, secretly imagining Gerry installed there with his laptop, gazing out over the rooftops at the green and golden fields. And what a great story it would make: how, thanks to one errant email, we met randomly one languid summer evening in France, fell in love and decided to stay.

'I'll certainly be back to visit,' said Gerry.

'I hope so,' I said, trying to sound like it would be no big deal.

We returned the keys to Victor, who promised that he would phone as soon as he heard back from the owner. I would have been happy to pay the full asking price – the house would still have been a bargain – but Victor seemed confident that he could secure it for less.

'He didn't bloody well suggest that to me when I bought my house,' grumbled Dave as we left, having invited Victor over for dinner that evening.

As the aperitif hour approached, Gerry and I sat at the kitchen table, peeling potatoes, while Dave searched in his cupboards for his fish steamer.

'Do you think one of you could lay the table?' said Dave. 'There are some napkins in the bottom drawer there.'

'Consider it done,' said Gerry jumping up from the table with mock enthusiasm.

'I'll help,' I said, following him into the dining room.

'How do you think he would like the napkins folded?' asked Gerry.

'I don't know. I'd just sort of put them flat on the table, if I were you.'

'What? Not folded into fancy shapes or anything? Dave's probably got a special napkin-folding device stashed away in one of his cupboards.'

'Shall I check?' I said, laughing. It was certainly true that Dave had a gadget for every culinary eventuality. 'Or shall we just use our initiative?'

'OK, but you take the rap if we get it wrong,' he said.

Side by side we finished laying out Dave's best silver and crystal wine glasses.

'Your knives aren't straight,' said Gerry. 'And I'm not impressed by your napkin folding.'

'Oh really?' I said. 'Well, I don't think you've spaced the water glasses evenly.'

Gerry narrowed his eyes in faux scrutiny and then flashed a disarming smile, causing my heart to perform a pole vault of excitement. We headed back to the kitchen for a drink. Dave, looking a little pink in the cheeks, stood near the hob, scrutinising a recipe book displayed in a special plastic recipe book holder.

'What do you think I should do with the green beans?' he asked.

'What do you normally do with them?' replied Gerry, opening a bottle of Bordeaux.

'Boiling them in water is always good,' I suggested.

'Unless you've got a special green bean steamer?' volunteered Gerry.

'What?' asked Dave, looking mystified.

'How about just lightly boiling them and sprinkling a little chopped garlic on top?' I suggested.

'Good idea!' said Dave. 'In fact, I think I've got an electric garlic press somewhere.'

Gerry winked at me and I smiled back at him as Dave started to rummage around in the cupboards again. As he did so, I spotted a box containing a 'stainless steel egg pricker' and a brand new crème brulée kit complete with blowtorch, and had to stop myself from laughing. It was as if Dave had equipped himself with all these gadgets ready to embark on a bachelor's life.

Through the kitchen windows we could see villagers emerging for an early evening stroll, having hidden away from the boiling sun all afternoon. The sun was still shining brightly and every now and again the scent of jasmine would drift in through the window. Occasionally, one of Dave's neighbours would stick their head through the open window to say a cheery '*Ça va?*' or wish him '*Bonne soirée*'. I knew without a doubt that I was doing the right thing in buying Maison Coquelicot. I, too, wanted a slice of life in this little village and, with Dave two minutes away on the other side of the church, I had a guest pass to an instant social life.

It turned out that Dave had also invited an English friend, Miranda, to dinner. 'I think you'll like her,' he said. 'She's been living out here for about ten years and she's hilarious.'

'How do you know her?' I asked.

'She's helped me out a lot with translation. I met her in the estate agent's office when she was doing some translating for Victor.'

I heard Miranda before I saw her. A voice as melodic as wind chimes shouted '*Coucou!* Anyone at home?' and then a small, delicately boned woman in her early fifties appeared, clutching a bottle of wine. She had dark, bobbed hair, twinkling eyes and was wearing sequins and high heels – in the French countryside! I liked the look of her immediately. Here was a woman who wasn't going to sacrifice glamour for *la vie rurale*.

'My darling boy,' she cried, planting two rosily glossed lips on Dave's cheeks. 'It's been too, *too* long.' She did the same to Gerry, saying 'Gosh, isn't he handsome! Where did you find him?' And then she turned her attention to me, brushing her lips against my cheeks. As she moved, I detected a hint of something heady and expensive, which I recognised as Guerlain's Shalimar.

'I'd love a Scotch please. No ice,' she said, though Dave had not yet asked. 'So,' she said to me, 'I hear you bought a house this morning. Will you live out here?'

'I hope so.'

'And where is it?'

'Here. In Villiers.'

'Darling girl, that means we're going to be almost neighbours! I live in the next village. How marvellous. I'm thrilled skinny for you! Here's to us being almost-neighbours.' She raised the tumbler of whisky that Dave had just handed her. 'So,' she said, turning to him. 'How was Victor?'

'Fine. He's coming this evening,' said Dave.

'He *is?*' said Miranda looking surprised. 'You do know what's happened?'

'No?'

'Well, you didn't hear it from me, dear boy, but *quel scandale*! His wife ran off with the local butcher about two months ago, taking their five-year-old daughter with her.'

'Bloody hell!' said Dave.

'Yes, he completely went to pieces. He was off work for over a month. Went completely doolally. The last time I saw him, in the supermarket, he looked dreadful. He was wearing carpet slippers and looked like he hadn't shaved for a week.'

'Well, he wasn't wearing carpet slippers today,' said Gerry. 'That's the sort of detail I would have noticed.'

Miranda threw her head back and laughed, her brown eyes twinkling, her wide smile revealing perfect white teeth. 'Well, maybe he and his wife are back together,' she said. 'Or maybe he's met someone else. I wouldn't put it past him.'

'Come to think of it, he did seem a little distracted,' said Dave.

'Well, he's playing the injured party in all this,' said Miranda, her voice conveying disapproval. 'But I've heard that his wife didn't just run off without good reason. Apparently, he'd had quite a few affairs – some of them with women that he'd met on the Internet.'

'Blimey,' said Dave, looking impressed.

The discussion of Victor's love life was cut short by his arrival. Dressed in pale cotton trousers and a crisply ironed blue shirt (and thankfully not carpet slippers) he did not look like a man on the edge. He was carrying a bottle of champagne and a box of cakes tied up with ribbon. He planted three kisses on my cheeks, his bushy moustache tickling my skin; and then, after a moment's hesitation, he did the same to Miranda. '*Bonsoir*, Meer-rranda. How are you?' he asked, quietly.

'Still alive,' she replied.

When Dave announced that it was time to sit down, Miranda assumed pole position at the dining table, in between Dave and Victor and directly opposite Gerry. 'Isn't he a handsome boy?' she said to me, nodding towards Gerry. 'I bet you're taken, aren't you, darling?' I couldn't quite believe the directness of Miranda's approach, but I have to admit that I waited with interest for the answer.

Gerry looked at her intently. 'What makes you think that?' he asked.

'Good-looking chaps like you are never single,' she replied. 'Not that I'm interested myself you understand. I'm through with men and *tout ça* and quite happy on my own, thank you very much. I've got my cat Napoleon for company and I'm entirely self-sufficient. The last thing I want is a man queering my pitch.'

Despite her small frame, Miranda was an athletic drinker. After limbering up with neat whisky, she moved on to white wine and continued drinking at a steady pace for the next few hours, before moving into a sprint finish with a glass of champagne (which Victor opened with dessert) followed by two whiskies by way of a nightcap. You had to admire her form. She was also an accomplished flirt and a brilliant and funny raconteur. She told us a hilarious story about how she had been banned from quiz night at a bar run by Brits in a nearby village. 'But I deserved it,' she said. 'I was so badly behaved that I would have banned me, too. Apparently, I told one woman that she had a face like a bag of spanners. And that wasn't even the worst of it.'

I didn't mind that she was dominating the conversation – thereby depriving me of the attention that I felt I rightly deserved having bought a house that morning – as she was so entertaining. She was also very interested in other people and not at all competitive with me. 'Now, my darling girl,' she said, at one point. 'What do you do that is going to allow you to live out here?'

She became very excited when I told her that I was a fashion and beauty journalist.

'Oh, how wonderful! Does that mean that you get lots of free beauty products?'

'Not as many as I used to get, but yes.'

'Oh, aren't you lucky!' she said. 'Now, *écoute*! If ever you are looking for a guinea pig for cosmetic surgery, be sure to let me know, because I wouldn't mind an eye lift.' I told her that it was unlikely but I would bear it in mind. 'Oh isn't she just darling?' she said, looking directly at Gerry for affirmation, and I couldn't help but warm to her.

But she was, I noticed, very scathing about *les Anglais*. 'Honestly, present company excepted, I can't bear them,' she said. 'Polluting the French countryside with their bad haircuts and washed-out looking clothes. Fortunately, most of them go a bit crackerdog after two years and run back home.'

'Crackerdog?' asked Gerry.

'Yes, they love it at first – *la vie française et tout ça* – but then, when the novelty of it has worn off, they get bored and depressed. Some of them develop a drink problem. Others go a bit mad. Or get divorced. Or else they die. We've just lost a whole load recently. I'm not joking. I bought a discount pack of condolence cards from Lidl a few months ago – there must have been at least half a dozen – and they've all gone.'

This was news I really didn't want to hear. I was hoping to move to the French countryside and live happily ever after – not end up mad, dead or with a drink problem. At least divorce wasn't on the horizon. 'So crackerdog or six feet under! Either way, it's good news for you, isn't it, Victor? All those houses to sell,' continued Miranda.

Victor was very quiet, probably because the conversation was mostly in English. While Miranda held forth with Dave and Gerry, I took the opportunity to practise my A-level French on him and, as if that wasn't torturous enough for the poor man, I bombarded him with questions about my house. Who were the current owners? How long would the paperwork take? Was it connected to mains drainage? (I hoped so, as I wasn't sure I could handle a *fosse septique*.) On a few occasions when I couldn't follow what he was saying – for Victor spoke very quickly – Miranda would come to my aid. Although she liked to be the centre of attention, there was something very warm and lovely about her.

'Victor is very impressed by your decisiveness,' she told me at one point. 'He says he has never had a client like you, who made a decision after only seeing one property.'

'I bet,' said Gerry.

Victor nodded. I noticed that he hadn't eaten much. He poked around suspiciously at the overcooked salmon and Dave's limp green beans, and he left a mound of new potatoes on his plate. But by the time we reached dessert, I was confident that he would not dare sell my house to anyone else. (Until he had heard from the owner, I was terrified that another interested party might come along and snatch my future away in front of my eyes.)

Miranda had turned the conversation around to her ex-husband, a barrister. She described how she had danced around the hotel bedroom on the first night of their honeymoon, wearing a very expensive set of lingerie. 'I was so thrilled to be married,' she recalled. 'I was dancing round the room in my new lace knickers trimmed with rosebuds and little blue ribbons at the side, shouting 'I'm married! I'm married!' and can you imagine what my husband's response was?'

Victor and I stopped talking about drains in order to find out. Miranda paused for dramatic effect.

'He said...' She took a gulp of wine and looked around the table. 'He said... for God's sake, pull yourself together, woman.'

Gerry looked at a loss as to what to say. Victor stared at his plate of untouched beans. Dave shook his head in sympathy. I wasn't quite sure of the appropriate response, but fortunately, Miranda was laughing as she delivered the punch line.

At the end of the evening, Victor offered to drive Miranda home – to everyone's relief, as she had drunk her own body weight in alcohol. 'That's awfully nice of you, Victor. I'm going to say yes,' she replied. And then, with a peal of laughter: 'I always knew you were a gentleman – despite what other people say about you.' Fortunately, Victor did not seem to understand.

'Now listen, sweet girl, I hope to see you again before I'm very much older,' cried Miranda as she teetered out of the house, a blur of cobalt-coloured sequins, her tiny frame struggling to balance on spindly heels. 'And don't forget, darling, if ever you're looking for a guinea pig for cosmetic surgery, I'd definitely be up for an eye lift…'

'She seems like quite a character,' said Gerry, as we watched her swaying up the street, like a small, colourful bird, on Victor's arm.

'How does she survive out here?' I asked Dave.

'She lives on an allowance from her ex-husband. I think she was once an actress or a dancer, but whether professional or not, I don't know.'

'It sounds like she and her husband were very mismatched,' I said.

'Yeah,' said Dave. 'I think she got drunk once too often at his firm's dinners. But she's a good laugh. Anyone for a digestive?'

'Oh, go on then,' said Gerry.

Dave took an opened bottle of wine from the table and the three of us sat down in front of the fireplace. We talked for well over an hour, mostly about life in France and my new house. 'Are you sure you don't want to look at any other houses?' Dave asked. 'Just to see what's out there?'

'It's a bit late now,' I said. 'I've already signed the contract.'

'Why bother?' said Gerry. 'If this house has fallen into your lap – and it looks like a pretty good deal to me – why waste your time? The best things in life are usually effortless.'

'I agree,' I said, thinking how the house wasn't the only good thing to have fallen into my lap this weekend. Here I was, at 2.00 a.m. in France, sitting in a candlelit room and drinking wine with a man who was gorgeous, successful and, so far as I knew, single. If only Dave would go to bed, so that I could have Gerry to myself. But Dave showed no sign of flagging. Each time we came to a pause in the conversation he would light a cigarette or pour himself another drink. In the end – and to my extreme disappointment – it was Gerry who bowed out first. 'I'm beat. I'm going to have to turn in,' he said. I followed him shortly afterwards and fell asleep planning the colour scheme for Maison Coquelicot, which was as good as mine.

The following day, Dave drove the three of us into Poitiers. We went for a stroll and visited Notre Dame cathedral, roaming around the cool, dark interior and admiring the painted columns. It all seemed so romantic that I began to wish I could hang out with Gerry and Dave forever. Then we had lunch at a cafe overlooking the cathedral. Dave went to the loo while we were waiting for the bill to arrive, leaving Gerry and me on our own. 'You know, I've really enjoyed this weekend,' he said, looking at me intently.

'Me too,' I said. 'It's a shame I've got to back this afternoon.'

'So is there someone waiting for you at the other end?' he asked, his voice low.

'No,' I replied. 'What about you?'

He looked into the distance, before not answering the question. 'I'm probably going to stay on for another week,' he said. 'Help Dave with the house a little and do some more writing.'

I toyed briefly with the idea of altering my TGV ticket, but I thought it better to leave on a high. And anyway, I was absolutely certain that I would see Gerry again. The conversation was cut short by the arrival of the bill – which Gerry insisted on paying.

At Poitiers station they both accompanied me to the platform.

'I can't wait to hear how it goes with the house,' said Gerry, kissing me on the cheek.

'I'll arrange for us all to meet up for London when I'm back,' said Dave.

As the TGV pulled away from the platform, I watched Gerry and Dave waving goodbye in the sunshine and felt a surge of happiness. The future, for the first time in ages, seemed like something to look forward to.

The final signing, or *acte final*, took place on a Friday afternoon towards the end of August in the peach-painted offices of Monsieur Guillon, the local *notaire*. It was exactly a month since I had first set eyes on the house. Victor had exceeded all my expectations by negotiating a significant discount on the asking price for the house so that, altogether, including legal fees, it cost €42,000, which amounted to just over £30,000. I went to the signing alone, straight from Poitiers station, and to be honest it was a little depressing. The owners, the Chevreuils, a dour-looking couple in their sixties, did not even manage a smile as I shook hands with them. Instead, they looked very anxious that I might duck out of the deal. While Monsieur Guillon gathered his dossiers, I asked about Madame Mauboussin, the former tenant, who had been forced into an old people's home through ill health. 'She was a spinster,' said Madame Chevreuil, with glee. 'She never married.' I had a sudden vision of myself as an eighty-year-old spinster, being carted off to an old folks' home in four decades time. But at least in a French nursing home I could expect foie gras and a decent bottle of wine for lunch rather than boiled potatoes and barley water.

Only when the *acte final* was signed and stamped did the Chevreuils allow themselves a smile. I noticed on the *acte de vente*, or deeds, that they had paid €7,000, less than £5,000, for the house six years ago. So they were getting a good return on their investment. As if reading my thoughts, Madame Chevreuil said, 'We did a lot of work on the house, you know.'

'Of course,' I said, thinking of poor Madame Mauboussin living there without heating or an indoor lavatory, with damp climbing up the walls and the kitchen floor in danger of collapse. The Chevreuils had already stood up to leave and did not invite me for the customary drink to celebrate. But I considered it a lucky escape. I picked up my travel bag and walked out into the sunshine, towards the square. I felt a surge of pride as I saw the cluster of French flags flying about the *mairie*. This was now *my mairie* and I now belonged somewhere other than west London. *I was the owner of a house in France!* As I passed the Café du Commerce and a group of flat-capped old men sipping cloudy pastis outside, I felt like I was on the threshold of a very big adventure. For financial reasons, I wouldn't be able to move to France for at least a year, but I had taken the first, very big step towards My New Life in France.

I arrived at Dave's house as the church bells struck 7.00 p.m.

'I'm now a member of the French property owners' club,' I said, with a grin. 'Let's go and celebrate. The champagne's on me.'

'OK,' said Dave, sounding a little reluctant. 'But my son's here at the moment. I'll have to bring him with us.'

'That's cool,' I said, trying not to look surprised. Dave had not mentioned that he had a son. I followed him into the dark *salon*, where a spotty, feral looking teenager was slouched on the sofa.

'This is Jason,' said Dave.

'Hi there,' I said, holding out my hand. The spotty teenager did not take it.

We went to the local crêperie and sat in the courtyard, at the same table that I had sat at with Gerry and Dave on my very first night in the village. There was no champagne on the menu so I ordered a glass of rosé and Dave ordered a bottle of Sauternes, a sugary yellow dessert wine. Jason did not want anything and sat slumped in the chair, his arms folded defensively across his body.

'I still can't believe that you've actually done it,' said Dave, sitting back in the sunshine. I noticed that he had put on quite a bit of weight since I last saw him.

'Dad, I'm bored. How long are we going to be here for?'

'Shh,' said Dave. 'Gerry didn't think you'd actually go through with it.'

'How is he?' I ask.

'Well, I'm a bit pissed off with him, now you mention it. I sent him a couple of emails when I was trying to arrange drinks in London, but he didn't even reply. I also left a few messages for him on his phone, but nothing.'

'Yes, I remember,' I said. I had gone along to meet Dave and a few other people from our writing course in a wine bar in Mayfair, but Gerry, disappointingly, had not shown up.

Dave suggested getting some food and asked for an English menu for his son, who immediately pushed it back across the table. 'I'm not hungry,' he said.

'Come on, Jason, have something to eat,' his father cajoled, but Jason just shook his head defiantly. Dave went ahead and ordered him an omelette and frites anyway, but it remained untouched. Jason sat in hostile silence as I picked at a goats cheese salad and Dave ate his way through a starter (*salade du périgord*), two main courses (a ham and cheese crêpe, followed by a smoked salmon crêpe) and dessert (an enormous chocolate ice-cream sundae). 'Did you say this was on you?' he asked when the bill arrived.

I paid without hesitation. After all, it was thanks to Dave that I had found the house. Also, over the next several months, I'd be returning to Villiers often as the work began, and Dave and I had come to a financial arrangement whereby I paid him €25 a night, the same rate as the pilots, for renting a room in his house. I did not want to take advantage of his hospitality. My house was a long way off being habitable, and staying at Dave's was likely to be far more fun than staying in a hotel – especially if Gerry came out to stay again. By paying his going rate I could stay with him whenever I wanted without worrying that I was exploiting our friendship.

We walked back to his house in the evening sunshine and I took my bag up to one of the guest rooms, decorated in the obligatory floral wallpaper that Dave had inherited from the previous owner. It had an en-suite bathroom, shared via a door on each side with the other guest room, which was occupied by Jason. I could hear him moving around in his room.

When I went back downstairs Dave had opened a bottle of wine and lit a few candles on the mantelpiece. Jason, thankfully, stayed in his room. I took a seat by the old stone fireplace and we sat and chatted. 'I won't have the money to do the house up at once. I'll have to do it step by step,' I said.

'At least you've always got somewhere to stay when you come out,' said Dave.

'Is everything OK?' I asked, after a while, for I had noticed that Dave seemed a little down.

'To be honest,' he said, lighting a cigarette (something he only did when drunk), 'things aren't going well between me and Linda.' He inhaled deeply. 'I think we've just grown apart,' he said, reaching over to top up my wine glass. 'We just don't have that much in common any more. I want to spend more time in France but she hates it. She can't stand the food and doesn't speak the language.'

'But didn't you buy the house together?'

'Yeah, we did. But it was more me that wanted to do it than her. This is really my project,' he said, indicating the flowery brown three-piece suite, the old-fashioned mahogany dining table and the huge carved wooden sideboard (all, he had proudly revealed, bought as a job lot from a *dépôt-vente* or second-hand shop, for €500.) 'But it runs deeper than that. Intellectually, I'm beginning to realise that we are just not on the same wavelength.'

'Really?'

'It's like with you, I can have all these deep discussions – politics, writing, whatever – and I can't do that with her. I just feel like I'm at a crossroads,' he continued. 'Maybe it's a mid-life crisis or something. I'd really like to quit my job and go freelance like you, come and live out here full-time, finish the house off, but I'm just not sure that I'm brave enough.'

This was all a revelation. 'But enough about me,' he said suddenly. 'I want to know more about you. I've spent quite a bit of time with you now but you don't give much away about yourself, do you?'

'How do you mean?'

'Well, for a start, it's a pretty bold thing to do, to buy a house out here on your own. Not many people would consider it.'

'Well, I've always been a Francophile and I've always wanted to live in France. And I know a lot about Marie-Antoinette...'

'Come off it,' he said, blowing his cigarette smoke sideways and jutting his chin upwards. 'I don't know why, but I get the impression that you are running away from something,' his voice low and gentle, his eyes kind, 'But if you don't want to tell me, that's fine.'

Dave, I realised, was a very unusual being: a heterosexual man who was able to talk with ease about his emotions, as well as tap intuitively into other people's. He was definitely blessed with a superior emotional intelligence. For a moment I was tempted to tell him everything, but stopped myself.

'It's a long story.'

'It's up to you,' he replied, pouring himself another glass of wine all the way up to the brim.

'No really, I... can't. I'm sorry.'

'I'm not going to force you,' he said. 'But I think it would do you a lot of good to talk about it.'

'It's nearly three in the morning,' I said, feigning a yawn. 'Time for bed.'

'Listen, there is something that I have to tell you...'

'What's that?'

'It's a bit embarrassing. Don't take this the wrong way...'

'What?' I was stricken with sudden fear as to what he is going to say.

'It concerns Victor.'

'It does?' I was swept by a huge feeling of relief.

'It was Miranda who noticed it first, but apparently he's quite taken by you.'

'What?'

'You know that his wife left him and ran off with another bloke and they're getting divorced.'

'Yes, poor guy.'

'Well, he's been going around saying that he is going to marry an Englishwoman next.'

'That doesn't necessarily mean me.'

'I'm afraid it does. He keeps asking Miranda – and me – when you are next coming out. He also asked me whether you were with someone. And were you looking for a French husband?'

'Oh come on!'

'I'm serious. Miranda said to warn you to tread carefully, as he is very emotionally vulnerable and a bit unstable, since his wife left him.'

'Poor Victor,' I said. 'I promise I'll do my best to let him down gently.'

Feeling somewhat disturbed, I made my way upstairs and opened the bedroom door. Lying on my bed, its head nestling on the pillow, was a large axe (the axe that Dave used for chopping wood). The only person who could have placed it there was Jason.

Before I got into bed, I made sure that the door to the shared bathroom was locked from my side.

The next morning I went round to Maison Coquelicot. It seems so ridiculous, given all the work that needed to be done on the house, but I spent a couple of hours dusting all surfaces and mopping the wooden floors using cold water from the dilapidated kitchen sink. It was my way of claiming the house as my own.

Just before midday Dave appeared at the open window as I was applying Farrow & Ball tester pots to a small patch of exposed wall above the fireplace.

'Hmm, prison grey,' he said.

'Actually, it's Farrow & Ball's Light Blue,' I replied, but I had to admit, grudgingly, that he was right. On first impressions, it was definitely more battleship grey than light blue.

'I don't think your son likes me very much,' I said, replacing the lid on the tester pot.

'Oh, ignore him. He's just being a typical teenager.'

'He left an axe on my bed last night. It sort of seemed like an act of aggression, or a statement of intent.'

'Oh, he wouldn't have meant anything by it,' he said. 'He's just a kid. He was probably just playing around with it.'

'It's a scary thing to play around with,' I said.

Dave wanted me to go with them to a *vide grenier*, the French equivalent of a car boot sale, in a nearby village. 'Maybe it's best if just the two of you go,' I said. But Dave insisted.

'I just need to stop at the market and get some seafood,' he said. 'I thought I'd make a paella this evening.' He bought prawns, mussels, squid and scallops from the very handsome fishmonger. Unfortunately, he had forgotten his wallet, so I paid.

The *vide grenier* was very busy. It had taken over the square in front of the *hôtel de ville* and spilled into the narrow surrounding streets of the village. There were stands selling ice cream, crêpes, chilled rosé wine, and hot sausages in baguettes. A *mélange* of aromas – sugar, vanilla and frying onions – filled the air. But it took me all of ten minutes and a quick walk around the square to establish that the various stands offered nothing of interest to me. The legacy of my fashion editor training and all those years scanning clothing rails means that I can case a joint in seconds. Mostly it was people getting rid of old children's toys, piles of comics and polyester clothes. A good many of the stall holders, I noticed, were ex-pat Brits selling off their old biscuit tins and broken ornaments. Dave, however, took his time, examining everything. He seemed particularly interested in unidentifiable metal objects and old pieces of farming equipment. 'Possi-bili-tay doon reduction?' he would ask, and then turn to me to translate the answer. Progress was slow and the sun was so hot that it hurt the eyes.

After hovering with Dave for a painfully long time, I went and sat at a cafe on the corner of the square and ordered a *diabolo menthe* – lemonade with mint-flavoured syrup. I spent a happy hour people-watching and playing a private game of 'spot *l'Anglais*'. There seemed to be lots of them in the market. Two of them sat down next to me and started to argue about whether or not they should have bought two willow log baskets. Not realising there was a fellow *Anglaise* in their midst, they spoke with abandon and it was fun eavesdropping on their argument – which subsequently evolved into whether or not they had bought the right house and whether or not they should have married each other.

Entertaining though this was, after I'd been sitting in the cafe for an hour I started to grow restless. There was no sign of Dave, so I went to look for him. I found him examining a World War Two gas mask. Dispiritingly, he wasn't even halfway round the fair. 'There you are,' he said. 'I was wondering where you'd got to. I don't suppose you could lend me twenty euros could you? Only, I'd quite like to buy this gas mask.'

I reached into my bag and gave him the money. 'I'll wait for you at the cafe over there,' I said. I went back to the cafe and ordered another coffee. Fifteen minutes later Jason came loping over. 'Dad wants to borrow another twenty euros,' he said, avoiding eye contact.

'Where is he?'

He pointed to where his father was examining a large clump of unidentified metal. I went and found a cash point and gave Dave the twenty euros. In addition to the gas mask, he had bought an old-fashioned iron, a big metal jug, and what looked like a rusty old plough. In order to fit it all in the back of his estate car, he was forced to put the back seats down and Jason had to sit perched in the back next to the plough, which was gratifying.

That evening, I helped Dave to cook paella, chopping chillies and de-bearding the mussels. 'I don't think Jason will eat this,' he said. 'I'll have to make him a pizza and chips.'

'Why don't you at least get him to taste it?' I suggested, for I had already noticed that he cooked a separate meal for Jason every night.

But there was no reply when he called his son's name. Dave went to see if he was in his room but he wasn't. He searched the garden, the attic and the cellar but there was no sign of Jason. 'Has he ever disappeared before?' I asked, not sure what to suggest.

'No, never,' said Dave, pulling a handkerchief from his pocket and mopping the sweat off his brow. 'He's been acting a little strange recently, because he's caught in the crossfire between Linda and me. I'd better go and see if he has wandered off into the village.'

As Dave went off into the balmy evening to search the square, I poured myself a large glass of red wine and went to sit on the sofa in the dark coolness of the sitting room. I opened my book and began to read until, suddenly, I heard a creaking noise behind me. I almost spilt my glass of wine in fright as Jason jumped out of the enormous carved sideboard, which ran along an entire wall.

'Fooled ya!' he cried, a sly grin on his ratty face.

'Yes, you did. Well done,' I said. He flashed a malicious grin. I thought again of the axe and suddenly I was very glad that I was returning to the UK the next day.

Chapter 4

Full Moon

IN THE YEAR that followed the signing of the *acte final*, Dave and I became really good friends. I realised that we actually did have a lot in common: we both loved France and we also shared a passion for *dépôt-ventes* – although I learned to always take a good book with me, as Dave could spend up to three hours looking at bits of old metal and furniture. He was the only heterosexual man I had ever known who liked to shop more than a woman.

That winter, we spent several weekends in France together. Often, if Ryanair was offering cheap flights, we would fly out together at a moment's notice. It meant I could meet up with contractors and get quotes for the electrical rewiring, plumbing, replastering and the new kitchen floor. We would take day trips to nearby villages, sitting in cafes having long, deep conversations or enjoying cosy lunches and dinners in small bistros. We spent many nights by his crackling log fire, discussing our plans for our respective houses and poring over paint charts and books on French country interiors together. He loved to sit and drink Sauternes until the early hours of the morning, discussing his wife's increasingly wayward behaviour. She was having a mid-life crisis, he said, and had started partying hard, going out to clubs every night and taking drugs. I lived in hope that he would bring Gerry along again but there was no news on that front – whenever I asked, Dave said that he hadn't seen or heard anything from him – and so most of the time it was just the two of us and, occasionally, another male friend or two of Dave's.

Dave seemed to have a limitless supply of male friends, all of them attractive and with good jobs – an architect, an investment banker, a commercial airline pilot and an advertising campaign director among them. Nearly all of them were single and they shared Dave's love of deep conversation and seemed to have bonded with him on a very profound level. Yet, despite appearing to have successful careers and attractive personalities, I noticed that they were all a little morose, like they had been through the mill in some way. And when I asked Dave how he knew so-and-so, he was always very vague and it was difficult to get a straight answer.

We met up in London for drinks too, always with other people. Then one evening, we stayed rather too late in the usual wine bar in Mayfair and Dave missed his last train home to Kent. His problems with his wife had worsened by then and I got the impression that he had missed his train deliberately. He was very drunk. 'You can come back to mine and crash in my spare room if you like,' I said.

'Can I? That sounds like a good idea,' he said.

We took a taxi back to my place, saying very little. Then he looked, or rather wobbled, around the flat. 'Christ,' he said. 'You've got such great taste.'

'Here's the spare room,' I said. 'The bed's already made up, so you can just crash in here.'

'Stay up and have another drink with me,' he said, reaching for my wrist. 'I don't want to go to bed just yet. I want to talk to you.'

Another drink was the last thing either of us needed, but I always enjoyed our conversations, so, against my better instincts, I went into the kitchen and opened a bottle of red wine. When I returned to the sitting room, he had taken off his jacket and shoes and was sprawled out on the sofa. I sat down opposite him.

'So Gerry was a no-show again tonight?' I said

''Fraid so,' said Dave. 'His girlfriend is six weeks pregnant.'

Girlfriend? Pregnant? Six weeks? This was a triple hammer blow. Not only had my only potential love interest been snatched away from me, but he was about to become a father. There was absolutely no chance of installing Gerry and his laptop in my French attic now.

'That was fast work,' I said, trying to hide my disappointment. 'I thought you said he didn't have a girlfriend.'

'He didn't. It was someone that he was friends with in the therapy group and it all happened very fast.'

'Therapy?'

Dave put his hand to his mouth and looked very embarrassed. 'Oh Christ,' he said. 'Look, I really didn't mean to tell you that. It just sort of slipped out. But now you know. That's where Gerry and I met.'

'You were in therapy too? Was it a drink problem?' I asked. 'Or drugs?' I knew that both were rife in the advertising industry.

'No. I was under a lot of pressure at work. Life was just getting on top of me.'

'And Gerry? Why was he there?'

'Depression.'

'Ah.' Suddenly, Dave's gang of disparate but emotionally literate friends made sense.

'That's why I tried to warn you away from him,' Dave continued. 'He's racked with self-doubt and constantly battling depression. He's not ready for a relationship, let alone fatherhood. I'm worried about him to be honest.'

'So all those other male friends of yours, did you meet them in therapy too?'

'Most of them, yes. It saved some of our lives. You can't help but form close bonds with the people that you meet there. The clinic encourages you to stay in touch afterwards, sort of as a support group, because we all know what each other has been through.' This explained a lot.

'So there. Now you know,' said Dave. 'So tell me, what secrets are you hiding?'

'Nothing I want to talk about,' I said. 'I'm sorry.'

'Listen,' he said, suddenly sliding off the sofa and onto the floor, so that he was closer to me and almost suppliant at my feet. 'I really think you should talk to someone.'

'Why?'

'Because you seem so… emotionally unavailable. I honestly think it would do you good to talk about it.' Dave's face was a picture of concern and, for a moment, I was worried that he was going to put his arms around me.

'So what's going on with Linda?' I asked, embarrassed by the intensity of his gaze. Fortunately, he took the bait.

'It's really bad,' he said. 'I've got to the stage now where I actually hate her. There's no going back for us…'

He made several more attempts to turn the conversation back to me that night but I managed to deflect the questions, no matter how astute they were. Eventually, I said I was going to bed. He said he wouldn't be able to sleep just yet, so I left him in the sitting room with a half-full bottle of wine, flicking through my books of fashion photography. Before I went to bed I put a bottle of Evian and some headache tablets in the spare room. I figured he might need them the next morning.

A month or so later, I was sitting at my desk in London when I received a call from Dave. 'Linda wants a divorce,' he said, his voice shaky.

'Are you sure?'

'She's taken out a restraining order on me and wants me to move my stuff out of the house by the end of the week.'

'Oh God! It's that bad?'

'She claims that I hit her. In fact, she attacked me with a table lamp. She's crazy. She's doing everything she can to get me out of the house.'

'And what about Jason?'

'He's staying with her for the time being. Though she doesn't give a damn about him. All she cares about is clubbing and her new bloke. Jason might have to come and live with me once I've got myself sorted out.'

'That's terrible news,' I said (and not just because I wouldn't wish Jason on anyone).

'We've decided to sell the house and split the profit,' he continued. 'If there is any. Most of the equity has already disappeared up her nose.'

'Where are you going to live?' I asked, suddenly worried that Dave might want to come and stay with me in London.

'I suppose it will have to be France,' he said.

'But what about your job?'

'Fuck the job. Anyway, I'm on compassionate leave.'

Dave's lack of concern for his job was a little worrying. It was no secret that his debts were stacking up. In addition to the loans he had taken out to buy and furnish his house in France, he had also amassed significant credit card debts. The more miserable he felt, the more money he seemed to spend. 'It seems to me there's no point in working at all,' he continued. 'I'd be better off claiming unemployment benefit since anything I earn will just go to Linda in child support.'

This sounded like bad news for Gerry, from whom Dave had recently confessed to borrowing £5,000. 'So the thing is, I need to hire a van and move my stuff out to France as soon as possible,' he continued. 'I was wondering if you would like to share it and split the cost?' It seemed like a good idea. I had recently bought two bedside tables and a leather tub chair and they were currently obstructing the communal staircase.

'OK. When were you thinking of going?' I asked.

'Tomorrow. Can you book the ferry?'

Dave picked me up the following morning, behind the wheel of a big white van. He was wearing beige cotton trousers and a black polo shirt with a large toothpaste stain on the front. 'I'm really sorry but the van's already pretty full,' he said. 'I didn't realise how much stuff I had.' When he slid back the side door I was expecting to see books and furniture but to my astonishment, it was almost entirely filled with board games.

'Bloody hell, Dave, what's all this?'

'I collect vintage board games,' he said, a little defensively, as a box toppled off the pile, scattering plastic soldiers everywhere. 'And battle memorabilia. Some of this stuff is quite valuable.'

'But where are you going to put it when we get to France?'

'I've just bought my neighbour's barn. It was only five thousand euros,' he said. 'A bargain.'

'*You've bought a barn?*' I repeated, incredulous. 'Where did you get the money?'

'I borrowed it. I think we might just fit in your bedside tables but there isn't going to be room for the tub chair.'

We were allocated a complimentary cabin for the crossing (earlier in the year Dave had insisted that we join the Brittany Ferries Property Owners Club, pretending to be a couple to save on buying separate membership). He said he was tired and went off to the cabin to sleep. I sat in the cafe with all the retired fifty- and sixty-somethings heading for their second homes and read a book for most of the seven-hour journey. Dave only emerged when the ferry docked at Caen and I noticed for the first time how dreadful he looked – unshaven and crumpled, as if he hadn't slept for a few nights. 'It's a long drive in the dark,' I said. 'Are you sure you're going to be OK to do it?'

'We don't have any option. I've got to turn around and bring the van back tomorrow,' he replied.

It was a full moon that night as we headed south towards the cathedral town of Sées. Dave talked about the sadness of love turning to hate – silently I envied him as I wished I could hate Eric – and his general disappointment at how his life had turned out. 'This is not how my life was supposed to be at forty,' he complained.

'I'm *so* with you on that,' I said.

'So what did happen between you and Eric?' he asked me, somewhere between Sées and Alençon.

'It's a long story.'

'We've got five hours.'

Maybe it was the influence of the full moon or perhaps because I felt bonded with him in misery, but as we drove along in the moonlight, I finally told him – not the whole story but an edited version. Deep down, I think I had wanted to confide in him for a long time. As we hurtled through the darkness, past the war graves of Normandy and with soft music playing on the radio, I explained how Eric had pursued me with breathtaking audacity and ruthless Gallic determination. A few days after our first date, he handed me a letter, which said, among other things:

'I'm sorry to be so insistent in saying what I feel for you, because I know I have no right to say it but I find it very difficult to keep it to myself. I am in love with you.'

I remember cringing at his flowery prose and throwing the letter in the bin. How having just split from my boyfriend of seven years, I wasn't interested in anything serious. I tried to finish with Eric several times but he refused to accept that the fledgling relationship was over, declaring on the verge of tears that he had never loved anyone the way he loved me.

'Was he a good shag?' Dave asked, suddenly, accelerating past a huge lorry.

'Being in bed with Eric was like winning the sexual lottery,' I replied, though I spared Dave the details (the beach in Thailand, the tree in Windsor Great Park, the cliff top in the Great Orme and the car park of Watford Gap services on the M1). I told him how Eric's persistence – the phone calls, the letters and the tearful pleas – finally wore me down. How, six months after we met, I capitulated and invited Eric to move into my flat 'on a temporary basis'. I recalled the joy of returning late from my job on the hideously bitchy magazine to find that the lights were on and someone was home – with a bottle of wine and dinner waiting.

It's funny how, looking back, it is the not the glamorous stuff – the Christmas shopping trip to New York, Kirs in the Hôtel Costes in Paris or skiing in the French Alps – that makes me miss Eric the most, but the more mundane moments: bike rides on a Sunday afternoon, walking home from the local pub in the evening, standing side by side at the kitchen sink, chatting while we did the washing up. We even survived a trip to IKEA together – the true test, I once read, of whether a couple are compatible. He even managed to look like he enjoyed the experience, unlike my previous (public school) boyfriend, who emerged shaking with anger and muttering darkly about his dislike of 'chavs'.

For a short while the balance of power must have been in perfect equilibrium, and for a brief period we both loved each other equally. He used to talk about what our children would be like and joked that if we had a girl it would be trouble for him, as he would have to deal with a miniature version of me. By that time he had grown on me to the extent that I had decided to spend the rest of my life with him. Somehow he must have sensed the shift in the balance of power. And cruelly – having begged me to marry him countless times – that was when he started to pull back.

He had started to work occasionally for a friend with a tour company, shepherding American tourists around France. The tours were always themed: Chateaux of the Loire, Vineyards of Bordeaux, that sort of thing. The evening he returned from 'Van Gogh's Provence' he was in a very strange mood. He gave me a perfunctory kiss on the cheek – strange in itself as he always kissed me full on the lips – sat down at *my* laptop, logged on to his emails and spent the next couple of hours typing furiously. I had planned for us to go out to dinner since we hadn't seen each other for a week and as I sat watching him type, I grew more and more angry. In the end, I ordered in pizza and we ate in sulky silence. This was followed by a huge argument. It was only a few days before he told me (in bed) that it was over between us and he was planning to move out. There are moments that change your life for ever. This was one of mine. 'You can leave right now then,' I said defiantly, knowing that the decision and the power no longer lay with me. And so he left in the middle of the night. I have no idea where he went but he returned with a minicab to move his stuff out the next day.

After he left, my heart and my body were overwhelmed, swamped by grief, my eyes permanently red and swollen. I was plagued by a recurring dream in which I am alone and driving down a long, dark country road. I drive and drive, thinking, hoping, that I am going to arrive somewhere but I never do. I am stuck on this dark road and there is no way to escape.

A few weeks after he moved out, he came back to collect his post. I watched from the upstairs window as he walked away and told myself that if he looked back, this would be a sign. Well, he *did* look back. He looked up and saw my tear-streaked face in the window. For ages, I took comfort in this, told myself that it meant something, but it didn't. I never saw him again.

I remember the bitterness spilling over into everyday life. Total strangers bore the brunt of my anger and misery: the British Gas customer services department; call centres too numerous to mention and the cold caller who phoned trying to sell me plumbing insurance. My life seemed to be a constant round of conflict and anger. Friends, who couldn't cope with the scale of my grief, melted away like the polar ice caps. For the first time in my life, I felt truly alone.

For weeks, I was immobilised by illness and misery, barely able to leave the flat. Then, almost a year after he left, I received an email from him. He hoped I was well but wanted to warn me that he was going to close our joint email account – one of the few things he paid for during our relationship – as he no longer used it. If I still needed it, I would have to switch it to my name within forty-eight hours. It was signed 'Best wishes, Eric.' It was sent on my thirty-sixth birthday.

For the first time, I felt a flash of anger rather than just sadness and regret: he *knew* that I relied on that email account for work. How could he give me just forty-eight hours' notice before closing it down? And choose my birthday to do it? I phoned the Internet supplier and discovered that since Eric's was the master name on the account he could not be removed. However, I could take over the payment and they gave me a new password. It was a couple of days before it dawned on me, with a sickening sense of excitement, that I could access his old emails. Intuition told me that this was a dangerous thing to do, but nothing prepared me for what I found. For the past six months, Eric had been corresponding with a woman called Suzanne Dance, a schoolteacher he had met on a 'Provence, Grasse and Fine French Perfumery' tour. From the passionate nature of the emails, it was clear to me that they had been having an affair.

'Fucking hell,' said Dave, the whites of his eyes widening in the moonlight.

I checked the dates of the emails against my diary and found out that the night he came home from 'Van Gogh's Provence' and sat down at my computer typing furiously, he had sent the following email to Suzanne Dance:

'*Coucou*,

Well it is not easy to return here. The next few days are going to be very difficult for me. This evening I ate my booring [sic] pizza and had to talk to her. It's not very cool. But I send you big, big kisses and will try and call you tomorrow. E.

PS: Have you seen the full moon? When I saw it in the sky this evening, I wondered if you could see it too? And I told it to tell you I am thinking of you.'

At what point, I wondered, did he fall out of love with me enough to let this other woman in? What did I do that contributed to that decision? The discovery of his betrayal, even though it was a year later, left me devastated and mired in self-doubt. In my innocence I never imagined that he would cheat on me. I trusted him completely.

To be left alone in my mid-thirties, after being promised marriage, children and regular holidays on the Île de Ré, made me feel I had been cheated not just by Eric but by life. It was like I'd set out on a journey expecting a lush, beautiful country and had washed up on a rocky, barren shore. And then the anger turned to obsession. I thought about him hundreds of times a day and I yearned not just for him but for my old self, the light-hearted, happy-go-lucky person I used to be when I was with him. Above all, I had an overwhelming desire to know where he was and what he was up to.

At this point I turned to Dave, whose face was a picture of compassion and concern as he drove steadily through the darkness towards Villiers. 'I know he behaved like a total bastard,' I said by way of a summary. 'I know I should be over him by now, but the sad fact is that I am not. I would take him back tomorrow.'

'So he was a scumbag but you're still in love with him,' said Dave. 'And you are not going to meet anyone else until you deal with that.' Dave, to his credit, did not repeat any of the usual platitudes, such as 'It was for the best' or 'You're better off without him'. Instead, he told me a story about how he had become obsessed with a beautiful girl he had gone out with as a teenager and how he tracked her down and turned up on her doorstep ten years later. 'She was fat and wearing fluffy pink carpet slippers,' he recalled. 'I had wasted ten years of my life being in love with a person who no longer existed, except in my mind.'

The story at least made me laugh – it was typically Dave – but I doubted Eric would be fat and I knew he wouldn't be wearing pink carpet slippers. 'But if I knew his address, I would turn up on his doorstep too,' I admitted.

As we drove past Alençon, Dave became serious and said I had to really try and move on.

'I am moving on,' I said. 'I'm moving to France.'

'But you have to remember,' said Dave, 'that you can't run from unhappiness. You just take it with you.' I can't remember all of Dave's advice that night, but he did point out that living in the past I was blocking opportunities in the present. 'There haven't been any opportunities,' I said.

'There have definitely been opportunities,' said Dave. 'It's just that you haven't noticed them.'

I loved Dave as he drove us south in the moonlight that night. He had listened to every word of my story. I loved him for his empathy, his emotional intelligence, his honesty and his ability to take on another person's problems when facing a barrage of his own. It was helpful for me to be able to talk about Eric with another man. After our French road trip, I added a new dream to my repertoire. In it, I was sinking up to my knees in quicksand while my friends watched from the shore. Only Dave waded in to try and rescue me, but unfortunately, before he could reach me, he ended up sinking more deeply into the mud than me.

It was 5.30 a.m. and still dark when we finally arrived in the village. Dave's house was cold and damp and smelt faintly of cat urine but he lit a fire and we sat up talking until the darkness faded into the brittle grey light of morning. Then we unpacked the van in the freezing cold, the air scented with the smell of wood smoke and damp earth. There were, I noticed, some new purchases. Despite his financial problems, and the fact he was still off work, Dave had bought a bread maker, a chrome-plated pasta machine and a device called a 'Flavour Shaker' for making marinades. I watched as he unpacked a new pair of wooden candlesticks for his mantelpiece along with a selection of other decorative objects that he had recently bought from Laura Ashley. 'Still spending then?' I said.

'Yeah,' he said sheepishly. 'But it's your fault. You shouldn't have told me about Laura Ashley.'

Villiers seemed very austere in the winter light but my heart still jumped with joy at the house that lay waiting for me around the corner – even though I was months away from living there.

After a few hours' sleep Dave set out in the late afternoon for the long drive back up to the ferry port with the empty van. When he returned the following afternoon by Ryanair, he opened another bottle of wine, sat down by the fire and we carried on talking, almost exactly where we had left off. He said that he had come to accept the Buddhist belief that we had no right to expect happiness in this life. Instead, it was best to view it as an endurance test, and the aim was to get through it while causing as little hurt as possible to other people. I had never seen him so down.

A few days later I had to fly back to London for a work assignment. I left Dave sitting by the log fire with a glass of sweet white wine, surrounded by Risk, Kerplunk, Operation and a vintage 1960s version of Monopoly. Only much later did I find out that he took the hire van out of the country illegally and, as a result, we were not insured for our road trip. But even then it was hard to be cross with him. Dave and I were two lost souls, swimming around in separate fish bowls.

For New Year's Eve, I suggested that Dave come over to mine for a few drinks and crash in my spare room. It made sense since he lived in Kent and we were both booked on the same Ryanair flight to Poitiers on New Year's Day. That way we could share a taxi to the airport together. I had invited my friend Charlotte, one of London's top libel lawyers, over to join us for drinks. Since Dave was newly divorced and Charlotte was also attractive and single, I thought they might hit it off.

Charlotte arrived at 7.00 p.m. with a bottle of champagne, looking fabulous in jeans and a black sparkly top. 'This is such a great idea,' she said. 'Low-key but much better than staying home alone.' (She was about to be proved wrong on both counts.) Dave showed up almost two hours later than advertised, unshaven and crumpled. I put this down to the pressure of his recent divorce, in which his wife, he claimed, had taken almost everything (including, by the looks of it, his clothes). He had just about managed to hold on to the house in France. He arrived accompanied by a friend called Matt, an architect, and his sulky teenage son Jason, who loped straight into the flat without saying hello, head down and earphones the size of saucers clamped over his ears. Still, it was gratifying to see that his acne had worsened and he had more spots than a Dalmatian.

'I know this is a bit unexpected,' said Dave, nodding in the direction of his son. 'But Linda and that new bloke of hers suddenly decided to go to Lanzarote at the last minute and there was nowhere else for him to go.'

'That's OK,' I lied. 'The more the merrier! Who would like a glass of champagne?'

'Yes please!' said Dave.

'Why not?' said Matt, with so little enthusiasm it was as if I'd just suggested a nice cup of cocoa and a game of Monopoly. (Neither he nor Dave had brought a bottle of any kind, I noticed.)

'Can *he* have a drink?' I asked, nodding at Dave's objectionable son, who was sitting on the sofa, legs apart and arms crossed defiantly, staring straight ahead. His presence dominated the room. I knew I should have felt sorry for him – after all, his world had no doubt been torn apart by the break-up of his parents' marriage – but it was hard to have sympathy with someone so charmless.

'Nothing alcoholic,' said Dave.

'Jason,' I shouted, so that he could hear me above the violent rap music that he was listening to. 'What would you like to drink?'

He shot me a look of contempt. 'Nothing.'

Determined not to let a surly teenager ruin the final few hours of the year, I went into the kitchen to take the canapés that I had made earlier out of the oven. And in a sudden rush of goodwill towards Jason I made him a special non-alcoholic cocktail – Angostura bitters, lime juice cordial and soda water. After all, it wasn't his fault that his cocaine-snorting mother had dumped him on his father on New Year's Eve. In fact, I was even tempted to add a secret shot of vodka. The poor kid probably needed it: abandoned by his mother and forced to spend New Year's Eve with his father and his friends rather than his own mates.

Dave was asking Charlotte about her job when I returned to the sitting room – 'Bloody hell, I bet that pays well, doesn't it?' – while Matt and Jason sat on the sofa next to each other in silence. I handed Jason the cocktail, which, served in a tall glass with ice, a slice of lemon and a stirrer, at least looked like an adult drink. 'Here you go. I made you a special cocktail,' I said.

He took it reluctantly, as if I was offering him rat poison, and put it straight down, without trying it. He didn't say thank you. Charlotte gave me a meaningful look, while Dave – who was gulping back expensive champagne as if it were Diet Coke – appeared not to notice his son's rudeness.

'There's a really good gastro pub on Brook Green – about a fifteen-minute walk away from here,' I said, after a while. 'We could go over and get some food.'

'I'm in,' said Dave, beaming.

Matt shrugged his shoulders in a non-committal way. All my attempts to make conversation with him had ended in a cul-de-sac. He was, I quickly realised, a clear-cut case of PGL (pointless good looks). He had decided to come to France with us at the last minute, which made me wonder what New Year's Eve tragedy had befallen him. Divorce seemed like the most likely scenario, since Dave, embittered by his own split, had told me that many of his friends were also in the process of getting divorced or being 'taken to the cleaners' by their wives. Matt, like Jason, looked like he would rather be anywhere than in my flat. But, on the bright side, his ex-wife obviously hadn't taken his Porsche, which was parked outside, and he was going to give us a lift to the airport tomorrow, though I wasn't sure how the four of us were going to fit into it.

The pub wasn't exactly rocking when we got there and it had stopped serving food. There was a forlorn banner saying 'HAPPY NEW YEAR' above the bar. The residents of west London clearly had better things to do. As Matt and Charlotte went to the bar to order the drinks, I asked Dave what he thought of Charlotte. 'Yeah, she seems quite nice,' he said, and then guessing the real meaning behind the question added, 'but not my type. I don't fancy her, if that's what you mean.' He turned pink and looked annoyed that I had even suggested it.

Surveying the depressing surroundings, I thought back to my best ever New Year's Eve – spent in a ski resort in the Italian Alps with Eric and a group of friends. Still, I forced myself to cheer up as Matt and Charlotte returned with the drinks. After all, I would be living in France before the year was out. I was on the brink of a new and exciting life.

Dave, at least, was in a jocular mood, asking everyone what their goals were for the coming year.

'To become a partner at my law firm,' said Charlotte. 'And have more fun.'

'So, Karen, what about you?'

'Huh?'

'What are your goals for this year?'

'Move to France. And finish renovating my house.'

'That's all?'

'You don't think that's enough?'

'What about personal stuff?'

'Like what?'

'Like find a bloke?'

Before I could reply, Jason beat me to it, with a comment that was gratuitously nasty – even for him.

'What did you just say?' I asked, thinking I must have misheard.

'I said, they'd have to be dead or drugged,' he repeated, his scrawny rodent features contorted with malice.

I bit my lip and did not react. Instead, I tried to put myself in his shoes and feel sympathy for him. I said nothing, but gave Dave a very pointed look, waiting for him to make his son apologise. He didn't. Charlotte raised an eyebrow.

'I couldn't believe what that obnoxious brat said to you,' she said a little later when Dave had gone to the bar. 'Or that his father didn't pull him up on it.'

'Well, I guess he's going through a tough time,' I said. But I had already decided that there was no way the toxic teenager was spending the night in my flat. I thought back to the axe he once left on my bed when I was staying at Dave's house in France. He had obviously identified me as the enemy. Fortunately, I had a solution since I had the keys to the rental flat below, which was vacant. (My American banker neighbour Kim was in New York for Christmas and had given me the keys, saying I could use the spare room over the festive season if I had guests.)

I was pleased when midnight finally chimed and Charlotte suggested that we go home.

'We'll follow you out,' said Dave. But they didn't. Charlotte and I stood outside in the rain on Brook Green for about twenty minutes. 'Let's just go,' she said, finally. 'They can find their own way back.'

We waited up. I called several times to ask if they needed directions back to the flat. But Dave's mobile was switched off. Two hours later we were still waiting. 'How rude,' said Charlotte. 'Especially since you have an early flight tomorrow.'

'Look, there's no point in you staying up half the night too,' I said. 'Let me call you a cab.'

But Charlotte, loyally, refused to leave.

Four hours into the New Year (and three hours before we were due to leave for the airport) the doorbell rang. I buzzed it open and Jason came running up the stairs and tried to push past me into the flat, without so much as a hello. There was no sign of his father or Matt.

'Hold on a minute! Where do you think you're going?' I asked. 'You wait here while I get the keys to the flat below.'

'What?' He looked at me blankly.

'Look,' I said. 'I know you're going through a tough time with your parents' divorce and everything but you insulted me in the pub tonight and I don't want you in my flat. There's another flat downstairs. I'll give you a sleeping bag and you can sleep there.'

Jason looked for a second like he was going to spit at me. Instead, he said, 'Fuck you. I didn't want to stay in your poxy flat anyway.' He ran back downstairs and slammed the door. Charlotte went after him and found him sitting on the doorstep in the rain, hood pulled up, earphones on. She spent half an hour trying to persuade him to come in, but despite her best efforts, he wouldn't.

It was another hour before Dave and Matt returned. I buzzed them in. Dave was drunk and very angry. 'What's going on?' he shouted. 'What's my son doing on the doorstep in the rain at four a.m.?'

'He chose to sit there.'

'He said you wouldn't let him into your flat. That you left him outside.'

'Let's not talk about this now.'

'We *will* talk about it now,' he said, slurring his words. 'This concerns my son.'

'Dave, you're drunk. I am not discussing it now. I have keys to my neighbour's flat. You can all sleep in there.'

'So, come on then, what's he done that's offended you so badly that you won't let him into your flat?' sneered Dave as he lurched unsteadily towards me. Fortunately Charlotte, having heard the commotion, appeared in the doorway

'Hey, come on,' she said, in her even, lawyerly voice. 'Let's all calm down here.'

'Yeah, come on, Dave mate, just chill,' said Matt, who looked like he was struggling to stand upright.

'You can shut up,' shouted Dave, at Charlotte. 'It's *her* (he jabbed his finger in my direction) that I'm speaking to. I want to know exactly what her problem is with my son.'

'Your son refused to come in. He said he wanted to sit on the doorstep,' said Charlotte.

'That's not true, Dad. She wouldn't let me in.' He pointed his finger at me.

'How could you let the poor kid sit shivering on the doorstep in the rain?'

'That's not what happened.'

'Are you calling my son a liar?'

'I am not discussing this now.' Behind his father, Jason was now snivelling.

'He's just a kid. I can't believe that you left him out in the rain.'

'I told you. I didn't! But you're not exactly a model of responsible parenting, sending him back here on his own.'

I regretted this almost before I'd finished saying it. Questioning Dave's parenting skills was bound to prove a flashpoint and it did.

'WHAT DID YOU JUST SAY?' he bellowed.

'Look, Dave, please calm down and let's all discuss this tomorrow,' said Charlotte. The torrent of abuse that followed was not pretty. Dave persisted in shouting louder and becoming more threatening until finally, pushed to the limit, I shouted:

'Look, you're not doing your son any favours by letting him get away with such obnoxious behaviour. He even left an axe on my bed once. That's not normal behaviour. The kid's really messed up.'

You should *never*, I know, criticise someone else's progeny, no matter how obnoxious they might be. Dave's face was now as red as a slice of watermelon and the effect of my last sentence was explosive. 'How DARE you,' he yelled, jabbing a finger centimetres from my face.

'That's enough!' said Charlotte suddenly, her voice raised but her face a picture of steely calm. 'Leave right now or I am calling the police.'

I was truly scared. This was a side of Dave that I could never have imagined. But thankfully, after much more shouting and swearing, he started to back away. 'Come on, Jason, we're not spending the night here,' he yelled. They stumbled noisily down the stairs, Dave still hurling random insults, Jason whimpering in his wake.

Charlotte stood in shocked silence for a minute or so as we waited for the front door to slam.

'Welcome to the New Year,' I thought, as I closed the door to the flat. I was about to move alone to a small village in France and my only friend in the village was no longer a friend but an enemy.

Chapter 5

Let My New Life Begin....

AND NOW, HERE I am, just over a year since I signed the *acte final*, standing outside Maison Coquelicot, feeling panicked by what I have taken on. I have a feeling that she – for I have decided that the house is definitely feminine – is going to be quite a handful. It doesn't help that what I know about DIY could be written on the back of a button and that my practical skills start and end at unscrewing lipsticks and spraying scent onto tester strips.

I stand in the fierce afternoon sun of the Poitou-Charentes and try to visualise the facade re-rendered with lime plaster and painted creamy white, the dull brown shutters transformed with a coat of pale blue-grey, and hot pink geraniums in terracotta pots lined up on the windowsills. My mission, I remind myself, is to restore this unloved little house to a thing of beauty – to turn Maison Coquelicot into the quintessence of *le style Français*. I will give this sad little house back its soul and, in the process, I will learn to lead a simpler, less superficial and more connected life (and stop buying so many pairs of shoes).

In contrast to the fashionably minimal decor of my old flat in London, I plan to fill Maison Coquelicot with colour and rustic comforts. The *petit salon* will be decorated with chintz curtains, colourful rugs and fat sofas piled high with faded floral cushions. The kitchen will have open shelving crammed with storage jars, colourful old china and wooden bowls filled with plump aubergines, lemons and bell peppers. And in the bedrooms I will have cream-coloured iron beds covered with linen sheets and flowery patterned eiderdowns, while the dressing table will overflow with antique perfume bottles and bath oils.

I will fill the small courtyard with scented roses, orange-pink geraniums, climbing jasmine and herbs growing in terracotta pots, as well as beaten-up wicker chairs and an antique wrought iron table. I will string a row of twinkling fairy lights along the stone walls, and on summer evenings I will drift around the courtyard with a watering can in one hand and a glass of ice-cold rosé in the other. Maison Coquelicot will burst with colour and pattern and pieces of furniture that look like they have been there for ever. There will be stacks of colourful books at every turn, jugs of sweet peas, roses and peonies placed on every surface and candles and antique mirrors in every room. And, most importantly of all, there will be a roaring fire (and willow baskets overflowing with logs) in the *petit salon*, so that in the evening the house will glow with warmth.

But this is all some way off yet, as at the moment I don't even have hot water or a kitchen floor. In the stone passageway, I am hit by the overpowering smell of gloss paint. Turning on the light in the *petit salon*, which is in pitch darkness with the shutters closed, I am met with a sight that makes me gasp. The walls are no longer brown. Neither are the dado rail, skirting boards or doors. *Pas du tout*. Instead, everything – and I mean *everything*, apart from the wooden floorboards and marble fireplace – has been painted glaring, unremitting, glacial white.

As requested on my last visit, Alain, the local lad who has been helping out with the redecoration, has stripped the walls of flowery brown wallpaper and has given the slatted wooden ceiling – formerly a dirty beige colour – a new coat of gleaming white gloss. Unfortunately, he hasn't stopped at the ceiling: he has painted *everything* – walls, skirting boards and even the fire surround – in shiny, bright white. I feel as though I am standing in an igloo. I throw open the shutters and, with daylight to amplify it, the effect is even worse. I have no idea how this happened – or what was lost in translation – but my French is obviously not as good as I thought it was.

'*Coucou!*' My neighbour Claudette appears at the open window. '*Dis donc!* What's happened here?' she says, peering into the blinding white space.

'I don't know. It's a mistake,' I say. 'I only asked for the ceiling to be painted white. But as you can see, everything is white.'

'Oof,' says Claudette, shaking her head. 'What a mistake to make! *Ça brille.*'

She's right. It is indeed shiny.

'I'm going to have to get it all removed.'

She shakes her head. 'I bet that's cost you.'

'Yes,' I say, thinking of the €200 that I left Alain to buy the paint, French paint being very thin and very expensive.

'So have you moved here now?' asks Claudette, eyeing the car piled high with stuff outside.

'Yes.'

'Permanently?'

'Yes.'

Claudette looks sceptical.

'In this house?'

'Yes.'

She looks even more sceptical. 'Oof, I think there is work to do before you can live here,' she says, squinting into my glacial sitting room. 'Have you got someone to help you?'

'Not yet.'

'You need to make one room habitable. And then you can do the rest.'

'Yes, that's what I am hoping to do.'

'But you are not planning to live here yet?' she says.

'Yes, I am.'

'On your own?'

'Yes.'

'*Ah non!* Karen,' she says, pronouncing my name, as the French always do, with a flourish of 'r's. I much prefer *Karenne*, or even *Kar-reen*, to the English pronunciation. She points at the kitchen in horror. 'You do not even have a floor!'

'No, but one is coming soon,' I say, sounding more optimistic than I feel.

'Who is doing it?'

I tell her the name of the carpenter I have hired and she nods her head in approval. 'Monsieur Picherou, he is very conscientious. You need not worry about him,' she says.

'Oh good,' I reply. 'I also need to find a good plumber.'

'To do what, exactly?'

'To install a bathroom sink and a toilet.'

'Yes, very important,' says Claudette. 'When do you need him?'

'As soon as possible.'

'Listen! If you need a plumber, I have one who is very good.'

'Oh superb. Can you give me his number?'

'Yes, of course. Are you here tomorrow?'

'Yes.'

'*Bon,*' she says, with a finalising nod of the head. '*Alors, je te laisse pour le moment. Mais bon courage, eh!*'

Claudette bustles off and I imagine word spreading round the village about the *Anglaise* and her bold taste in interior decor. But at least I have a functioning phone, I tell myself. I pick up the futuristic *Star Trek*-like gadget in the corner (the only phone I could find in the local electrical store) in order to call Monsieur Picherou. Unfortunately, the phone is dead. The line, not for the first time, appears to have been cut off. I decide to go and visit Dylan and Lola in the Liberty Bookshop on the square. If the house has any other nasty surprises to spring on me they will have to wait until this evening, when I return (oh joy) to sleep on the bare floorboards of the upstairs bedroom. As I close the shutters, the doorbell rings. It is Alain, furiously dragging on a cigarette. News travels fast in a small French village. He stamps out the cigarette and, after the usual handshakes and greetings, waves a hand towards the white walls of the *petit salon*. 'Does it please you?' he asks.

I am tempted to tell him that it makes me want to fling myself on the ground and wail like an infant. Instead, I say, 'The ceiling is very nice, thank you.'

'Ah good,' he says. 'And the rest?'

'I am a little… *disturbed*,' I say, searching for the right words in French, 'as to why you also painted the walls in gloss paint. It is not precisely what I wanted.'

'No?' he says looking surprised. 'Why not?'

'Well, I didn't ask you to paint the walls – only the ceiling,' I say.

'Oh,' he says. 'I thought you wanted me to do it all.'

There doesn't seem to be much point in arguing – or trying to figure out how the misunderstanding occurred. Instead, when he hands me a bill for €700 for making my walls resemble a fridge, I just write out the cheque. He also asks me for another €50 in additional paint costs, having spent the €200 I gave him. It's galling to have to pay for this disaster – but not quite as galling as having to ask him how much it will cost to undo it all.

I drive around to the Liberty 'English Bookshop and Organic Tea Room' on the square. Many of *les Anglais* who move to France suddenly profess a profound abhorrence of their fellow countrymen and a desire to avoid them as much as possible, but I bear no such prejudices. One of my biggest fears about moving to France alone is that it will be difficult to make friends, so I am not going to start ruling people out by nationality. Dylan and Lola Liberty, both former youth workers in their late thirties, are lovely. They arrived in Villiers six months after I bought my house, but in the time that I have been shuttling back and forth from London for meetings with artisans, they have turned a cavernous shell of a shop (once an electrical wholesaler's) into a pristine and carbon-neutral Internet cafe and bookshop with solar panels. They have also become experts on *la vie française* – and a support system for every newly expatriated *Anglais* in the area. And because they are so charming and generally helpful to everyone, the Liberty tea room also has a very loyal following among the French people in the village, many of whom visit regularly for a cup of PG Tips and a slice of Lola's lemon drizzle cake.

Since I bumped into the Libertys in the estate agent's office a year ago, they have really gone out of their way to help me. A few months ago, they even managed to stop bailiffs from entering the house and seizing goods to the value of €34 (although at that point the only thing they could have taken was my Laura Ashley iron bed). The problem arose because France Telecom sent the bill to the wrong address, and when I first became aware of the arrears the matter was already in the hands of bailiffs. Dylan and Lola stepped in at the last moment and very kindly paid the bill, thus ensuring I had a bed to sleep on when I arrived. They have also offered to let me leave my sofa and my clothes (and anything else that would benefit from a dust-free environment) in their vast back room until the work at my house is finished.

Dylan comes out to greet me, wearing a T-shirt with a rainbow on it, faded jeans and flip-flops. 'Now listen,' he says. 'Lola and I have been giving it some thought, and we don't think you should move into your house just yet.'

'You don't?'

He shakes his head. 'Apart from anything else, it's dangerous having to leap over the hole in the kitchen floor to reach the staircase. We think it's better that you stay in our spare room for a week or so, until you have at least sorted out the basics.'

I want to fling myself on the floor and kiss his gnarly, dolphin-tattooed feet.

'So, no arguments,' he says. (Did he really think I was planning any?) 'It's totally cool for you to stay here. I'll just call Lola down and help you in with your stuff.'

I was hoping we could put this off for a while, but Lola emerges from the kitchen, where she has been making carrot cake, to take over the shop for half an hour. She is wearing a beautiful red and cream printed sarong tied around her hips as a skirt and her dark, curly hair is wrapped up in a floral scarf.

'You made it then?' she says, giving me a hug. 'Finally! We thought you would never come.'

'Yeah,' adds Dylan. 'What took you so long? We were expecting you in June and it's now August.'

'I know. That was the plan. But it took longer to wrap things up in London than I expected.'

'Come on then,' says Dylan. 'Let's unload the car.'

And so, in the August heat, we divest my car of its contents, including the 15 kilos of organic dried fruit that I have brought over for Lola to make fruit cake with. Dylan and I ferry my possessions up to the apartment above the shop and pile them in a large, sunny room with wooden floors and windows overlooking the *mairie* and the square.

When all my possessions have been brought upstairs, I plug my mobile phone into its charger and immediately it starts to flash with messages, several of them from one of the newspapers that I write for in the UK. 'We were hoping you could write something for us today,' says the commissioning editor, who fortunately has not realised from the ringing tone that I am abroad. (I haven't bothered to tell any of my editors that I have moved to France, for fear they will stop commissioning me.) 'We need a really bitchy, cutting 800-word piece on Victoria Beckham's new hairstyle and thought you'd be the perfect person to do it… in the next couple of hours… for tomorrow's edition.'

I call her back. 'I am so sorry,' I say, realising that I don't even know where my laptop is. 'I don't think I'm going to be able to help this time.'

Surveying my possessions piled up against the wall – most of them thrown into black bin bags in the rush to leave – I realise the enormity of what I have done. After so many years of fiercely cultivating my independence and a comfortable lifestyle in London, I have thrown myself on the mercy of virtual strangers. It is not an easy feeling for me. But there is no going back now. The question is: how on earth am I going to be able to function as a freelance journalist from here?

I wake up at the Libertys' wondering where I am. This is the moment I have been planning and dreaming of ever since I bought the house a year ago. So why do I feel so strangely deflated? Although I have had nine hours sleep, I feel like I have just limped across the finishing line in a marathon. I cannot believe how tired I am. The last frantic week of packing up in London, followed by the (almost) sleepless night in Caen and the long drive from the ferry have taken their toll. I am tempted to stay under the duvet until tomorrow. But this is not the moment to lie in bed like a giant *escargot*. This is the first day of My New Life in France.

There is no sign of Lola and Dylan but I am pleased to find the bathroom unoccupied. Inside there is a very futuristic-looking shower unit with numerous knobs and dials and shower heads. When I finally figure out how turn it on, jets of ice-cold water pummel me from every angle. I jump back in shock and try to turn the shower off, but whatever I do has the opposite effect and the hydra-headed beast assaults me with more icy water. As I fiddle with the various levers and knobs embedded in the plastic torture chamber I am alternately scalded and then pounded by glacial jets. I am not good at staying in other people's homes and feel a pang of longing for my former flat in London and the well-behaved shower, with its simple chrome controls. Back in my room, cheered by the sight of sunshine streaming in through the open windows, I rummage through my pile of black bin bags for something to wear. It doesn't take long to realise I don't own any clothes suitable for renovating a house.

Lola is in the pristine kitchen and laying out ingredients to start baking as I leave. 'Morning!' she says, brightly, looking me up and down quizzically. 'I thought you said you were going to start working on the house today.'

'Yes,' I say. 'I am. Why?'

'Oh! Well, it's just that you look a bit... dressed up, that's all.'

'I know, but I can't find anything else to wear,' I say, with a shrug.

'Why don't I lend you a pair of dungarees? They'd be much better for decorating.'

Dungarees! I don't wear dungarees. Under any circumstances. 'Um... maybe tomorrow. I think I'm mostly going to be organising stuff today anyway,' I say. And so, in my flower print dress and gold gem-encrusted sandals, I set off to renovate a house, stopping at the bakery to buy some breakfast. The smell of vanilla and sugar and sweet pastry is so comforting that I am tempted to curl up in a corner and sleep for an extra couple of hours.

At Maison Coquelicot, I open the tightly closed shutters and, perched on a cardboard box, eat my *pain au chocolat* in the brilliant white sitting room, wondering if I have taken on too much. I have no idea where to start. If only Sarah Beeny would walk through the door and tell me what to do. The problem is that almost everything that I could feasibly do myself, such as painting walls or plastering in holes, must wait until the major works such as the electrical rewiring and plumbing are done.

And since my phone is out of order, I can't even make calls to chase up the various artisans – *'artisan'* being the rather poetic term used in France to describe any skilled workman. I feel very unanchored and alone. Where there was once calm and order and hot running water in my life, there is now clutter and chaos.

On paper at least, my life in London was a success. I had a packed social diary (if I wanted to I could have attended fashionable parties every night of the week), I owned so many handbags I could open my own boutique and I earned enough money to pay off the credit card bills in full at the end of the month. And yet at thirty-five I was bereft of responsibility. I was the centre of nobody's universe. My life felt shallow and materialistic – as empty as the spare closet after Eric left. I'd spend the money I earned in order to compensate for the emotional void in my life. But, as I learned, you cannot buy your way out of unhappiness. And so I tried other routes. I did courses – lots of them. At least it would fill up my weekends: salsa dancing, poetry writing, Keralan cooking and learning to swim the Alexander Technique way – I signed up for them all. I even (on the ill-judged advice of a friend) submitted myself to a weekend of abseiling and fell-walking in Wales with members of the British military. This included a fully clothed walk up a gorge, up to our necks in ice-cold water, and culminated in a jump off the top of a waterfall. That, let me tell you, was almost as traumatic as splitting up with Eric.

After quitting my job on the magazine, for the first year it was a huge relief to be my own boss again, with no petty office politics or unpredictable editors to deal with. Instead, I had a calm, very predictable life working from home. Evenings I would either go to yoga or the gym, or meet up with friends for drinks or dinner. Then the next day I did the same thing all over again. It should have been the ideal lifestyle but it wasn't. My life lacked any goal or clear purpose. And that's when I started to have the dream, where I am lost on a dark country road, running out of petrol and with nowhere to turn off. I drove and drove, hoping that morning would arrive and it never did. It didn't take a psychologist to work out that the dream was trying to tell me something.

The house in France offered me an escape route and gave me a new focus. After buying Maison Coquelicot, I continued to live in London for another year, earning the money to do the house up. But I didn't waste that year. I signed up for twice-weekly French classes in the evening and I read every book I could find, fiction or otherwise, on moving to rural France. Most of them were plodding, middle-aged memoirs about septic tanks, elusive artisans and epic meals. But I devoured every word, and loved their soporific, calming effect. I fell asleep each night dreaming of sunflower fields and rustic interiors. Sitting at my desk in London, I wrote lists of the work that needed to be done and the furniture that I needed to buy. I spent evenings and weekends studying paint charts and ripping pages out of country interiors magazines for inspiration. The house became my hobby and suddenly I had a goal, something to work towards.

It meant that I would always have something to do at Easter and on Bank Holidays, when the spectre of Eric, and the loneliness of life without him, loomed largest. It also served another purpose: it gave me something to talk about, and suggested that my life had moved on in some way, when friends or acquaintances I hadn't seen in a while asked the inevitable question: 'So, what have you been up to?' I would listen to their news – that they'd got married, reproduced or met their soulmate – and, while I wasn't able to match any of that, I was at least able to say that I'd bought a house in France and was planning to move there soon.

Meanwhile, I set about acquiring the accoutrements of the rustic French lifestyle with a passion. It became my favourite Saturday morning pastime. Laura Ashley, I discovered, had an interesting, souk-like approach to pricing, suddenly, with no warning, offering thirty to fifty per cent discounts. And from time to time they sold off the old display furniture. I even went so far as to befriend the manager of my local branch, hoping for advance tip-offs. In this way I acquired a wrought-iron bed, a distressed leather sofa, two velvet tub chairs, a huge wooden refectory dining table with benches and a mirrored chest of drawers – all at hugely discounted prices, and then shipped them out to France at vast cost, since there was nowhere to store them in my London flat. I also bought, among other things, floral eiderdowns, willow log baskets, an old-fashioned cake stand, an enamel breadbin and watering can, and tasselled curtain tie-backs. I was kitting myself out for My New Life in France. And with every purchase it seemed a step closer.

And now, here I am, a year of acquisitions later, with all these carefully chosen purchases sitting in boxes around me. I am living the moment that I dreamed of for so long. And I am more than a bit scared. What if I start to miss my London life? There is no going back now, and I won't even be able to go and take solace in Selfridges shoe department or call up a friend on the spur of the moment and go out for a glass of champagne.

Having finished my breakfast, I leap over the hole into the kitchen floor and climb the narrow, dusty staircase to the main bedroom. I open the tightly closed shutters – a struggle, as if the house does not want to open up to me – throwing sunlight into the brown room. I imagine Madame Mauboussin sleeping here, reading, possibly lying in bed all day as illness and old age eventually got the better of her. Did she have a lover? I wonder. I really hope so. I can't bear the idea of her growing old here, alone and unloved. I go into the bathroom, looking for clues as to the former occupant. There is no natural light, and the speckled beige floor tiles are reminiscent of a particularly unappealing public lavatory. I open the bottom drawer of the old, surgical pink bathroom cabinet half hanging off the wall above the wash basin. Inside, there is a half-used pink Guerlain lipstick and a gold powder compact. I am struck by the poignancy of this. Madame Mauboussin was keeping up appearances right until the end. Did she like clothes? I wonder. Was there a reason why she didn't marry? Did she have a happy life?

The doorbell rings, taking me by surprise. I stick my head out of the bedroom window and see Claudette standing in the sunshine with a man in a flat cap and blue overalls. '*Coucou, c'est moi!*' she calls. 'And this is Monsieur Joffré, the plumber.' I'm suddenly immensely cheered. Who needs Sarah Beeny when they've got Claudette as a neighbour? '*Alors*, you can tell him everything that you need doing,' she says, after the usual civilities. And so I show Monsieur Joffré up to the dingy bathroom and explain that I need a new boiler, loo and washbasin. (The shower and retiling will have to wait for the time being as I do not have the money to do everything at once.) My spirits soar each time he says '*d'accord*' or '*pas de problème*'. Before leaving, he tells me he will post a *devis* through my door in the next day or so, detailing the exact work and the cost. After years of dealing with London builders, who shake their heads as if you are asking them to recreate the Pyramids of Giza or suck in their cheeks and tell you 'It ain't gonna be cheap', Monsieur Joffré is as refreshing as a *citron pressé*.

'Thank you so much,' I say to Claudette, after he has gone.

'Oh, it's nothing,' she replies. 'And don't you worry. He will do a very good job. Or he'll have me to answer to. *Et voilà*. I must get going too.'

'Claudette, did you know Madame Mauboussin?'

She nods her head. *'Oui.'*

'What was she like?'

'She was very nice,' says Claudette, clearly not wanting to discuss her. 'Now *écoute*. If you want, my husband can help you clear the rubble in the backyard and also the garage.'

Once Claudette has gone, I am seized with a sudden desire to do something, so I go upstairs and rip up the brown carpet in the main bedroom. It is nailed down at the edges but I manage to yank it up, releasing alarming clouds of thick dust into the air in the process. I roll it up into a giant sausage, reminiscent in colour of raw *andouillette*, the famous French delicacy made from pig colon. Whenever I imagined My New Life in France, I saw myself floating around the local market dressed in a selection of splashy floral prints, a straw basket swinging over my arm, not wrestling with a giant carpet sausage. This is not so much self-actualisation as self-flagellation. With great difficulty, I drag the rolled-up carpet into the rear bedroom and stuff it through the window so that it lands on top of the rubble heap in the courtyard. Just as I am brushing the dust off my clothes, the doorbell rings again. I rush downstairs to find Victor the estate agent standing on the doorstep, his bushy moustache obliterated by a profusion of brightly coloured flowers and cellophane.

'Victor, hello. How are you?'

'Not bad,' he says, looking shy. He thrusts the flowers towards me.

'They are very beautiful. What a surprise!' I say, hoping the fact that I am sweating and covered in dust and grime might cool his ardour. Instead, he invites me out for an aperitif that evening. 'But I am very busy with the house,' I say, mindful of Miranda's earlier warning. I do not want to give Victor false hope but he looks so morose that I find myself adding: 'But I will call you when I am free.'

'When?' he asks. 'Tomorrow?'

'I am not sure,' I say. 'But I will call you soon.' As I close the door I feel bad for him. Nothing, I know, hurts like rejection.

I put the flowers in a plastic Evian bottle with the top crudely cut off and then go back to the Libertys' to phone France Telecom and get my phone reconnected. Even though the debacle is France Telecom's fault for sending the bill to the wrong address, I am forced to pay a 'safety deposit' of €150 to get the line reconnected. It is galling but at least it means that my phone will be working within twenty-four hours, which feels like a huge achievement. Tomorrow, I will be able to phone around and chase Monsieur Picherou and the other artisans.

But what to do for the rest of the day? The truth is that I would like to lie down in a dark, cool room and seek refuge from the afternoon's heat. But, since I am staying with Lola and Dylan, I must look busy – like I am getting on with things – so I walk back round to Maison Coquelicot and wonder what to do next. Alain arrives just after lunch with an apology.

Scrupulously polite as ever, he asks me if I have dined well. 'Yes,' I lie, as I don't want to upset him by telling him I haven't had any lunch. He tells me that he couldn't come this morning as Chantal, his girlfriend, is pregnant again and had to go to the hospital for a scan. Chantal is about 15 stone and fierce, with a permanent scowl, so I don't blame him for dropping everything to do her bidding. He puts on a mask and starts to sand away the gloss paint that he so carefully applied to the walls a few weeks ago. The noise is deafening, there is white dust everywhere and it soon becomes apparent that this is a job that could last a lifetime.

I decide to escape for half an hour and go over to Intermarché to buy some basic supplies. Crossing the square in the fierce afternoon sun, I do not see a single soul and when I arrive, the supermarket is closed. I look at my watch – it's 1.45 p.m. – and then remember that in rural France all the shops close between 12.00 and 2.00 p.m. *Bloody marvellous*. I stand in the fierce sun for fifteen minutes, tapping my heels in frustration, worried that I am too much of a type-A personality to live here.

When the supermarket finally opens, I search in vain for an 'organic' or 'bio' section but there isn't one. Instead, there are rows and rows of junk cereals and biscuits. It's very depressing. In London, I only shopped in M&S food hall and I scrupulously ate five (organic) fruits and vegetables a day. In France, I might have to let standards slip for a while. I throw a couple of bottles of Evian into the basket along with a packet of biscuits, a large bar of chocolate and some Brie. Then I join the checkout queue, which is very long. There is only one cashier, and even though there are other staff around, they do not bother to open any more tills. Again, I tap my feet and force myself to breathe deeply. But my fellow shoppers

– all comfortably over sixty – do not seem to have a problem with the slow-moving queue. It's a similar story over at the newsagents, where I stand in line behind ten people buying lottery tickets. There is absolutely no sense of urgency. Despite the fact that the queue is out of the door, several customers linger for a long chat with the proprietor, oblivious to the line behind them. I return to Maison Coquelicot thinking that perhaps I have opted out of my dynamic London lifestyle a decade too early. And since most of the local population is comfortably over sixty, it is already obvious that I have more chance of climbing Everest in a pair of Manolos than meeting the man of my dreams here.

By the end of the day, Alain has made negligible progress in blasting the white gloss off the walls and I have a headache from the noise of the sander and not eating lunch. What I would like most right now is comfort food: roast chicken and mashed potato with lots of organic vegetables. But I am a guest in someone else's home. The Libertys have very kindly allocated me a shelf in their larder for food but I do not want to mess up their spotless kitchen. And since they are both vegetarian, it's probably not very diplomatic to start roasting a chicken. To cheer myself up, I stop off at La Cave Poitevine, the wine shop on the square, and buy a bottle of wine. The owner, Gérard plants a generous four kisses on my cheeks. *'Ah bonjour, Ka-renne,'* he cries, throwing his hands in the air as if it has been an age since he last saw me, when in fact, it was the previous evening. (He has, I think, already identified me as potentially a very good customer.) I ask him to recommend a good red wine for around €6. 'What are you going to be eating with it?' he asks.

'Er… pizza,' I say, since it sounds marginally less tragic than a cheese sandwich.

'OK. This one is very good,' he says, pulling a Médoc off the shelf. 'And I see your husband has now arrived too?'

'Husband? I don't have a husband.'

'Yes, yes, your husband,' Gérard persists. 'The tall man who lives on Rue du Bac and sometimes wears a hat.' I realise that he's talking about Dave.

'Ah no, he is not my husband,' I say, horrified. 'I do not have a husband.'

Gérard looks unconvinced. He gives me a knowing wink as he hands me the bottle of wine. And right on cue, as I am crossing the square to return to the Libertys', I bump into my 'husband'. I am dismayed to see him but not as dismayed as he is to see me. 'Hi Dave,' I say, trying to sound as cheerful as possible. He turns pink, mumbles something inaudible and walks away. My one hope of a social life in the village cannot even bring himself to say hello to me.

Chapter 6

Camping Out

WHEN RENOVATING A house in France, the standard advice is to make one room habitable, and then camp out in it while you do the rest. But I am planning to do some camping of the real kind, as I have to vacate the guest room above the Liberty Bookshop. There are two reasons for this. The first is that Lola's mother is coming to stay for a month; the second is that Lola and Dylan have been lovely to me but I am in danger of becoming the house guest from hell. A few days ago, I crumbled at the idea of bread and cheese for dinner again and, while Lola and Dylan were out at a French lesson, cooked a steak. Unfortunately, they came home early and I was caught in the carnivorous act, thereby offending their vegetarian sensibilities. Lola rushed to find a 'detoxifying' aromatherapy spray, which she sprayed intermittently for several hours afterwards. It didn't help that I carbonised their frying pan in the process. For my part, I have still not mastered their terrifying pump action shower and I cannot wait to have heating (the Libertys are so concerned about global warming that they *never* have the heating on) and to cook real food again.

So I pack up my possessions and prepare to move to the campsite in Beauchamp, 12 kilometres from Villiers and on the banks of a tranquil river. At least I won't have to worry about bumping into Dave and him blanking me again. A couple of evenings before I leave for *le camping*, I arrive back at the Libertys' after a day of sanding floors to find him sitting at a corner table, chatting to Lola and Dylan. My first instinct is to keep on walking, to the back of the bookshop and up the narrow staircase to my room. Instead, I boldly (or, as it turns out, stupidly) go over to join them. Dave carries on talking – recounting some funny story about bringing his microlight over on a trailer – and does not stop to acknowledge my presence.

'Hi Dave,' I say, pulling up a chair next to him. 'How nice to see you.'

He looks pained but mutters 'Hello' in a strange, strangulated voice.

'So how are you?' I persist, determined to make him talk to me. (I figure that with Lola and Dylan present he doesn't have a choice.)

'Fine thanks,' he says, and carries on with his anecdote. Lola and Dylan looked extremely uncomfortable but I stay for another ten minutes and in that time Dave manages not to look at me once. Instead, he converses solely with Lola and Dylan. Every now and again, I ask him a direct question – I must admit, I am enjoying the challenge of making him talk to me – and he answers in one, possibly two words, as if speaking some binary language.

'So how have you been?' I ask, as cheerily as possible.

'Fine thanks.'

'And how's the job going?' I persist.

'Not bad,' he replies, staring pointedly straight ahead at a wall of bookcases, marked 'romantic fiction'.

'How long are you here for?' I ask at another juncture in the conversation. I'm particularly interested in the reply to this, as I want to know how long I've got to avoid him.

'Don't know,' comes the economical reply.

After about ten minutes I give up with a cheery: 'Well, really nice to see you, Dave. Hope to see you again soon.'

His reply is inaudible but his look tells me everything I need to know. From it I deduce that there is no chance of reinstalling myself in Dave's affections (or his flowery guest room) anytime soon.

And so, to the campsite I must go. But camping can be very glamorous with the right accessories. I feel suitably equipped for this experience, since, somewhere, in one of my hastily packed bin bags, there is a floral tent, sent to me several years ago by a fashion PR. And in a strange, masochistic way, I am quite excited by the impending exercise in self-sufficiency. I will, at least, have access to hot water, showers and a loo at the campsite – all still sadly lacking at Maison Coquelicot – and I will be experiencing *la vie rurale* at very close quarters. Even if I do have to rough it a bit, it will only be for a week or so and it will give me a powerful incentive to get things moving on the renovation front.

The Libertys, however, are a little sceptical when I tell them the plan. 'Are you sure that's a good idea?' says Lola. 'Wouldn't you be better off in a *chambre d'hôte* or B&B?'

'Have you ever been camping before?' asks Dylan, looking doubtful.

'No, but how difficult can it be?' I reply, rummaging in another bin bag for my Tiffany penknife (also a gift from a PR).

'Anyway, it's only for a week, while the boiler and plumbing works are being carried out at the house.' And even though it is late September, the weather is on my side and unseasonably warm.

In the end Dylan accompanies me to the campsite on Friday evening to put up my tent, neatly ending my delusions of self-sufficiency. 'Are you sure that's meant for real camping?' he asks, as I pull my tent from its nylon casing.

'Yes,' I say. 'Here's a picture of what it will look like when it's up.'

'Well, at least you won't have any problems finding your way back to it,' he says. I can tell that he disapproves of my tent because it is made from nylon and is not biodegradable.

'Now, have you got a wooden mallet?'

'A wooden mallet?'

'To hammer the tent pegs in.' Dylan reaches into his rucksack and pulls one out. 'Fortunately, at least one of us planned ahead.'

The campsite, by the side of a river and accessed by a stone bridge and a narrow country track, is very peaceful – and, since it is late September, mostly unoccupied. There are just a few camper vans dotted around, mostly occupied by middle-aged French couples making the most of the unseasonably warm autumn weather. I have been given a plot next to one such couple, both sporting khaki shorts, matching fleeces and a tan. They are camping *à la française*: a big camper van with a separate, designated dining area under an awning, from which a delicious smell drifts my way. They are also, I note, drinking wine out of proper wine glasses and are about to eat dinner at a little table laid with real white china and a tablecloth. *Madame* watches as Dylan and I unfurl the small, flower-power tent and whispers something to Monsieur, who looks over with a wry smile.

'Now are you sure you are going to be OK?' says Dylan, packing his mallet back into the rucksack. 'Remember, if you change your mind you can always book into Le Vieux Chateau for a few nights.'

'Oh no, I'll be fine,' I say. 'It's so peaceful here.'

Less than half an hour later I am sitting inside my sleeping bag, taking alternate bites out of a lump of Brie and a stale baguette, when the peace of the campsite is shattered. A camper van draws up in such close proximity to my tent that I fear it is going to park on top of me. Amid much shouting and laughing, at least half a dozen men roll out and proceed to have a party. They are not the only newcomers. In less than an hour, the tranquil campsite becomes the equivalent of an all-male Glastonbury, with a sudden influx of camper vans, motorbikes and men. Most of them seem to be travelling in large groups. The countryside rings to the sound of male laughter, and the persistent beat of my neighbours' ghetto blaster, regularly interspersed by the sound of cans of lager being opened and someone peeing in the bushes nearby.

Lying in my sleeping bag and attempting to read by torchlight another memoir of someone living the good life in France, it occurs to me that some might view this as a marvellous opportunity. Miranda, for example, finding herself camped out in the middle of what appears to be a stag party, would no doubt put on some lipstick, grab a beer and join in. Me, I lie in the dark wondering why they have all decided to converge here off-season.

The answer presents itself the next day. A huge 'TRIATHLON' banner has been erected across the campsite and there are racing bikes everywhere – propped against bushes or tents or hung on the side of camper vans. Emerging stiffly from my tent, I see lots of men in cobalt-blue Lycra, already up and about and performing muscle stretches in the early morning sunshine. My neighbours, dressed in form-hugging sunflower yellow, are frying sausages on a small gas stove. One of them waves a cheery *'Bonjour'* as I pass by on the way to the shower block. *'C'est jolie, votre tente!'* he declares.

'Merci,' I reply, not sure if he is being facetious.

In the shower block – fortunately *not* unisex – I encounter yet another irritating shower. Unlike the Libertys' high-tech monster, this one does not take you by surprise with cold jets from odd angles but it does require you to push a button every ten seconds in order to keep the water going. I perform a curious hopping routine to try and get dressed in the small cubicle without dropping or trailing my clothes on the wet floor and, once again, think longingly of my former bathroom in London with its power shower, pale limestone tiling and ladder radiator with warm, fluffy towels.

The manager of the campsite rushes over as I leave the shower block. 'Madame, you have paid for this evening also?' he asks. 'Because there is a sporting event happening today and I must tell you that access by car will not be possible later. The campsite entrance will be closed all day.'

'That's OK. I am leaving now and won't be back until this evening.'

'And tonight there will be a big barbecue but you must buy a ticket.'

'Thank you, but I already have plans for this evening.' *I have plans for this evening.* The campsite manager has no idea what pleasure it gives me to be able to say those words, for tonight

I have my first real social engagement since moving to France. It's a dinner party at Miranda's, and the opportunity not only to dress up but to socialise with some *real* French people. Miranda hasn't told me exactly who is coming – 'It's a surprise, darling' – but has promised that at least two of the guests will be French, both of them male and single. As you can imagine, my expectations are high.

I drive to the outskirts of Poitiers and spend a useful hour in Castorama, looking at wood stains and varnish for the wooden floorboards, before visiting the DIY store Leroy Merlin, where I am accused of shoplifting. This is because I did not declare my electric toothbrush charger (for which I was seeking an adaptor) on entering the store. Fortunately, the girl at reception remembers me revealing my charger on entry and asking for help, so I am eventually allowed to leave, but I am bristling with indignation at the idea that I would steal something of such low net worth. Still, it teaches me a valuable lesson: in France, the customer is always guilty until proven innocent.

Afterwards, I drive into the centre of Poitiers and walk to the main square. There is a food market taking place in the shadow of Notre Dame Cathedral and, unlike the few stalls that pass for a market in Villiers, this appears to be the real French deal. People are bustling around with baskets or pull-along shopping trolleys, squeezing, sniffing or sampling the goods. Many stalls sell just one product – goat's cheese, artichokes or exotic looking breads, for example – and the shopping process, I notice, is rife with flirtation: 'Did you make those yourself, Monsieur?' one elegantly dressed woman asks a man selling fluffy white goat's cheeses.

'Yes, with my own hands, Madame. Would you like to taste a little piece?'

'Oh, but they look lovely, your pears!' I hear another woman cry.

The produce itself looks very alluring: purple-green cabbages sprouting like big flower brooches, small black prunes glistening like jet beads, heads of purple and white garlic strung together like a necklace. There are aubergines, the same opulent shade of purple-black as a YSL *smoking*, piles of large mushrooms, their undersides pleated like a Vionnet gown, and stalls selling pungent frills of parsley and basil or velvety green leaves of sage, while plump and shiny red and green peppers nestle in wooden boxes. Unfortunately, none of this is much use to me as I am weeks, if not months, away from a functioning kitchen and mostly living on bread and Brie.

As I contemplate this depressing thought, a man pushes a plate of *saucisson* towards me. Would I like a little taste? Why not? I spear a disc of the claret-coloured sausage and savour its salty deliciousness.

'Yes, it's very good,' I say. 'I would like one please.'

Smiling, the stallholder wraps a *saucisson* in wax paper and hands it to me. 'Thats thirty-two euros,' he says.

'How much?' I gulp, thinking that I have misheard. 'That seems a little expensive.'

He explains that the *saucisson* has been dried and left to mature for several years, that the pigs that produced it were fed a very good diet and it has been handmade to a recipe passed down from his grandmother. It seems churlish to argue. (I later discover that many an *Anglais* makes this mistake, assuming that all market produce is cheap and not bothering to check the price before being hit with a €40 bill for a small wedge of rarefied cheese.)

The sight of all this food is making me hungry. The cafes around the cathedral are packed with couples and groups of friends enjoying the autumn sunshine – and lunch. I think how nice it would be to have someone to eat lunch with: a leisurely Kir, followed by *steak frites*, or even an omelette and a glass of red wine. I think back fondly to the days when Dave and I were still friends. One of the great things about him was that he was always up for a long lunch.

I buy a *pain au chocolat* and a bag of chocolate-coated nuts in the Cordeliers shopping mall and eat my lunch alone sitting on a bench outside the *hôtel de ville*.

The cycling stage of the triathlon is reaching a culmination when I return to the campsite early that evening. I park my car on a grass verge half a mile away and pick my way back into the campsite through a crowd of cheering spectators and past groups of men pedalling furiously in shiny Lycra. Miranda has very kindly offered to pick me up at 7.30 p.m., as she says it would be very difficult to find her house on my own. I call from my mobile to warn her about the triathlon. At least she won't have any problems finding my tent. I perform a strange series of contortions inside my tent in order to change into a green swirly print dress and sparkly black sandals. I crawl back out and wonder what to do with myself until Miranda arrives. The 'must-have' accessory on a campsite, I realise, is a camping chair. The couple in the camper van next to me look very comfortable as they sip aperitifs in theirs. Rather than face the ignominy of sitting on damp grass, I crawl back inside the tent and wait and think to myself, What a waste! The campsite is wall-to-wall men – hundreds of them, all fit, buff and primed for action. I am surrounded by more eligible men than I have met in a lifetime of living in London and here I am hiding in a pod of floral nylon.

'*Coucou!* Anyone home?' I am thrilled to hear Miranda's voice. 'My word, isn't this just darling? And so clever of you to put up a tent all by yourself...'

I crawl out on my hands and knees to meet her.

'Oh *dis donc*, look at you! You look divine. It's so important to maintain standards, even when camping,' she says, kissing me through a cloud of Shalimar. She is wearing a purple satin dress, a feathered headband and high heels. This campsite, I think to myself, has probably never seen such kit.

'So you weren't tempted to don a Lycra suit and join in the triathlon then?' she says.

'Tempting, but no.'

'Well, darling, this is definitely what I would call integration. You're completely surrounded by Frenchmen. If I had a tent, I'd come and join you.' We head back out of the campsite, Miranda teetering along in her high heels. '*Allez, Monsieur!*' shouts Miranda, at one particularly handsome athlete, who turns around and gives her a little wave.

Miranda is right. I would never have found her house on my own. It is tucked away on a dark, narrow track leading from a dirt road. There are a few other barn conversions dotted around nearby, but Miranda's house feels isolated and alone. The front door opens immediately into a windowless kitchen and dining area. It is dark, sombre and chilly. There is a wood-burning stove (unlit), with two very scary looking swords placed above it, and a rather stern, dark wood dining table, which is not laid. Nor is there evidence of any cooking activity, which is disappointing as I am starving and looking forward to my first home-cooked meal in weeks.

Miranda lights a solitary candle and places it on the dining table. 'So, darling girl, what can I offer you to drink? What about a glass of white wine – though I'm afraid it's nothing fancy? Job lot from Lidl!'

'Lidl?'

'Discount store. Fabulous value!'

'That would be nice,' I lie. Cheap white wine always gives me a headache.

She pours us both a glass of wine and then says, 'I know! What about some fairy lights? It would brighten the place up. I do so love fairy lights.' She runs upstairs and returns with a string of red, flowery lights that between us we string across the rear wall, Miranda balancing on a chair in her high heels. 'There,' she says taking a large gulp of wine. 'What do you think? Do they look OK?'

'Very nice.'

'Really? You're not just saying that?'

'No, they definitely add something.'

'Now I must just quickly paint my nails.'

'Is there anything I can do to help?' I ask.

'Oh no, darling. It's all under control.'

I sit opposite Miranda at the table and watch as she produces a bottle of Chanel nail polish and proceeds, in a leisurely fashion, to paint her nails.

'So who else is coming this evening?' I ask.

Miranda looks hesitant, embarrassed almost.

'Well, let's see… there's Desmond and Elinor. You'll love them. Elinor teaches yoga. Desmond is retired but he used to be a bank manager – I think. They're both strict lacto-vegetarians and very into healthy living, but don't worry, they're good fun.'

'Right,' I say, thinking that I have yet to meet a strict lacto-vegetarian who was really good fun.

'Now, darling, I have to tell you that I also invited Dave.'

'Dave? You did?'

'Yes. I've no idea what's going on between you and I don't want to know – but he was absolutely adamant that he wouldn't come when he found out that I had invited you.'

'He said that?' I say, surprised at how hurt I feel at this news.

'Yes,' says Miranda. 'It's a shame, as I always thought he was a bit of a dish. And now that his divorce has come through, he's single and, word has it, very much looking for a girlfriend. I rather thought that you two might... you know.'

'We were good friends,' I say. 'But now he won't even talk to me.'

'What a shame,' says Miranda. 'Perhaps he'll come round eventually.'

'Perhaps,' I say, feeling doubtful. 'But I'm really sorry that it's causing other people problems because they can't invite us both to the same thing.'

'Well, it's his loss entirely, darling. But I had to make up the numbers somehow, so... I hope you don't mind, but I've invited Victor.'

'Victor!' The news is lurching from bad to worse.

'Yes, darling. But don't worry. I think he's got the message that you're not interested. And he's promised me that he'll be terribly well-behaved.'

'Right.'

'Oh, and I also invited Jacques, one of my neighbours. A farmer. Single! He's *darling*, though he's on antidepressants at the moment. I thought a little outing would cheer him up. Don't be put off by his slightly brusque manner. Underneath it all, he's got charm to spare.'

'ANYONE HOME?' shouts a cheery male voice, as he opens the door. Miranda jumps up. 'Desmond!' she says. As she does so she spills the bottle of Chanel polish, pouring a little pool of plum liquid onto the dining table. 'Oh *merde!*' she cries.

'Don't move,' says Desmond, marching confidently into the room in crisp, pale cotton trousers, pink polo shirt and sand-coloured corduroy jacket. 'I'll deal with it.'

He hands Miranda a bottle of champagne and then finds a cloth and some white spirit to clean up the polish, negotiating his way around Miranda's kitchen with ease. Job done, he briskly washes his hands and then takes charge of the drinks.

'Isn't he the perfect gentleman?' says Miranda, as Desmond expertly pops a champagne cork.

'I like to look after my ladies,' he says with a wink.

'Have you met Karen?' Miranda asks.

'No,' says Desmond, 'but I'd like to.' He grabs my hand, shaking it firmly and pressing his lips to my cheeks. His wife – an elegant blonde in her late forties – greets me with a friendly smile. 'So you've just moved to Villiers?' she says. 'How lovely! Are you going to be based here full-time?'

'Yes,' I say, explaining that the plan is to write from home for British newspapers.

'She's a fashion and beauty journalist,' declares Miranda. 'Isn't that wonderful?

'And I hear you're a yoga teacher,' I say to Elinor, who bears the markings of every yoga teacher I have ever met: clear skin, lustrous hair and a lean, bendy looking body. Even her fragrance

– I recognise it as Green Tea by Elizabeth Arden – smells clean and wholesome. 'Well, yes, but only on an informal basis now. I do voluntary work for a charity for the bereaved, which takes up most of my time.'

There is another knock at the door and Victor arrives, also clutching a bottle of champagne. He seems to know everyone – Desmond and Elinor, it transpires, bought their house from him – although he looks slightly sheepish when he sees me.

'And are you busy at the agency, Victor?' asks Elinor in perfect French.

'Ah non,' he replies. 'Things are terrible at the moment. Terrible! All the English, they are selling up and leaving. And no one is coming to take their place...'

'Good,' says Desmond. 'The less English there are out here, the better.'

Jacques, the depressed farmer, is the last to arrive. He is very short (like most men in the Poitou-Charentes, it seems to me) with cheeks as pink as pomegranate pips. Miranda greets him enthusiastically, flinging her arms around him, and introducing him as 'my very good friend Jacques'. She says this in a very meaningful way. He hands her a bunch of flowers and looks embarrassed.

'So you're a farmer, are you?' says Desmond in English.

'Yes.'

'Agriculture or livestock?'

'Livestock,' says Miranda.

'What kind?'

'Cows.'

'For beef?'

'Yes.'

'Ah,' says Desmond.

'Oh let's not go there,' says Miranda. 'We know you're a vegetarian, Desmond. But no need to force it down everyone's throats. Yes, Jacques slaughters cattle for a living. This is the countryside, you know, and that's what people do here. Aren't these flowers lovely? Thank you so much, Jacques.'

'What about CAP?' says Desmond.

'*Comment?*' asks Jacques.

'The Common Agricultural Policy,' Desmond continues in English. 'I must say you chaps get rather a good deal out of the rest of Europe. All those brand new combine harvesters.'

'Oh do shut up, darling,' says Elinor.

'Generous subsidies, interest-free loans to buy hundreds of thousands of pounds worth of farm machinery... No benefits like that for English farmers, you know...'

Fortunately, Jacques doesn't seem to understand.

'And what really makes me mad,' continues Desmond, 'is the way the French turn their noses up at British beef. Not that I eat the stuff, you understand, but we weren't the only ones to have mad cow disease you know...'

'Darling,' says Elinor. 'That's enough.'

Personally, I can think of nothing nicer than tucking into a big juicy steak right now, with or without mad cow disease. But there is still no sign of any food, not even nibbles, and I am beginning to think that I misinterpreted Miranda's invitation to 'come over for a bite to eat'. The conversation limps painfully on, until eventually Miranda announces that dinner is about to be served. I am intrigued, as there are no delicious food aromas and no sign of any cooking activity. Not even the ping of a microwave.

'I'll lay the table, shall I?' says Desmond, opening a drawer and producing cutlery.

'I'll help you, darling,' says Elinor, moving towards her husband and placing her arm around his waist, the metal bangles on her wrist jangling as she does so. They make a striking couple. Elinor, in a pea-green cashmere sweater and tight jeans tucked into knee boots, dresses more youthfully than most ex-pats I have seen – shapeless jeans and fleeces in washed-out colours being the uniform of *l'Anglais* abroad.

'Oh, *please*! No public displays of affection, thank you!' says Miranda, swaying towards the fridge with her glass of champagne and producing a glass bowl covered in cling film.

'What is that?' asks Jacques.

'Chilled strawberry soup,' says Miranda, placing it down on the table, a little clumsily, so that some of the pink liquid slops over the side.

The strawberry soup is not unpleasant – rather like eating melted strawberry sorbet – but as a starter for a chilly autumn evening, it takes everyone by surprise. Jacques is unimpressed. 'Miranda [he pronounces it *Meeranda*], I cannot eat this,' he says with startling honesty after one spoonful. 'It will give me indigestion.'

Desmond fixes him with a cold, hard look. 'This is delicious,' he says, loudly and rather too enthusiastically. 'Absolutely delicious. Isn't it Elinor?'

Elinor nods her head in agreement. 'Absolutely,' she says. 'Well done, darling.'

'Honestly?' Miranda's face lights up. 'You're not just saying that? I thought I would try something a little different. And it's got hardly any calories in it. I used a low-cal sugar substitute. I've never tried it before but I saw the recipe in a Californian diet book and thought it sounded quite interesting.'

'Yes,' says Victor. 'It's interesting.'

We eat the soup in silence. Miranda, I notice, does not eat, but refills her champagne glass several times, which is worrying – not least because I am relying on her to give me a lift back to the campsite. The main course is vegetarian couscous dotted with sultanas and served cold with a sweet, caramel-coloured sauce. No one bothers to ask what it is. Jacques, I notice, rummages in his jacket pocket for a bottle of pills and swallows several between courses. For pudding, Miranda serves cucumber sorbet, which Jacques declines, saying that he has sensitive teeth. By now, the two bottles of champagne have been drunk, mostly by Miranda, who has steered the conversation around to whether French or English men make the better lovers. Victor and Jacques both look uncomfortable, as does Elinor. Only Desmond seems at ease, leaning back in his chair and laughing. 'Well, perhaps you can tell us what *you* think?'

'How should I know?' says Miranda. 'I've been on my own for nearly thirty years.'

Desmond sits back in his chair and laughs. 'Is that so?' he says.

'Yes it is, thank you very much,' says Miranda. 'As you well know, after my ex-husband I need another man in my life like I need a railway line in my back garden.'

'I must be going soon,' says Jacques in French. 'I am hunting tomorrow morning.'

'Oh, you can't leave yet,' says Miranda, looking hurt.

'What did he say?' asks Desmond.

'He says he must go soon as he is hunting tomorrow.'

'Oh you hunt, do you?' says Desmond, bristling, his lips pursed in disapproval. 'What exactly do you hunt?'

'Tomorrow, wild boar,' replies Jacques in French. 'But deer, rabbits, hares – in fact, everything that the forest offers, when it is the right season.'

'What is he saying?' asks Desmond, and I sense we are heading into dodgy territory.

'I know!' says Miranda, suddenly. 'Let's dance!'

She puts on a Johnny Cash CD and starts to dance to 'Ring of Fire', pulling Jacques up to join her. 'Come on, my old firework, I know how you love to dance.'

'No,' says Jacques. 'It is time for me to go.'

'I'll dance with you,' says Desmond gallantly getting up from the table.

Victor picks up the bottle of wine and tries to refill Elinor's wine glass, but she extends her hand to stop him. 'No thank you, darling,' she says, softly. 'I'm driving.'

To my relief, Elinor and Desmond offer to drop me off at the campsite on their way home.

'I didn't like that farmer chap,' says Desmond, as we pull away.

'Oh, I thought he seemed rather nice,' says Elinor.

'He was a jerk,' says Desmond. 'No manners whatsoever. Did you hear what he said about the soup?'

'Darling, you don't like him because he kills animals.'

'It's not just that. I'm worried he might try and take advantage of Miranda. You know how vulnerable she is.'

'Yes, darling, but Jacques didn't strike me as that sort of man. Now, Karen, I'm a little worried about you staying at this campsite tonight. Are you sure you won't come and spend the night in our *gite?*'

'It's kind of you,' I say. 'But I've put up my tent and now I'm going to lie in it.'

'You know there is a storm forecast for tonight?' says Desmond.

'No, I didn't, but I'll be fine,' I say.

'Well what about all those noisy athletes that you told us about?' says Elinor.

'Maybe they'll be too exhausted to make any noise tonight,' I say.

'Well, I insist that you take our telephone number just in case you change your mind,' says Elinor.

The barbecue is in full swing when Desmond and Elinor deposit me in darkness outside my tent. But at least the action is taking place on the other side of the campsite. The distant hum of people enjoying themselves is actually quite comforting as I try to make myself comfortable on the cold, hard ground. I've been trying to go to sleep for about ten minutes when suddenly the air is rent by a very loud noise and I sit bolt upright in my sleeping bag as the sound of 'Ra-Ra-Rasputin' by Boney M thunders over the loudspeakers. (DJs in the French countryside, I've noticed, are very fond of Boney M.) Then, just to compound my misery, it starts to rain. And rain. Water pours down from the sky, rebounding off the top of my tent while, inside, condensation drips off the inner lining. How, I wonder, did my life come to this – lying in a tent in the middle of nowhere, cold and alone and being rained on?

Surprisingly, I manage to fall asleep – to the sound of Phil Collins singing 'I can feel it coming in the air tonight...' But this happy oblivion does not last long. At around 3.00 a.m. I am woken by a terrifying bang. I sit bolt upright in my sleeping bag for a second time. Bright white light flashes around me and for a moment I think my tent has somehow relocated itself to the dance floor. But then there is another loud crash, followed a few seconds later by rain hammering down. This is the storm that Desmond predicted. The bangs become louder and louder, interspersed by flashes of lightning at ever-quickening intervals. It is unlike any storm I have ever experienced in the UK. I think of Desmond and Elinor lying in bed in their safe farmhouse. I think of Miranda, probably bedded down with a bottle of wine; of the Libertys, cosy under their thick (ethically produced) Mongolian wool blankets; and of my neighbour Claudette and her husband, safe from the storm behind closed shutters. I also think of Dave and his flowery guest room, in which I could now be safely tucked up if we hadn't fallen out.

And I decide that rather than lie here waiting to be struck by lightning, I will go and sit in the car. Condensation dripping from the roof of the tent, I grope around in the dark for my glasses, pull on my clothes and bolt towards the car. In the few seconds that it takes to unlock the door, I am completely soaked. It's like standing in a freezing cold power shower with your clothes on. I hurl myself inside and sit, hair dripping, glasses steamed up, wondering what to do with myself until dawn.

The storm rages for over three hours. I sit in the darkness in my sopping wet cocktail dress and ruined Prada shoes and watch, terrified, wondering if it is possible to be struck by lightning while sitting in a car. This is *so* not a situation that a woman my age should find herself in. When morning finally comes, and as soon as there is a gap in the rain, I take down my soggy, muddy tent, chuck it in the back of the car, drive back to Villiers and book into Le Vieux Chateau.

Chapter 7

Moving In

LE VIEUX CHATEAU costs €50 a night, which seems extravagant when I am not earning, but if it means that I don't have to fall asleep listening to Phil Collins, it's worth it. The room itself is very basic but there is a bathtub and a hot meal to look forward to at the end of the day, since I manage to persuade the staff of the attached restaurant to deliver *steak frites* or *le plat du jour* and a glass of red wine to my room in the evening. It seems like utter luxury (a concept that has been radically redefined for me since moving to France: where once it was a hot new handbag, now it is hot water and a bed).

I stay at Le Vieux Chateau for a week, since, with the synchronicity of swallows arriving in their winter grounds, the artisans have suddenly turned up en masse: Monsieur Joffré the plumber, Monsieur Picherou the carpenter and a team of Gitane-smoking electricians from *Gattelier et Fils* all arrive within days of each other. I pop in occasionally to make sure they are still there and I haven't imagined it, but mostly I keep a low profile. I can't see much through the fug of cigarette smoke anyway.

Late on Friday afternoon, after a pleasant day spent in Poitiers looking at large electrical appliances, I go over to check on the house. It is clear that the curtain has dropped on summer. The days have started to shorten now and the tables and chairs outside the Café du Commerce have been put away until next year. As always, Marie-Claude's beauty salon is busy with a constant stream of well-groomed French women coming and going, while the Liberty Bookshop looks warm and inviting, lit up like a cruise ship in the autumn gloom. I am tempted to pop in for coffee and a chat with Dylan but I know that if I do I will bump into someone I know and end up staying for over an hour. (Though if it's one of the villagers, I can always justify it on the grounds that I am improving my French.)

I turn into Rue St Benoit feeling nervous. After the episode with the white gloss paint, I am always wary as to what I might find. Most of my neighbours have already closed their shutters for the evening – in very cold or very hot weather, some of them don't open their shutters at all – and I see Claudette, in her floral apron, coming out to perform the nightly ritual of closing hers. '*Ça va?*' she shouts, looking very excited to see me. '*Ecoute!*' she says, kissing me on both cheeks. 'Have you seen the new baker?'

Have I seen the new baker? I have been going in there every day since he arrived and have even started putting my contact lenses in especially.

'Yes,' I reply. 'I went in this morning to buy a baguette. His bread is very good.'

'Oh, his bread is *magnifique*,' agrees Claudette, kissing her hand for emphasis. 'And his pastries. He only uses pure butter, you know. *Mais, écoute!* What I wanted to tell you is this: the new baker, he is single! He does not have a wife.' She nudges me and gives me a wink. 'It could be good to have a *pâtissier* for a husband, no?'

I agree. A pastry chef – and *surtout* a French one – would make an excellent boyfriend. But I have seen the new baker, who is a big, handsome bear of a man with a dark, stubbly chin. I cannot believe that he is single. Claudette must have made a mistake.

'Are you sure he is single?' I say. 'I cannot believe that a man as handsome as him and so good at making cakes is not already taken.'

'I am certain that he is not married,' says Claudette, 'because I asked him.'

'Well, that's very exciting.'

'Yes, and he is already very popular. Everyone is queuing to get his bread.'

'What happened to the other baker and his wife?' I ask, because the change of ownership at the *boulangerie* was all very sudden.

'They have gone back to Paris,' says Claudette, performing an exaggerated sniff and flicking her hair back. 'They felt they were too grand for our little village.'

This explains a lot. I had started to take their dour demeanour and constant look of disapproval personally until I discovered that they were equally unfriendly to everyone in the village. And now I know why: after the bright lights of the city, they had felt Villiers was beneath them. We were country bumpkins in comparison to the *beau monde* of Paris.

'*Et voilà,*' says Claudette. 'So, everyone has been very busy at your house this week.'

'Come and have a look,' I say, turning the key in the lock.

Claudette follows me into the dusty sitting room, and we pick our way through the various cardboard boxes, cans of paint and other decorating equipment. *'Oh, il est beau!'* she says, on seeing the new oak kitchen floor. It is not quite what I expected; the oak is pale and untreated and looks anaemic – not the rich chestnut colour I envisaged. Still, it represents a real advancement on the health and safety front – no more having to jump across a cavernous hole to reach the staircase – and the first step towards a proper, fully functioning kitchen

'Oh he has worked very well, Monsieur Picherou,' says Claudette. 'With a little wood stain and some wax to protect it, this floor will be perfect.'

Monsieur Joffré, meanwhile, has installed a toilet and wash basin in the bathroom, as well as a new boiler in the garage adjoining the house and an enormous white plastic 1,000 litre oil tank. As soon as I can arrange an oil delivery, I will have hot water. A real breakthrough! The electrical works also seem to be progressing; there are new sockets and power points in all the places that I marked with pink Post-it stickers although, rather disconcertingly, there are wires hanging down from the ceiling where the light pendants and light bulbs should be. Claudette and I make a tour of the house, my neighbour scrutinising everything much more closely than me. She is a little disapproving of the electrical works. 'This could be better,' she says, pointing to plastic casing that covers the wires. 'Monsieur Gattelier's apprentices would be better to work more slowly and with more care. They are very young and lack concentration.' But I am overjoyed at the progress that has been made. If I set my mind to it – and with a final push on the bedroom over the weekend – I could move in by Monday.

'Oof! I had better go as my husband is waiting for his dinner,' says Claudette, when we have finished our inspection. 'But don't forget what I told you about the *boulanger*!'

Feeling energised, I call Alain and offer him a fixed sum to get the bedroom floor sanded and varnished by Sunday evening. 'I will help you myself,' I say, and there is silence at the other end of the phone. But this doesn't deter him. He arrives early on Saturday morning and starts to sand the bedroom floor with enthusiasm, while I play around with wood tints in the garage. By lunchtime, the floorboards have been sanded back to a pale, nude state. The next step, according to the enormous DIY tome that I brought over from the UK, is to clean the boards with a cloth soaked in methylated spirits. While Alain is at lunch, eager to press on, I get to work with the meths. It's a deeply unpleasant job and the fumes make me feel light-headed and nauseous, like I'm suffering from a hangover but without any of the fun beforehand. By the time Alain returns there is a cloud of concentrated alcohol lingering in the air – I warn him not to light a cigarette as we could both go up in flames – but he seems impressed by my efforts and we are ready to move to the next stage.

I've narrowed down the choice of wood tints (having bought at least a dozen different colours from pale oak to dark walnut) and decided on a rich chestnut brown. Alain and I set to work in companionable silence, starting at opposite ends of the room and painting the colour onto the boards as evenly as possible with a wide brush. It takes an hour for the tint to dry and with almost perfect timing Claudette arrives at the front door, bearing a tray with two cups of coffee and two slices of home-made apple tart. We eat it perched on crates in the *petit salon*, and it tastes, at that moment in time, as good as a lunch in an Alain Ducasse restaurant.

'Come and look at the bedroom,' I say, leading her upstairs and showing her the floor.

'*Oh, c'est magnifique!*' she exclaims. 'You did this yourself? With Alain? Since yesterday evening?'

'Yes,' I say, proudly. 'But it is not finished yet.'

'Oh you have worked well, the two of you. *Ecoute!* When this floor is done, we will put up your bed and move in your furniture and then you can be totally calm and tranquil in this room. Just tell me when you are ready, and my husband and I will help you.'

'Thank you so much. It's very, very kind of you,' I say, thinking how lucky I am to have Claudette as a neighbour. In west London your neighbours were more likely to run off with your bag or steal your car wing mirrors than knock on your door with cake and offers of help.

'It's nothing,' she replies, waving away my thanks. 'It's normal.' But I have done nothing to merit the kindness of my neighbour and it is incredibly humbling.

While Alain returns to the thankless task of removing the tenacious white gloss, I apply the *vitrificateur*, or satin finish varnish that I brought with me from the UK (where for some reason paint and varnishes are much cheaper and far better quality than their French equivalent) to the floorboards. This is a very slow and painstaking process since, according to the instructions, you must do no more than a couple of boards at a time to avoid overlapping. It also releases another toxic burst of volatile compounds into the bedroom. And since it is too cold to open the windows and ventilate the room as advised on the tin, I inhale a concentrated dose of the noxious, sickly smelling vapours. The other problem with this task, I realise, is that if you are not careful, you can end up stranded in the middle of the room surrounded by newly varnished boards and with no escape route.

Alain and I work late into Saturday evening, listening to some of my old Ibiza CDs, which he seems to like. Before leaving, he shakes my hand, scrupulously polite as ever, and wishes me *une très bonne soirée* – even though there is only an hour left of it. I walk back to my little room at Le Vieux Chateau, feeling exhausted but happy, the tiredness, brought on by hard physical labour, a pleasant one. The air is cold and scented with wood smoke – the scent of rural France in winter. I inhale deeply: it is a pleasure to breathe the night air after the potent *mélange* of chemicals in an enclosed space. The village is deserted, as it always is at this hour. In the summer that I first saw the house, Dave told me that there was a set of secret underground tunnels running underneath the village, which is why you never saw anyone in the heat of the afternoon. (He was joking of course, but for a while I believed him, thinking they were old war tunnels or something.)

It's a similar story in winter. After 7.00 p.m., Villiers is as impenetrable as a fortress, with not even a chink of light visible from the surrounding houses. Everything is closed for miles around; no nipping down to the corner shop for an emergency supply of Quality Street as I once would have done in London. Instead, there is a real sense of closing the shutters, lighting the fire and climbing into one's burrow with a bottle of Bordeaux. I cannot wait to be able to do the same at Maison Coquelicot. As I head back to my hotel room, I think of the lives unfolding behind those closed shutters: the families and the elderly couples gathered around dinner tables or chatting around a roaring log fire. I think of Dave, who is still in residence on the other side of the church. I figure he must have quit his job in the UK but I wonder how he is surviving financially. I have tried to casually extract information from Lola and Dylan, but they are far too discreet to give anything away, although Lola did let slip that Dave had invited them over for dinner this evening. Back in my hotel room with just French TV for company, I picture him in his cosy, terracotta-tiled kitchen with his comprehensive selection of cooking equipment and his roaring log fire and I wonder who else he has invited this evening. Dave always liked to entertain in large numbers. If I'm honest, I cannot bear the fact that I am no longer part of it.

I return to Maison Coquelicot the following morning to apply another coat of lacquer (eight hours' drying time is required between each one) and then late in the afternoon, I repeat the procedure for the third and final time. When I've finished, I look at the smooth expanse of glossy chestnut and feel something akin to euphoria (although it could just be the effect of all the chemicals I have ingested over the past forty-eight hours.) There is, I realise, a sense of achievement from physical labour that you don't get from sitting in front of a computer all day. Still, I must be patient and wait another twenty-four hours for the lacquer to dry before moving in the furniture. Downstairs, Alain is finally winning the battle with the white gloss.

Monday morning arrives – a momentous day. I arrange an oil delivery, and in the afternoon I check out of Le Vieux Chateau and return to Maison Coquelicot, stupidly excited, but also nervous at the thought of spending my first night there. I head straight upstairs to admire my handiwork and spend a happy ten minutes gliding across the smooth, lacquered floor in my socks, as if on a skating rink. *I'm in! Finally!* The bedroom, with its newly primed chestnut-coloured floor and walls stripped back to plaster and painted in Farrow & Ball's creamy-coloured

New White, is unrecognisable from the gloomy brown room that I inherited.

An hour or so later, a small tanker arrives and deposits 1,000 litres of fuel in my oil tank. After months of inactivity, now everything is happening at once. Claudette comes round to help unpack my clothes and hang them on a clothing rail. '*Oh, ce sont jolies,*' she exclaims again and again as we unpack an embarrassing amount of shoes, handbags and laughably impractical clothes. Where in the French countryside, for example, am I going to wear a silver sequinned micro-skirt (where, for that matter, did I wear it in London?), a full-length black plissé silk evening gown or a pair of leopard-print court shoes? But My New Life in France will be vastly improved by not having to rummage around in a pile of black bin bags in order to get dressed in the morning.

Later that afternoon, with the help of Claudette and her husband, I move my desk into the bedroom (on a temporary basis until the *petit salon* is finished) and assemble my Laura Ashley bed. '*Oh, qu'il est beau ton lit,*' says Claudette, when the white iron bed is in place. It takes quite a while to assemble the bed, mostly because I cannot find the bolts (despite putting them in a white envelope in London, saying NB: BED BOLTS). I finally locate the envelope stuffed inside a champagne glass – no, I don't know what I was thinking either – in one of the cardboard boxes in the sitting room.

It is already dark when Claudette and her husband leave, not before enquiring about my dining arrangements for the evening and asking if I would like them to bring me some home-made soup. But I am too excited to bother with dinner. Instead, I unpack the new pillows and make up the bed, using the new, crisp Egyptian cotton sheets and duvet cover that I bought all those months ago in London in anticipation of exactly this moment. I put a cardboard box next to the bed to act as an impromptu bedside table, cover it with a pillowcase and plug in a night lamp on top of it. *Et voilà*. I have a bedroom.

I then give the bathroom a good clean, removing the mound of plaster, rubble, electrical wiring and piping that has been dumped in the shower tray. I scrub the bathroom floor using liberal amounts of bleach and attack the grimy 1970s tiling on the walls with a determination once reserved for the Prada sample sale. And then I take my first shower in my new home and wash my hair, marvelling at the simple but remarkable fact that I have hot water.

A strong smell of chemicals lingers in the bedroom but as I climb in between the sheets, everything is clean and all seems perfect. I am looking forward to a relaxed evening reading my book – another 'good life in France' memoir, in which the author cooks and eats lots of delicious meals – followed by a tranquil night's sleep, with no triathletes or Phil Collins for company.

Unfortunately, I am woken in the middle of the night by pests of a different kind. The first manifestation of this is an intense, unbearable itching sensation around my ankles. I switch on the bedside light and discover that my ankles, legs, arms and even my stomach are covered in big angry bites the size of buttons. I have been bitten by mosquitoes many times before – it's as if my blood is made of honey as far as insects are concerned – but *nothing* compares to these bites. I feel ill just looking at the big berry-coloured blotches, and am alarmed as to what kind of creature has caused them. Unable to sleep for scratching, I lie in bed, waiting for morning to come so that I can rush out and buy some calamine lotion.

At around 5.00 a.m. I finally stop scratching and drop off to sleep – only to be woken up thirty minutes later by someone frantically ringing my doorbell. Outside, I can hear the engine of a truck running. Throwing open the bedroom window, I peer into the darkness below and see a man in a fluorescent yellow jacket and trousers pointing at my car, which is blocking the progress of the refuse truck down the narrow cobblestoned street. I run downstairs in my floral print silk pyjamas and try to find my car keys in the chaos of furniture, dust and cardboard boxes in the sitting room. The truck outside toots its horn impatiently, ensuring that my neighbours are also woken up by my misdemeanour. As I search in a panic for my keys, the stress only makes my spots itch more furiously. This is not the peaceful start in my new home that I had imagined. Eventually I find the keys (in the door – where else?) and rush out into the dark street to move my car. I am expecting angry recriminations, but the man in the yellow suit politely informs me that the refuse collections are on Tuesdays and Thursdays and I must not leave my car outside on those days. The truck driver, meanwhile, raises his hand to say thank you as he drives by.

I return to bed, but am woken again at 7.00 a.m., this time by the prolonged and deafening ringing of the church bells on the other side of the courtyard wall. It is, I imagine, what a Butlins holiday camp must have been like in the 1950s: the bells are the cue for everyone in Villiers to get up. The campsite in Beauchamp is starting to seem peaceful by comparison. I lie in bed scratching until the bells strike 9.00 a.m. and then I drag my itching, pox-covered body over to the pharmacy in order to identify the cause of my affliction. The pharmacist looks at my bites and immediately diagnoses fleas. The people queuing behind me listen in with interest. 'But how can I have fleas in my house when I don't have any animals?' I ask, appalled at the idea that there might be fleas in my brand new bed.

The pharmacist shrugs. 'It is possible, Madame.' He then suggests a *bombe* and a tube of calamine gel. I am not sure what a *bombe* is (I later discover it is an aerosol spray) but it sounds extreme and I'm not sure my lungs can cope with any more chemicals, so I decline. I return home with the calamine gel and marinade myself in the stuff, but it has no effect on the bites whatsoever. Driven to distraction by the itching, I call Miranda, who tells me that flea bites are a common occurrence when you move into an old house. The insect larvae lie dormant between the floorboards, she says, until being woken by the movement or warmth. I'm not convinced by this theory. The methylated spirits that I so liberally applied to the floorboards would have seen off anything living or sleeping within.

And so I spend a second sleepless night, scratching at skin which is now, in places, bleeding and raw. I cannot bear the idea that I am sleeping with fleas. In the early hours of the morning, I manage to doze off, but I am jolted awake by the frantic ring of the doorbell again. It is not Tuesday or Thursday. Yet, through the bedroom window I can see another man in a fluorescent suit outside my door, another big truck with its engine running in the narrow street outside. What is going on? Confused, I run downstairs, practically vaulting over the cardboard boxes cluttering up the *petit salon* in the hurry to move my car. The truck and its crew watch intently as I run around in floral pyjamas in the darkness, and then one of them explains that the collection of *les sacs jaunes* or recycling takes place every other Wednesday, so I must be careful not to park my car outside.

The following morning, I make my way bleary-eyed and spotty to the Liberty Bookshop for a coffee. To complete my run of bad luck I bump into Dave, who comes in to use the Internet as I am sitting alone with a newspaper.

'Hi,' I say, unable to summon up any pretence of cheeriness.

'Hello,' he mumbles, avoiding eye contact. (This suits me fine given that my skin is covered in blotchy bites.)

'Look, Dave,' I say. 'This is really silly.'

'What is?'

'The fact that you refuse to speak to me. We were really good friends.'

His cheeks turn pink. 'I'm *not* not speaking to you,' he says.

It takes me a while to figure out the double negative, but I can tell by the expression on his face that he is not exactly seizing the olive branch. Instead, he keeps walking to the back of the bookshop, until he spots Dylan. 'Hello, mate,' he says. 'Can I use the Internet?'

Despite the wintry nip in the air, Claudette is outside cleaning her windows when I return to the house. She calls over to ask how I am. 'Not good,' I reply, unfurling the sleeve of my astrakhan-trimmed hippy coat to show her my bites. She takes one look at them and says *'Aoûtats'*. At first, I think she is saying the French equivalent of 'ouch' but she keeps repeating the word *'aoûtats'*. I have no idea what this is, but Claudette seems to know what she is talking about and I am relieved to find that it is a recognisable condition. She writes the word on a piece of paper for me and insists that I return to the pharmacy to ask for the appropriate pills and cream. 'Calamine gel!' she says. 'That won't do anything against *aoûtats*.'

By now I am on the point of being driven mad by these bites – the more I scratch, the more fiercely they itch – and my mind cannot focus on anything else. I am ready to try anything the pharmacist suggests. Chemicals? Pills? *Bombes*? Bring them on!

There are three women in white coats working behind the counter today and gratifyingly, they gather to exclaim in horror as I roll up my jeans to reveal my lower legs and backs of knees. By now, with all the scratching, the bites have melded into one big furious patch of redness. '*Oh la la*,' says one, before recommending antihistamine pills and a hydrocortisone cream, 'it's not very pretty.'

But at least I now know the cause of my affliction. Back at home, I apply the cream liberally to my bites (which takes about half an hour as there are so many of them) and then Google '*aoûtats*'. I discover that they are harvest mite larvae, which usually appear in late August or early September, but, with the increasingly muddled-up seasons, they have struck in October. I am not sure where I picked them up, though, it was possibly from a patch of grass near Le Vieux Chateau, as apparently these things have legs like pogo sticks and can jump really high. My Internet search also reveals that the horrible itching is caused by 'the powerful cocktail of digestive enzymes that they inject into your skin to liquefy the tissues before sucking them up.' Fleas sound almost desirable by comparison.

But the cream and the pills have an immediate effect on the itching and it's good to know that I don't have fleas in my bed. That night I eat my dinner of bread and slice of very expensive *saucisson* and then, taking no chances, I drive my car up to the square and park it next to the *mairie*. This way, I tell myself, lies a night of uninterrupted sleep. But no, for the third morning in row, I am woken in darkness by the sound of the doorbell ringing. I throw open the bedroom window (a ritual I will soon be able do to in my sleep) and this time, instead of a refuse truck and a man in a fluorescent jacket, I see Dylan standing on my doorstep in his pyjamas.

'Karen,' he says. 'It's the *foire* today.'

'Uh?'

'It's *foire* day. The big fair that takes place twice a month.'

I am confused. Is Dylan really waking me up to tell me about a fair?

'You need to move your car now, before the market people arrive.' he persists. 'I looked out of the window when I got up and saw your car by the *mairie*. But you're not allowed to park in the square today.'

I throw my hippy coat over my floral pyjamas and, still half asleep, follow Dylan up to the square. After thanking him for his trouble, I drive my car over to the car park of the local Intermarché and leave it there. This is not the peaceful life in France that I imagined. And I am beginning to think that Maison Coquelicot is fighting back at my occupation.

Fortunately, I have Claudette as an ally. She calls in regularly to check on the progress of the renovations and is particularly concerned about the lack of cooking facilities. (It seems pointless to buy a fridge or a cooker until the kitchen floor has been stained and lacquered, and I can't face another job of that magnitude just yet. I need to give my lungs time to recover.) As we head into November and the evenings grow colder, she knocks on my door regularly with a home-made soup or *potage*. 'You have to eat warm food,' she declares, 'or you will get ill.'

But mostly I am still living on bread and cheese and caffeine, and the stress and unhealthy diet are taking their toll. On Friday evening, my fifth night in the house, I am again woken in the early hours of the morning – this time with the worst case of migraine imaginable. My migraine pills could be in any one of thirty unpacked cardboard boxes, so there's no point in even starting to look. Instead, I lie back and wait for the worst. My head feels like it has a metal band with spikes in it tightening against my brain, while the nausea has me running into the bathroom every ten minutes, where I bond deeply with the newly installed toilet bowl.

I stagger back to the pharmacist the next morning – this is rapidly becoming part of my daily routine – and, clutching my temples, explain my affliction in front of the small but interested crowd waiting at the counter. I mime the extent of the pain to my fascinated audience, trying to convey that this is no ordinary *mal à la tête*. The best the pharmacist can offer is aspirin. Trying to treat migraine with aspirin is like trying to crack a walnut with a paperclip, so I spend the next forty-eight hours in bed, my head pulsing with pain and gloomy thoughts.

Lying there alone, and feeling super-sorry for myself, I again think back to the life I once had in London – the autumn weekends spent walking through Hyde Park with Eric, having breakfast at the little French cafe behind Kensington High Street, cycling along the Thames or sitting in the Haverlock Tavern, our local pub, reading the weekend newspapers. I wonder what Eric is doing right at this second, and it hurts almost as much as the migraine, like a Christian Louboutin stiletto stamping on my heart. On Sunday morning, I know *exactly* what he will be doing. It's just that he is no longer doing it with me. The truth is that, despite his behaviour, I still miss Eric madly. And it seems so shameful to admit it. I should be over him by now, but even the simplest things still have the power to trigger pain: the sight of a TGV pulling out of a station on a summer's evening; merry-go-rounds; the smell of madeleines and coffee – all remind me of some aspect of my life with him.

No doubt Eric is relieved that I never called, that I acted, as far as he knows, with dignity. But it still feels like unresolved business. Unlike Ben, my previous long-term boyfriend, with whom I have remained good friends, I do not even know where Eric is. For him, I am now a very distant memory, growing more distant with every passing day. But it's not like that for me. Moving to France has thrown the memories into even sharper relief. I am starting a new life but part of me, as Dave once pointed out, is still anchored very much in the past.

Chapter 8

Lonely in La Rochelle

I NEED TO start earning some money if I'm to be able to pay for the continuing work at Maison Coquelicot. So I email several of the newspapers I used to write for, pitching ideas for articles. One of the commissioning editors responds immediately with a feature that involves interviewing a well-known French perfumer about the holiday home that inspired his latest perfume. It's a dream assignment, particularly since I like and admire the perfumer in question, but when the details of the location come through, my immediate reaction is to turn down the job. The perfumer's holiday home, by appalling coincidence, is on the Île de Ré, and worse, it is in Bois Plage, the little village where Eric's father ran the post office.

I can't do it. I cannot cross the bridge that links mainland France to the Île de Ré. This bridge is a direct line to my past. I discovered the island through Eric and with him, and for me the two will always be inextricably linked. The narrow streets, the whitewashed cottages, the towering *rose trémières* growing against old stone walls – to see the island again is to see him. The very mention of the place causes me acute emotional pain. But I have to do this job. I can't let the newspaper down and, more importantly, I need the money. I call the PR agency that is marketing the fragrance, which is called – oh the exquisite irony – Je Me Souviens ('I Remember') and ask if there is any possibility of meeting the perfumer in La Rochelle instead. Although the picturesque port is also steeped in painful memories – La Rochelle is the gateway to the Île de Ré – it is not quite as painful as crossing that bridge.

So we reach a compromise and the plan is that I will meet him in a cafe in La Rochelle. And on a Thursday towards the end of November, I set out to drive to La Rochelle, just under 100 kilometres away. There is a pale winter sun in the sky, but the sun disappears on the way, wiped out by a morose white mist that drops suddenly down from the sky like a theatre scrim. I drive through dull, flat terrain towards the opaque white horizon, passing fields of ploughed brown earth and silvery green kale. The roads, already quiet, are almost deserted as I get closer to the coast, so that the headlights of oncoming cars seem ghostly and sinister as they emerge from the mist. La Rochelle had been so welcoming, so full of love and promise when I first arrived on that sultry August evening, which now seems like another lifetime ago. Today, it feels impersonal and threatening, like it is warning me away. I follow the directions for the *centre de ville* with a heavy heart. I feel a cruel stab of pain as I recognise the scenes from another life: the fort; the high masts of the yachts; the harbour front cafes with silver metal chairs.

I park the car in the almost empty car park near to the fort and walk around the harbour, replaying in my mind that lush

summer evening when I first arrived here. I remember the
moment as the TGV pulled into La Rochelle, just before 9.00
p m , the chic weekending Parisians spilling onto the station's
wide platform and the flattering glow that the evening sun
cast on everyone's faces. And Eric, waiting there on the
platform, dressed in jeans and loose white shirt, his gnarly
toes visible in surfer flip-flops. Healthy and tanned in the few
days that he had been away from me. We had planned to
travel down together, but at the last moment I had stayed
behind in London to finish a magazine article. He looked
quietly thrilled to see me, smiling shyly, pulling me towards
him and kissing me slowly, oblivious to the crowds around
us. 'My old man, he is waiting in the car park,' he said after
a while, picking up my bag and putting his arm around my
shoulder.

I remember the feeling of low-key (but in retrospect perfect)
happiness as we drove down the wide boulevard of the Avenue
Charles de Gaulle, and I first glimpsed the tropical palms, the
yachts in the harbour and the packed cafes lining the quayside.
I remember the sky, as turquoise as a swimming pool in St
Tropez, and the burnished light as we drove across the slender,
awe-inspiring bridge that led to the Île de Ré.

La Rochelle, which looked so beautiful, so exotic on that
summer evening, looks drained of colour and bloodless under
the white November sky. I notice ugly concrete buildings, like
bunkers, opposite the station. And there is graffiti on the walls.
I walk around the lifeless harbour, remembering the evening
when Eric's father drove us into La Rochelle for dinner –
nothing fancy, just a crêperie. Me in a silvery satin sleeveless
dress, wedge heels, long hair still damp from the shower. Eric
smiling at me. How protected I was then, wrapped in Eric's

love. His arm around my shoulder, his hand gripping mine, nearly always touching some part of my body. I couldn't have known then how badly it would end.

Those cafes are deserted now. No one sits at the silver bistro tables and matching chairs. There are no children on the merry-go-round, which is motionless and closed up for the winter. I'm over an hour early to meet the perfumer, so I take a seat outside a cafe overlooking the harbour, muffled up against the cold in my navy jacket, a big black scarf around my neck *'Bonjour, Madame,'* says the waiter, offering a menu. He is brisk, businesslike, makes no attempt to flirt. I order a *café crème* and sit for a long time, surrounded by a sea of empty chairs, listening to the plaintive cry of the seagulls.

Shortly before 2.00 p.m., I pay the bill and walk away from the harbour towards the hub of the town, past shops selling perfumes, postcards and tourist tat. I find myself subconsciously expecting to bump into Eric. It is very possible that, if he lives on the Île de Ré, he works in La Rochelle. When I arrive at the Café de la Paix, the huge windows are steamed up. Inside, the cafe is warm and old-fashioned with dark wood panelling on the wall and there are waiters bustling around in long white aprons. Inside, I spot the perfumer, waiting for me in a corner. We've met several times before, at fragrance launches in Paris. Like all perfumers I have ever met, he is handsome, charismatic and erudite. He is dressed in jeans and an open-neck shirt under a dark tailored jacket. He stands up to greet me, speaking in heavily accented English, and then over espressos and after some small talk he tells me about his latest perfume.

Je Me Souviens, he explains, was inspired by his childhood holidays on the Île de Ré and a curious *mélange* of smells:

the diesel of the fishing boats, the smell of Pineau (a sweet aperitif produced on the island) and of oysters (another of the island's specialities). Into this mix he has woven some fresh green notes to evoke spring and the pleasure of cycling through vineyards and along the many paths that criss-cross the island. He tells me also how the soft pink and green packaging was inspired by the colours of the Île de Ré: the green of the shutters and the paint originally used for the fishing boats; and the pink of the hollyhocks that blossom all over the island.

'The Île de Ré was, until very recently, a secret place,' he says. 'All the celebrities, the trash [he waves his hand dismissively], they went to the Côte d'Azur. The idea of Je Me Souviens was to evoke a secret island, a place that seduces the senses and where you can experience the very basic pleasures of life. I wanted to evoke damp skin behind closed shutters in the heat of an August afternoon, the smell of sea and oysters and sex.' I dutifully write all this down, but my mind is elsewhere. It is in a dark bedroom above the post office in the little village of Bois Plage, where Eric and I lie entwined under a poster of two crying clowns, listening to the faint hum of the nearby market through the semi-open shutters.

As the perfumer shows me a photograph of his holiday home – a white *pavillon* covered in wisteria on the outskirts of Bois Plage – memories flip through my head like a series of cinematic scenes. I remember the market in Bois Plage where Eric once bought me a straw basket for my bike, and where, another time, I kitted us both out in navy fishermen's jackets to go crab fishing in the rain. I remember the *boulangerie*, where I used to buy *pains au chocolat* in the morning, the bike rides to the little port of St Martin and the café overlooking the harbour where we would have aperitifs. And I think of the twelfth-century church, in pole position in the centre of Bois Plage, where I thought that Eric and I would one day get married.

'Have you ever been to the Île de Ré?' the perfumer asks me suddenly.

'Um, I've heard of it,' I say. I think back to the press dossier for the fragrance that I read this morning, describing it as 'The Island of the Beautiful People' and listing the celebrities who have recently been spotted there, Johnny Depp and Vanessa Paradis among them. I manage to stop myself from saying that I knew the island when it really was beautiful and an insider secret as I don't want him to ask how I discovered a place that until recently was, to Brits at least, a relatively unknown part of France.

Instead, I feel stabs of pain, as if I am being poked in the soul with a big electric prod, as he describes his house on the outskirts of Bois Plage and talks about cycling through vineyards and fields of sunflowers in the golden light of early evening, or watching the fishermen bring in their haul in the port of St Martin. I think of my beautiful, golden-haired former boyfriend and the summers that we spent there.

The perfumer is talking about damp skin and sweat again and how the 'dry down', the lasting impression of the fragrance, is of earthiness and sensuality. 'Enough already!' I want to shout. 'Stop talking about sex.' Instead, I nod sagely and continue to make notes that mean nothing.

'You know,' the perfumer is saying. 'My car is parked very near here. We could be across the bridge and on the island within twenty minutes. I think if you experienced it, you would better understand what I'm talking about...'

'Oh, I understand perfectly what you are talking about,' I say, declining his offer on the pretext that I've got a long journey home. 'You've described it very well.'

It's about 4.00 p.m. when I finally leave. Feeling alone and forlorn, I head back towards the harbour to collect my car in the grey winter half-light. The street lamps around the harbour are already lit. As I head towards the autoroute and the journey home, I wonder what Eric is doing at this very moment. And I think to myself: *I so need to move on from here.*

Chapter 9

Patisserie and Poetry

IN MANY WAYS, I moved to France at the worst possible time of year. Rather than timing my arrival to coincide with the poppies of early spring or the hollyhocks of high summer, I pitched up on the cusp of winter. The once smiling sunflowers have had their heads brutally chopped off and the long-armed irrigators that sent huge arcs of water soaring over lush green and golden fields in the summer now lie still. The countryside is flat and colourless; the fields brown and barren, the sky the colour of steel. On the days when the sun does come out, it hangs sheepishly over the fields, a pale imitation of its vibrant former self. The landscape of my new life is bleak and lacklustre. And yet I find the deadness strangely comforting – perhaps because I know it will not stay this way for ever. Flowers and fertile crops will soon be pushing through those muddy brown furrows and it's just a matter of time before the countryside pulses with beauty and colour and life again.

I love the feeling that I am living in sync with nature. In London, I measured the passing seasons in terms of bare legs or winter boots and whether or not to wear a coat. Here, the markers are more elemental and I'm much more aware of the passage of time. Even in the dying days of autumn, I have found much to love about my new life: the sense of space and timelessness, the new baker's melting chocolate macaroons, and the fact that no one cares about whether or not I'm carrying the latest 'It' bag. I have even learnt to love the church bells, jolting me awake at 7.00 a.m. every morning. I love driving along deserted country back roads surrounded by flat, open fields, past dilapidated stone barns and houses with pretty blue-grey shutters. I also love the old-fashioned courtesies that mark everyday life here – the fact that when you walk into a shop or restaurant you are expected to greet everyone with a friendly *'Bonjour, Messieurs, Mesdames,'* (it's considered the height of bad manners not to). I get a buzz from the fact that, just crossing the square to buy a newspaper in the morning, I will recognise and say *'bonjour'* to at least half a dozen people. In London, I would step out of my front door and be told to 'get out of the effing way' by a cyclist speeding up the road the wrong way.

Visiting the *boulangerie* at the end of my little road, meanwhile, is a highlight of the day. Dressed in pristine blue and white checked trousers and a white T-shirt, René Matout, the new baker, will often rush through from the kitchen at the back with a cake or dessert specially ordered by a customer. I love watching as he places it carefully in a box as if it were a precious Cartier necklace, before tying it up with a flourish of ribbons. And I love the way this big, macho baker flirts and jokes with the old ladies, handing over a cake big enough for a dozen people, with the stern warning not to eat it all at once. In London, like most fashion and beauty writers, I viewed bread and most carbohydrates as the devil's food. But since René Matout came to town, I have changed my mind. His *'tradition française'* – a baton of bread slightly denser and chewier than a normal baguette – is excellent, while his *pains au chocolat* are flaky, buttery perfection. And whereas his predecessor offered a fairly pedestrian choice of patisserie – mostly dense slabs of fruit tart and mountainous choux buns – René Matout's cakes are much more refined, betraying a delicate sleight of hand. Like the *boulanger* himself, they are perfectly formed and very easy on the eye.

The new baker is to desserts what Christian Dior was to dresses, with a constantly changing array of shapes, textures and pretty pastel colours to pique the curiosity of his customers. How can one resist the soft, pink, quivering mound of his almond rose biscuit topped with rose confit? Or his fennel-flavoured crème brulée, ready to go in its own little shot glass? Or the irresistible jade *ganache* topped by a frilly pale-green mound of absinthe cream? How to decide between his quivering *bombes* and luxuriant vanilla tarts? René has even introduced the delights of the mini macaroon and the *religieuse* (two cream puffs on top of each other with patisserie cream in the middle) to the good people of Villiers. No wonder the queue stretches out of the door and a visit to the *boulangerie* has become a social event.

Aside from the baker's delights, my tenure of the house so far has been marked by moments of self-doubt but also a euphoric sense of achievement. I find joy in small things that I once took for granted in London, such as a functioning broadband connection, which in my little village house seem nothing short of miraculous. Small achievements – getting a shelf put up in the kitchen for example – can carry you a long way. And even though I am essentially camping in one room, I feel as though I have turned a corner as far as Maison Coquelicot is concerned, as all the really big works have been done.

But some days are not so good: queuing in the post office, for example, behind someone who is counting out the contents of their piggy bank before the solitary cashier is never fun. And, although I did not expect life in the French countryside to be all pink champagne and Chanel suits, I do long for a little more glamour. The local Intermarché is a bit of a comedown after Planet Organic in Notting Hill or even the M&S food hall in Kensington, where I bought chocolate ginger biscuits and organic watercress alongside yummy mummies dressed more for clubbing than buying a pint of milk, in tight jeans and revealing tops.

At the supermarket in Villiers, with the notable exceptions of cheese and wine, the choice of food on offer is surprisingly limited and seems to revolve around biscuits, sugary breakfast cereals, junk food and animal innards, while 'sell-by' dates are so well hidden that several times I have returned home with products – including yogurts, dips and even pasta – whose shelf life has expired. But I am intrigued by Intermarché's choice of background music. This ranges from the husky strains of Barry White singing 'Get It On' or else rap music with explicit lyrics. Neither seem appropriate for an elderly population shopping for toilet rolls and cat litter, blissfully ignorant of the obscene music being piped through the store.

There are, I have to admit, many things that I miss about my life in London: my twice-weekly Pilates sessions; playing tennis in Holland Park at weekends; impromptu coffees with Kim, my high-powered banker neighbour, on Saturday mornings. I miss being able to meet friends for a glass of champagne or watch a movie at a moment's notice and I miss wearing high heels and cute dresses (there *are* opportunities for dressing up here – mostly when invited to other people's houses for dinner – but not so many as in London). I badly miss being able to pop round to my local gastro pub for sausages and mash on the spur of the moment or when the cupboards are empty. Perhaps I've been spoilt by living in London but contrary to expectation, dining out in the French countryside is not all pillows of foie gras, pungent dribbling cheeses and delicious carpaccios of this and that. Possibly it is in Peter Mayle country, but I seem to have landed in the only corner of France where the food is borderline inedible and the meat often tough enough to pull out your molars. I have found one restaurant where the food is half-decent but the menu never changes and vegetables rarely feature on it.

If I'm being really truthful, I also miss the shops – above all not being able to jump on a bus to browse around Selfridges. This surprises me, as part of the plan when I moved here was to lead a less consumerist life. But what I really miss, I realise, is *looking* rather than actually buying. There is a Zara in Poitiers and a Princess Tam Tam boutique, which sells wickedly sexy French lingerie (not much use to me at the moment), but that's about it.

In London, my day as a freelance journalist began with a twenty-minute walk to Prêt a Manger on Kensington High Street for a cappuccino (another thing I miss, for although it sounds sacrilegious to say it, the coffee in rural France is often bitter and acrid tasting). Then, after a quick browse around the shops, I would return home (as if arriving at the office) and spend the rest of the day working. Here in this French village (unless of course, there is a refuse collector banging on my door) I can wake up anytime I want, there is nowhere to walk to with a purpose, and frankly, the freedom is frightening. And so I establish a new routine. It's similar to the London one but without the twenty-minute early morning walk and without the work. Instead, I start each day with a two-minute stroll up to the square for either an organic, fair trade coffee at the Liberty Bookshop, or *une petite noisette* (an espresso with a splash of milk) at the Café du Commerce on the square. The Liberty Bookshop has become, in many ways, the focal point of my life. Dylan is my DIY guru – he has the answer to every dilemma I present to him and gives me advice on everything from the best broadband connection to gas bottles. Gas bottles, incidentally, are by far the most worrying thing about moving to France alone. Since mains gas does not exist in most French villages, it's necessary at least once a year to wrestle home an enormous gas bottle – even when empty they are as heavy as a slab of concrete – and then hook it up to the oven. (I'm not alone in worrying about this: a female friend recently confided that replacing the wretched thing was her chief concern when she split up with her boyfriend shortly after moving to France.) I still don't have an oven but when the time comes I have no idea how I will get the gas cylinder home, let alone connect it safely. The answer, I suspect, as with most things, is to ask Dylan.

As well as being the source of all my DIY advice, the Liberty Bookshop is, ironically, an excellent place to meet other French people, many of whom come from surrounding villages up to 25 kilometres away to sample British delicacies such as PG Tips and buttered scones. On Wednesday afternoons, the Liberty Bookshop hosts an informal Anglo-French conversation group. The people I meet here, French or English, are all lovely, friendly and invariably over fifty. They have all the time in the world to sit and chat.

There is one exception: Jon Wakeman. One afternoon in November I walk into the bookshop, hoping for Dylan's help slotting a tube of silicon filler into a metal gun, and find a guy I have never seen before, with long, unruly hair, chatting with Dylan at the counter. He seems to be relaying a funny anecdote and because he has a very attractive laugh I go and join them.

'Hi,' says Dylan. 'Have you met Jon?'

'No,' says the man with unruly hair, holding out his hand. 'Jon Wakeman.'

'Hi,' I say, with a (possibly over-eager) smile. I am thrilled to meet someone my own age. Unfortunately, the stranger's body language suggests that the feeling is not reciprocated. He shifts on his feet and crosses his arms defensively.

'Karen lives in the village too,' says Dylan. This is usually the cue for a mini-interrogation: How long have you lived in France? What made you move here? Are you here on your own? And so on. But the man with the long hair looks very uneasy, wary even. It's as if Dylan had said: 'This is Karen. She's got avian flu.'

'Excellent,' he says in an off-hand way, before continuing with the story he is telling. I hover by the counter for a few minutes but feel uncomfortable as Jon Wakeman does not make any attempt to include me in the conversation. Eventually, I take the hint and go and sit down at a nearby table listening to their raucous laughter as I wait for Dylan to come and take my order. I feel miffed and very left out. I want to be part of their conversation. Instead I pretend to read *Ex Pat France*, an amateurish news sheet filled with ads for British builders and *auberges* that have been taken over by Brits offering 'fish and chip evenings' or 'quiz and curry nights'.

'He's a nice guy, that Jon Wakeman,' says Dylan, when he has gone.

'What's he doing out here?'

'He's renovating an old farmhouse. He's planning to turn it into a B&B.'

'Really? Whereabouts?'

'I've forgotten the name of the village but it's about ten kilometres away from here. I'm not sure if he's got a girlfriend or whether he's out here on his own. But he goes back to the UK for work from time to time. I think he's an IT consultant.'

'Good for him,' I say. Touching though it is that Dylan appears to be carrying out such reconnaissance on my behalf, I don't want to appear too interested in Jon Wakeman, given that he was so uninterested in me.

Other encounters in the Liberty Bookshop are more successful. One rainy Saturday morning in late November, I am quietly reading the latest anti-cellulite tips in *Madame Figaro* magazine, when an attractive French woman in her forties approaches my table and asks if I would like to meet up to exchange French/English conversation. I am a little alarmed that she can so easily identify me as an *Anglaise*, but I agree readily to her proposal. Her English is already very good – she is training to be an English teacher and is clearly an Anglophile – so it looks like I will get the better part of the deal. She introduces herself as Mathilde and suggests that I come to her house the following Saturday at 12.00 noon. It seems like a strange time for a French person to arrange a rendezvous, being on the cusp of lunch hour, but I take down the directions and on Saturday morning drive the 8 kilometres to her village in crisp winter sunshine. I feel incredibly happy as I drive through the countryside. If I still lived in London, I would probably be wandering aimlessly along Kensington High Street right now, indulging in 'shop research' – my euphemism for mindless shopping – and steadily increasing my credit card debt.

In truth, I'm braced for some rather stilted conversation chez Mathilde but what I get is a very convivial lunch. Mathilde lives in a house converted from the old village school. Inside, it is an effortless homage to the shabby chic style that Londoners pay interior designers a fortune to recreate. The kitchen smells deliciously of something stewing in garlic and onions. She shows me through to a room with gloriously 'distressed' leather armchairs, a huge fireplace with log burner and crackling fire and a long wooden refectory table, unexpectedly laid for lunch. Everything in Mathilde's house feels warm and friendly and bears the patina of age and character.

She introduces me to her partner, Sebastian, an artist. He has a weather-beaten face, kind, laughing eyes and long grey hair that he wears in a ponytail. I like him immediately. He clasps my hands and greets me like an old friend. He is older than Mathilde – although it is obvious that he was devastatingly attractive when he was younger – and I later discover that they met when Mathilde enrolled on one of his art courses. Together they have created a series of paintings, based on a Mozart symphony, which add intriguing bolts of colour to the walls of their home. Their other artistic endeavours – sculptures, pottery and painted papier mâché vases – cover all available surfaces. The overall effect is utterly charming.

Mathilde has a ten-year-old son, Albert, but he usually spends the weekend with his father, her ex-husband. Sebastian offers me a glass of red wine and signals for me to take the place at the wooden trestle table, closest to the wood-burner. We speak in English at first, then switch to French and then after a while speak a *mélange* of the two, switching (in my case) from one to the other in the same sentence. Mathilde's English, though not perfect, is far better than my French. She is also an excellent cook – we have avocado salad followed by coq au vin and cherry charlotte. It is all the more delicious as it is my first proper meal in months. She asks why I moved to France and I explain about the unlikely set of coincidences that brought me here.

'Did you move on your own? Or do you have a boyfriend?' she asks.

'I'm looking for a French husband,' I reply, secretly thinking how ironic it would be if I met a British one instead.

'Good idea,' said Sebastian, throwing his head back and laughing.

It is 5.00 p.m. and dark when I leave. Our 'language exchange' has been so successful that Mathilde invites me back the following Saturday and I instantly accept. 'I would invite you to mine,' I say, 'but there is nowhere to sit.' Mathilde laughs. 'So we will meet here again,' she says. She also asks if I will be free on Wednesday afternoon as she has a friend, a poet, who will be giving a poetry reading at the Liberty Bookshop. 'That sounds great,' I say, though in fact I can think of few things – crossword puzzles and potholing maybe – that appeal to me less than a poetry reading.

On the way to the Liberty Bookshop for the poetry reading, with my head down against the cold, I bump, almost literally, into Victor the estate agent outside the *boulangerie*. I have not seen him since Miranda's dinner party, where he was surprisingly cool. Today, however, he ambushes me with two whiskery kisses on the cheeks. 'Ah, *Ka-renne*, how is it going? Where have you been hiding?' he says.

'Le Vieux Chateau,' I say. 'While work was being done on my house.'

But Victor is not interested in the work being done at my house. His voice low and furtive, he asks, 'And what are you doing this evening?'

'Um, nothing,' I say, desperately trying to think of something. The problem is that in a small French village it is difficult to claim a packed social life.

'Then I am inviting you for an aperitif,' he says.

I can't carry on avoiding Victor forever. What with trying to avoid him and dodging Dave, My New Life in France is starting to feel like an episode of *'Allo 'Allo!* or a French farce. So I accept Victor's invitation. It seems like the polite thing to do – after all, he did secure me a big reduction in the purchase price of my house – and I will make it clear that I am not interested in becoming his next wife.

'OK, where?' I say.

'My house,' he says. 'And I will make you dinner. I am a very good cook.'

The thought of a hot meal is very tempting but dinner alone with Victor – I'm guessing that there won't be any other guests – is not.

'Maybe we could meet in a cafe for an aperitif instead?' I say.

'I live near Beauchamp,' he says, ignoring my suggestion, 'but my house is quite difficult to find, so it's probably easiest if I meet you outside the church in the main square in Beauchamp, say at six-thirty.'

Since moving to France, every experience (even getting your telephone line connected or organising an oil delivery) feels like an adventure, but I am annoyed at the way that I have allowed myself to be bulldozed into this impromptu arrangement. But it's too late to backtrack. 'See you at six-thirty outside the church,' says Victor and he is halfway across the square before I have time to argue.

It's only 4.00 p.m. but already getting dark as I slip into the Liberty Bookshop, which is warm and brightly lit. A small group of people has already assembled for the reading. Mathilde and Sebastian are chatting to Dylan, who is dressed in a thick alpaca sweater, a purple scarf wound around his neck. With them is Henri, Mathilde's poet friend, who is tall and thin and wearing an anorak. He is in his mid-to-late thirties and smiles a lot, and when he does so his eyes have a wide, rather manic look about them. Sitting at a table in the window are members of the Anglo-French conversation group; an elderly contingent of mostly French people and a charming couple from Yorkshire, who have a problem with rodents in their roof. I am surprised to find Jon Wakeman sitting among them, although, judging by the expression on his face, he would rather not be.

'So you're a poetry fan?' I say.

'No,' he says. 'I came in to use the Internet but Dylan insisted that I stay.'

'Hello darling,' says a cheery voice behind me. It's Elinor, the glamorous yoga teacher that I met at Miranda's dinner party. She throws three kisses on my cheeks. 'Heard from your boyfriend recently?' she asks playfully.

'*Boyfriend?*' I say, mystified, as Jon Wakeman takes the opportunity to escape from the table and look at a new delivery of cookery books.

'*Victor!*' says Elinor. 'I hope you don't mind but Miranda told me that he had a crush on you.'

'Actually, I just bumped into him,' I say glumly.

'Ever since the dinner party, he keeps asking about you,' continues Elinor. 'And I thought you ought to know that he's started to monitor your movements. Apparently, he spotted you on the road to Beauchamp the other evening and wanted to know where you were going. I'm afraid he's rather obsessed by you.'

'Oh dear. I thought Miranda had explained that I wasn't interested in him like that.'

'Oh did she? Well, it hasn't cooled his ardour.'

I tell Elinor about his invitation for this evening and am surprised when her mood switches from jocular to outraged on my behalf. 'He invited you to his home for an aperitif did he? That's absolutely not on,' she says. 'In France, to invite a woman that you hardly know to your home for an aperitif suggests only one thing.'

'That's what I thought,' I say. I tell her about the plan to meet him in front of the church in Beauchamp.

'He will probably have a vicar waiting,' she deadpans.

'And the wedding rings…' I say.

'But really, what a bizarre plan, to make you hang around outside a church in the middle of winter.'

I look over at Jon Wakeman, but he is studying a book entitled *One Pot Cooking*.

'If I were you,' says Elinor. 'I would think very seriously about going there alone. I mean, why can't he meet you in a bar, for heaven's sake? Look, it's only an idea, but if you like I could wait with you in Beauchamp. We could pretend that we've just bumped into each other and that way, you can suggest that the three of us go for an aperitif.'

'Are you sure?' I say, thinking how nice it is of Elinor to take me under her wing like this (but then yoga teachers, in my experience, are always nice people). It would certainly take some of the pressure off if she came along. 'That would be absolutely brilliant, if you don't mind.'

'Not at all,' she says.

'OK, people, we're about to start,' shouts Dylan, banging a Tibetan gong. We all pull up seats around the big table in the window. Henri takes his anorak off to reveal a patterned sweater over a shirt and tie. My cheeks are flushed and I feel very nervous, for I have a pretty good idea of what is going to happen next. I really, really wish that I hadn't agreed to come to the poetry reading.

'This is a series of poems based on the emotions I felt when my lover left me,' he says, pushing his glasses up his nose and clearing his throat. I know I shouldn't, I know it makes me seem deeply immature, but the reading hasn't even started and already I am fighting back tears – of laughter. I don't know why but I always get very nervous and giggly in group situations where I am supposed to look serious and thoughtful.

The poetry is in English, but it might as well be in Punjabi. Dylan has been seconded into reading some of the poems and, although he starts off reverentially enough, he doesn't look too happy about it. A dozen very opaque poems later, he looks pained. I scan the faces of the assembled group. The couple from Yorkshire are a study in inscrutable blankness; Mathilde looks like she is concentrating hard; another elderly member of the Anglo-French conversation group has his eyes closed, and I realise it is because he has fallen asleep. Dylan is struggling with some of the words, which do not exist in English. I look at Jon, who is sitting directly opposite me. If I am not mistaken, the corner of his mouth is curling upwards and he too is trying very hard not to laugh. My face is flushed and my breathing is shallow, and suddenly I'm transported back in time to A-level English in the headmaster's office where my fellow classmates and I played a secret game of spotting the double entendres in Jane Austen. Week after week, I suffered physical pain trying not to laugh out loud at sentences that described a young man of twenty-six as 'very well endowed' – which to a group of hormonal seventeen-year-olds seemed like the last word in hilarity.

Suddenly, I can't help myself. The wave of laughter that I have been holding back comes out as a large snort and everyone looks at me. I lean forward and just in the nick of time manage to turn the snort into a coughing fit. Mathilde silently offers me a glass of water. Jon looks at me and raises an eyebrow. I am choking back laughter and it is excruciating. I am terrified of offending Mathilde and Sebastian and their friend. If I start to laugh, I won't be able to stop and will probably set everyone else off. So I breathe deeply and force myself to think the most miserable thoughts possible – my credit card debts, eighty-year-old spinsters being carted off to nursing homes, Eric married with two children. It does the trick.

When the ordeal is over, Henri comes up to me and in perfect English says, 'Might I ask what you thought?'

'It was very brave,' I say, choosing my words carefully, 'to write poetry in a second language.'

Elinor grabs me by the arm. 'See you at six-thirty outside the church,' she says. 'I'll be wearing my wedding hat.'

Elinor is waiting in the darkness, her car parked under the lime blossom trees in the square. She is muffled up against the cold in a Russian Cossack hat, long velvet coat and knee boots. She is wearing make up – normally she doesn't – and looks surprisingly glamorous for our assignation. 'No sign of him yet,' she says, getting out of the car. 'He's probably changing the sheets on his bed. Or out buying condoms.'

'Or trimming his moustache,' I say, getting into the spirit, although I am a little shocked at Elinor's suggestions, which seem a little out of character for a yoga teacher. At Miranda's party, Elinor had struck me as fairly reserved.

'His pubic hair more like it,' retorts Elinor, which causes me to clutch my stomach with laughter.

I feel guilty laughing at Victor's expense but when I mention this, Elinor becomes very angry. 'He deserves it,' she says, her kind voice now hard. 'The devious old rake. What kind of girl does he think you are? Oh, look, speak of the devil...'

A dark estate car draws slowly into the square. But even though we are standing outside the church as instructed, and Victor has clearly seen us, he drives on by.

'There is only one church in Beauchamp isn't there?' I say.

'Yes,' says Elinor, watching the car disappear over the bridge.

'Perhaps he didn't see us in the darkness.'

'Of course he saw us. What on earth is the daft bugger up to?'

We stand outside the church for another fifteen minutes and Victor reappears twice. Each time, he drives past the church really slowly but he doesn't stop. The third time Elinor gives him a cheery wave but still he drives on by. It's all very strange.

'I think it's because I'm with you,' says Elinor. 'He's probably hoping I will go so that he can have you to his predatory self.'

'Let's go,' I say. 'I showed up and I've waited fifteen minutes, so I kept my part of the bargain.'

'Why don't you come back to mine for a glass of wine?' says Elinor.

'That would be lovely,' I say.

I follow Elinor along dark country roads for a few kilometres to her farmhouse, parking my car by the iron gates. Struggling to see in the inky darkness, I follow her across the crunchy gravelled courtyard towards the house. Elinor lights the wood-burner in her cosy, sunflower-yellow kitchen and over a glass of red wine we discuss Victor's curious behaviour. 'He must have seen us,' she says. 'How very odd that he didn't stop.'

We have been chatting for about half an hour when the phone rings. I can tell from the face that Elinor pulls and the way that she gesticulates at me that it is Victor.

'I'm very sorry to hear that, Victor,' she says, in perfect French. 'But no, Karen is not here. I don't know where she is.' She is silent for a while, listening to whatever Victor is saying on the other end of the phone. And then, looking at me with a grin and a wicked glint in her eye she says, 'I don't know the answer to that but I do know that her boyfriend is arriving next week... Yes, he's in the SAS... back from serving in Afghanistan.'

She puts the phone down and with undisguised delight says, 'Well, I think the mention of an SAS boyfriend has done the trick.'

'I actually do have a male friend visiting next week,' I say. 'Though he's a literary editor and not in the SAS. And not my boyfriend.'

'Well, you'll just have to make him wear combat trousers and look mean as you parade him around the village,' says Elinor with a grin. 'If that doesn't discourage Victor nothing will. By the way, I hope you don't mind me asking this but—'

Before she can finish asking the question there is a firm rap on the kitchen window and Elinor's dogs, who are in the sitting room, suddenly go bananas.

'Good grief,' whispers Elinor. 'I hope that's not him.'

'Who?'

'Victor.'

She motions for me to keep out of sight and goes towards the kitchen door.

'Who is it?' she cries.

'It's me,' says a male voice that I instantly recognise.

Elinor opens the door and I see Dave standing outside in the darkness, wrapped up in a dark jacket and a scarf. He is holding a bunch of flowers and a bottle of wine.

This is a surprise; I didn't realise that he and Elinor even knew each other.

'I've come to say goodbye,' he says.

'Come in, come in!' says Elinor looking flustered. 'We thought you were someone else.'

Dave steps into the kitchen and his demeanour changes instantly when he spots me.

'Don't worry,' I say, getting up from the kitchen table. 'I was just about to leave.'

Chapter 10

Word Games

THE FOLLOWING MORNING Elinor calls. 'Darling, so sorry you had to dash off last night. I wasn't expecting a visit from Dave,' she says.

'I didn't even realise you knew each other,' I say.

'Yes, Desmond and I have known him since he first arrived in France. We met at a dinner party. Or was it through Miranda? I really can't remember. He just dropped by to say that he was leaving.'

'For good?'

'No. He's just got a new job. He came by last night, on the spur of the moment, to celebrate. Now have you heard from Victor this morning?'

'No,' I say.

'Good,' she replies. 'That was a very strange debacle last night. Let's hope he got the message.'

I want to know more about Dave's job but Elinor is vague and seems reluctant to volunteer information. Nonetheless, a little probing reveals that he has resolved his financial problems by declaring himself bankrupt (or something similar) in the UK but has somehow managed to hold on to his house in France. Now he is planning to go and work for a start-up advertising agency in Hong Kong.

'*Hong Kong?*' I repeat incredulously.

'Yes, that's what I thought. It's a strange move,' she says. 'I gather you two have had a bit of a fall-out.'

'Why, what did he say?'

'Nothing at all. But I could tell by the speed of your departure that something was wrong. It made me wonder if there was ever anything between you two?'

'No,' I say. 'Absolutely not.'

'Well, enough of Dave. The real reason I called was to see if you were going to games night at the Liberty Bookshop next Wednesday.'

'Games night?'

'Yes, you know, board games – Scrabble, Risk, that kind of thing. The Libertys are donating the one-euro entrance fee to Kharma Aid or some other Save Tibet charity. Miranda and I thought we'd go along and wondered if you'd like to come.'

'Yes, why not?' I seem to be spending a lot of time in the Liberty Bookshop, but it is just around the corner and has become a sort of rural French version of the coffee shop in *Friends* since I invariably bump into people I know in there.

'Great. We'll see you there at six-thirty then. We thought we'd have dinner at Le Vieux Chateau afterwards if you'd like to join us.'

It's cold, dark and raining when I set out for the short walk to the Liberty Bookshop. Inside, three tables are occupied.

I spot Jean-Claude, a stoic from the Entente Conversation group, playing cards with a garrulous old Brit called Florence Coppinger, who likes very much to talk about her health problems, as well as an American couple who live in a nearby village. A table in the centre of the room is laid out with a selection of board games. In total there are no more than nine of us, so our combined entrance fees won't be doing much for the Tibetan cause.

'*Coucou!*' shouts Miranda, who is wearing a fake purple hibiscus in her hair. 'We're over here.' She and Elinor are sitting at a table in the window and with them is Jon Wakeman, who looks, to my annoyance, very attractive. His hair is slightly less unruly than last time and he is dressed quite smartly for an evening of dominos in a dark tailored jacket and jeans. He pulls out the seat next to him for me to sit down. I notice that the Libertys have placed a little card on the table that says (in French and English) 'Gambling is not permitted. Thank you for your understanding.'

'I hope Florence isn't gambling away her pension over there,' I whisper as I sit down. Jon chuckles.

'Spoilsports!' says Miranda, looking at the card. 'I was hoping we could play strip poker later but I suppose that's banned too.'

'So have you been to any good poetry readings lately?' Jon asks.

'No, I've had enough poetry for a while,' I say. 'So what brings you here? You like playing games?

'Actually, I'm here to show support for Dylan and Lola,' he replies.

'And how's the B&B?'

'It's progressing. Slowly.'

'Are you out here on your own, Jon?' asks Miranda.

'Yes,' he replies and I feel inexplicably happy.

'I won!' says Elinor, putting down her last domino.

'Shall we play something else?' she says. 'What about Scrabble? I'll get the board, shall I? Or maybe Risk if everyone knows how to play?'

'Better not,' I say. 'I get very competitive playing Risk.'

'Do you?' says Jon, looking suddenly interested.

'Oh yes! I never settle for anything less than world domination.'

'Honestly?'

I nod.

'Me neither. Go on then, let's play Risk,' he says.

'I'm all for a bit of domination,' says Miranda with a wink, 'but I don't know how to play. So maybe we should stick with Scrabble.'

'Would anyone like a drink before we start?' asks Jon.

'Darling, I thought no one was ever going to ask,' says Miranda. 'A large glass of dry white please.'

'I don't think they serve alcohol,' says Jon, handing her the menu.

'We don't,' says Dylan coming over to serve us.

'Oh come on, darling. No one wants a cup of tea at this hour. You must have a bottle of Sauvignon Blanc stashed away behind the counter somewhere,' says Miranda.

Dylan shakes his head. 'I'm afraid we don't have a licence and it's not worth the risk.'

And so we order tea instead. If someone had told me a year ago that my social life would soon consist of Scrabble and an early evening cup of camomile tea, I would have thought them one paving stone short of a patio. Surveying my surroundings,

I realise that it is a far cry from cocktails in the *fumoir* at Claridges and yet… strangely, I find that I am enjoying myself. *Really* enjoying myself.

'So, Jon, what are you doing for Christmas?' Miranda asks, as we each take turns to pull seven letters from a bag. I wait for his reply with interest.

'I've been invited to lunch with my French neighbours.'

'Marvellous,' says Miranda, as I note his use of the word 'I' rather than 'we'.

And so the game of Scrabble commences. Miranda goes first, clapping her hands together with delight when she realises that not only does she have a word but it is a very high-scoring one. She spells out the letters S-A-P-P-H-I-C on the board.

Elinor starts to laugh, as using Miranda's 'S' she spells out the word S-M-I-T-T-E-N.

Jon goes next. 'Not many points for this,' he says, as he puts down just four letters: L-U-S-T.

'My goodness, maybe we should rename this "Naughty Scrabble",' says Elinor.

'Excellent idea,' says Miranda. 'Only rude words allowed.'

I blush as I follow Jon's LUST with the word S-H-A-R-E-D. (It was either that or SHED.)

'Steady on there!' says Miranda. 'We don't want this getting out of control. The Libertys probably have some rules about this kind of innuendo.'

Jon looks embarrassed. The game soon reverts to safer ground – though Miranda does manage to slip in E-R-O-T-I-C before the game is through. Jon also wins plaudits for interesting use of an 'X' with the word M-I-N-X. He looks at me as he puts the letters down and once again I find myself turning pink. And am I imagining it or is there a slight glimmer of a smile on his face?

In the end it is Miranda who wins and the game is brought to a close for the rest of us when Elinor looks at her watch and declares, 'Good grief, it's gone eight o'clock.'

'Good-o,' says Miranda, 'time for a drink.' And then, looking at Jon: 'Darling boy, why don't you join us for dinner? We're going over to Le Vieux Chateau.'

For a moment Jon looks like he is considering it. I shove my letters back into the bag, really hoping that he will say 'yes' but somehow knowing that he won't.

'I'd like to,' he says, 'but I promised some friends that I would drop in and see them later this evening.'

'*Tant pis!*' says Miranda. 'Another time.'

'Yes,' says Jon, looking hesitant. 'Another time.'

'Well isn't he just *darlingo*,' says Miranda as we walk down the hill towards Le Vieux Chateau. 'I've never met him before but he seems very charming.'

'Yes, possibly boyfriend material for you?' says Elinor.

'No, Jon Wakeman's not interested in me,' I say.

'How do you know?' asks Miranda.

'I can just tell. Whenever I meet him on my own he's never very friendly. And he never asks me any questions about myself.'

'Well, he seemed perfectly friendly this evening,' says Elinor. 'And he obviously doesn't have a girlfriend.'

Mathilde calls to invite me to lunch on Sunday. 'But that's Christmas Day,' I say. 'A family event.'

'Eh, *Ka-renne*, you are almost family now,' she replies. 'Anyway, it is very casual; in France we do the big family dinner on Christmas Eve.' She tells me that Henri the poet will be there, 'but don't worry. He will not be doing any poetry readings.'

In truth, I am delighted with Mathilde's invitation. Christmas seems to have crept up very suddenly and I haven't made any plans. The festive season really isn't happening at all *chez moi*. I haven't got a tree because there is nowhere to put one (the *petit salon* is still piled high with unpacked boxes) and I won't be cooking Christmas dinner for anyone as I still don't have an oven. I had dreamt of a cosy French *Noël* with a log fire burning, real mistletoe and holly decorating the hearth and a champagne-fuelled feast for my new friends, but that will have to wait until next year. I toy briefly with the idea of spending Christmas with my parents in the UK but they kick that idea into touch by telling me they are going to the Caribbean. My brother, an entomologist, beat me by many years to a new life abroad when he disappeared to Venezuela to do his PHD – a study in sand flies – and then landed himself a job as a government scientist helping to control the mosquito population in the Cayman Islands. Inexplicably, the promise of warm weather, the swimming pool at my brother's apartment and the company of my two little nieces won out over a half-renovated house in France. So, as a festive orphan, I jump at the offer to spend Christmas Day at Mathilde's.

The French countryside, meanwhile, more than makes up for the lack of festive touches at Maison Coquelicot. Every village has a Christmas tree and lights outside the *mairie,* and some have really gone to town on the decorations, tying big green and red metallic bows to lamp posts and railings, or suspending tinsel lanterns, like glittery earrings, from trees. Unlike the stylised lights and monochromatic colour schemes of London, the look in the French countryside is charmingly homespun. A neighbouring village has a display of Christmas trees made from patchwork outside its *mairie*, while in Villiers the nativity scene features a life-size Mary and Joseph, made from stuffed potato sacks with hand-drawn faces. My favourite decorations, however, are the cheeky inflatable *Pères Noël* that have suddenly appeared, scaling the walls of buildings all over the countryside. The sight of one always makes me smile. René Matout, meanwhile, has applied his artistic talents to the windows of the *boulangerie*, which are hung with three glass chandeliers and a profusion of twinkling white fairy lights, angels and gold cherubs. The effect is charming. I love driving into the square late at night and seeing the *boulangerie* all lit up.

On Christmas Eve I join the queue in the bakery to collect the *bûche de Noël* (A French Christmas cake shaped like a log) that I have ordered to take to Mathilde's. René himself is behind the counter, dressed in his baker's white jacket and blue and white checked trousers (an outfit that I find devastatingly sexy, perhaps because of the way it hints tantalisingly at the muscle-bound body within). When I tell him that I have come to collect my cake, I am rewarded (unexpectedly) with a big, spontaneous, lop-sided grin. A first! This is certainly news to tell Claudette, for I have been coming to the bakery every single day – dressed up in a selection of my most alluring outfits – since the new baker arrived, and this is the first time that he has smiled at me *ever*. Even my aubergine polka dot dress from Prada – always a winner with men – failed to elicit any kind of response. I have been smiling and speaking French and enquiring as to the differences between his *pains*, all to no avail. And today, René's attentions do not stop at a smile. 'Oh I adore the way you speak French,' he says and I melt like one of his macaroons, and almost have to be scooped up from the terracotta floor as he disappears into the back to fetch my cake. When he returns with a white box and opens the lid for me to look inside, it is very hard for me to concentrate on the *bûche* and not his biceps. '*Ah, c'est très jolie,*' I manage to say.

The cake is very pretty. It's iced in subtle shades of pink and cream and decorated with chocolate twisted to look like branches and a scattering of perky strawberries. What girl wouldn't melt at the idea of a man as macho-looking as René who can whip up a cake like that?

'Now, the important thing to remember,' he says, looking totally serious, as he ties the box with a flourish of ribbons. 'Is not to eat more than one slice at a time.'

'*Bien sûr,*' I say, heart palpitating like a massive sugar high. And, even better, as I scrabble in my purse to find the €23 to pay for it, I discover that I am three euros short. I will have to come back. A second opportunity to see René in one day!

'I will just have to go to the cash machine,' I say. 'But I'll be back.'

'Don't worry,' says René, with a dismissive wave of the hand. 'Just pay me next time. Don't put yourself to any trouble.'

Trouble? He must be kidding. I live for my visits to the bakery. My fridge is currently full of choux buns and custard-filled pastries that I will never get round to eating, that I purchased just to see his handsome features, his big hook nose and twinkly blue eyes. And then all of a sudden, a male voice behind me says, 'Monsieur, I will pay.' I turn around and am surprised to see that it is none other than Jon Wakeman. Before I have chance to decline, he has paid the three euros. He too is rewarded with a flash of the baker's disarmingly lopsided smile.

'Ah,' says René, handing me my cake. 'It is truly adorable that accent. I could listen to it forever. Now, what would you like, Monsieur?'

Although I am furious at being deprived of a second sighting of the baker in one day, I am forced to thank Jon. 'I can leave the money in the Liberty Bookshop,' I say.

'Don't worry about it,' he says. 'Have a good Christmas.'

'You too,' I say.

'We should get together and play Risk sometime,' he says suddenly – in the way that someone might say, 'let's have lunch sometime' when what they really mean is never.

'I'm always up for a game of Risk,' I reply.

'I'll call you,' he says. But he doesn't ask for my phone number.

During the fifteen-minute drive to Mathilde's house on Christmas Day, my spirits soar. The surrounding countryside is as crisp and pleasing as one of René Matout's millefeuille pastries. The fields and trees are covered in a fine white layer of frost for as far as the eye can see. But despite the frost and the drop in temperature, the sun is out and the sky is blue and dotted with clouds like little cream puffs. As I drive along the narrow, curving roads, surrounded by the glistening winter landscape, I think how very, very lucky I am to live here.

I park my car outside the twelfth-century stone church in Mathilde's village and walk the short distance to her house. Sebastian answers the door with a warm, *'Ah, comment vas-tu, Ka-renne?'* (I am always thrilled when a French person addresses me as *'tu'*.) Mathilde's kitchen, which is full of potted plants, herbs and copper cooking utensils suspended from the ceiling, is cosy and warm and filled with delicious cooking smells. I hand her the cake, which she admires with an *'Oh, c'est magnifique, ça,'* and a teasing, 'Did you make it yourself?'

'Hello Ka-renne. How. Are. You?' asks Albert, carefully enunciating each word. Unprompted by Mathilde, he plants a kiss on my cheek, while Henri hovers in the background with a big smile on his face. He is wearing a Fair Isle patterned sweater and corduroys the colour of French mustard. 'Hello again,' he says, while Sebastian organises aperitifs. 'I'm so glad you could come to lunch.'

We stand and chat for a while – a fine point of French etiquette, since it is rude to go directly to the table – before moving into the cosy sitting room where the log fire is roaring, the long trestle table is laid for lunch and it all looks so effortlessly comfortable. Mathilde's Christmas tree is white and artificial, but decorated with blue lights and tinsel, it looks very charming and – as with most things she does – stylish.

Over lunch Henri tells me that he is rereading Jane Austen's *Emma* and asks me about my favourite Shakespeare plays. Although he displays many of the characteristics of the classic nerd, Henri is very easy to talk to and we are getting along rather well. In fact, with better wardrobe choices and *sans* the Cliff Richard glasses, he could look quite attractive. While he expounds the view that Coriolanus was a victim rather than a villain, I secretly plan his route map to sex appeal, trying to imagine him restyled in jeans and a plain navy sweater.

'*Dis-moi*,' says Mathilde, with a mischievous wink, but her usual flair for judging a situation, 'if Henri starts to bore you.'

'*Ka-renne*,' says Albert, suddenly, a mischievous smile on his angelic freckled face, 'are you in love with Henri?'

'Why do you ask that?'

'Because Henri, he does not have a girlfriend at the moment,' he replies. 'And *maman* says that you are looking for a French husband.'

Sebastian throws his head back and roars with laughter. Mathilde, who is busy serving up the main course, a coq au vin pungent with herbs and garlic, shrugs apologetically at me and pulls a mock angry face at her son. I do not look at Henri to see his reaction.

After lunch Albert goes to play with a neighbour and Sebastian, Mathilde, Henri and I set out for a walk. The air is so cold that it makes my cheeks tingle as we walk down the narrow lane towards the forest. Over the low stone wall on either side of the road, the fields stretch crisp and white to the horizon, while, in the distance, the trees and hedgerows look like they have been dipped in icing sugar. 'Ah, superb!' says Henri, breathing in deeply. 'This is how winter should be. It makes you feel so... *alive.*'

We walk past the chateau, its antique metal gates and grey-blue shutters tightly closed. (Chateaux seem to pop up in the most unlikely places in my patch of France. This one, flanked by two round turrets and set in an expanse of neat green lawn, is well maintained, though its owners remain an enigma as I have never seen anyone living there.) As we take a deeply furrowed and muddy bridle path into the forest, Mathilde and Sebastian walk ahead, and it occurs to me that they have done this deliberately. Rambling through the dark, slightly sinister forest, I find out that Henri is thirty-nine, that he lives near Tours and that he met Mathilde – with whom he has been friends for a long time – on an English literature course. I also establish that he doesn't make a living from writing poems. He teaches English in a private school for girls.

We walk in the half-light of the forest for over an hour, picking our way around deep, muddy tracks that are partially frozen over. 'Look,' says Henri at one point, stopping under a tall tree, its branches bare but for a dense green ball high up its trunk. 'Do you know what that is?'

'A bird's nest?'

'No,' says Henri. 'It's mistletoe. And we are standing under it.'

'Oh,' I say, and step quickly away.

When I leave Mathilde's house in the late afternoon, it is nearly dark. Henri follows me outside to my car in his slippers. 'I've really enjoyed meeting you,' he says. 'I really hope we get to see each other again.'

'I'm sure we will,' I say, jumping into my car before he has chance to say anything else.

I drive home in the wintry darkness and check my phone to see if Jon has called. After all, he could easily get my number from Dylan in the bookshop. But he hasn't. And I fall into bed, wondering where and with whom Eric has spent Christmas Day.

Chapter 11

Miranda's Birthday

'MAY I SAY how utterly stunning you look today?' says Desmond, getting up from the table, where he is sitting with Elinor and Miranda, as Henri and I arrive at Miranda's birthday lunch. It's late January and the restaurant in Peyroux, a small medieval town close to Desmond and Elinor's farmhouse, is cold, in both temperature and ambiance, with only one other table occupied. But Miranda, who is wearing a cocktail dress decorated with colourful sequinned butterflies – this despite the fact it is lunchtime – and a feathery pink and fuchsia fascinator in her hair, radiates warmth and colour.

'Hello, my darling girl,' she cries. 'Who's this delightful fellow that you've brought with you?'

'You must be Henri,' says Desmond, gripping his hand sincerely and turning the full wattage of his charm on our French guest.

Henri, who cleverly inveigled an invitation to today's lunch when I bumped into him and Mathilde in the market the previous weekend, beams an enthusiastic smile.

'Karen told us you were coming,' says Elinor. 'It's very nice to meet you.' Dressed in jeans and honey-coloured cashmere, Elinor looks, as always, subtly expensive and, in contrast to Miranda, understated (in fashion-speak, her look is one of 'stealth wealth'). But although she is friendly, she seems rather subdued, not her normal cheerful self.

After ordering a round of Kir Royals, we each order from the €25 set menu. I choose a snail tart, followed by sea bream.

'Thanks so much for inviting me today,' whispers Henri after we've ordered, though in reality I didn't have much choice. I had happened to mention to Mathilde that I was going to a birthday lunch where the ratio of females to males would be three to one.

'Oh, well maybe you would appreciate another man to join you,' she replied. And before I knew it Henri, who was once again staying with her for the weekend, eagerly offered to escort me.

'It's a very simple restaurant – nothing fancy,' I said, while thinking that another male – and a Frenchman at that – would be a welcome addition to our little group.

'I would like that *very* much,' he replied, beaming. 'And it would be a good opportunity to practise my English. There is just one problem.'

'Yes?'

'I do not have a car. Can you pick me up and bring me back from Mathilde's?'

And thus Henri secured himself not only an invitation to Miranda's birthday lunch, but my services as a chauffeur there and back.

'So have you heard from Victor at all?' Elinor asks me suddenly. I tell her that the strategy she devised, of pretending to have a boyfriend in the special forces, seems to have done the trick. I made sure to introduce Jonathan, my visiting literary editor friend, to Gérard in the wine shop, describing him as 'my boyfriend on leave from Afghanistan'. Gérard looked confused at first (possibly because he is still convinced that I am married to Dave) but he must have spread the word around the village, because when I took Jonathan for lunch in the Café du Commerce, I felt dozens of pairs of eyes looking at me with a newfound respect. 'So no, I haven't heard or seen anything of Victor since that night in Beauchamp when we waited for him outside the church,' I say.

'Oh *good*!' says Elinor. 'You must be so relieved.'

'An imaginary boyfriend in the special forces, eh?' asks Desmond, and he leans back, his arm draped over the back of my chair, and laughs. 'But you know, there is just so much to love about you, I just don't understand why you don't have a *real* boyfriend.'

Desmond seems to think I lack self-confidence (as if!) and has made it his mission to bolster my ego. He is always lavishing me with compliments. For my part, I have come to see Elinor and Desmond – who have no children of their own – as substitute parents, while Miranda (for the three of them spend so much time together that I have come to think of them as a trio) is like a favourite mad aunt.

'You're making me blush, with all these compliments,' I say.

'It's true,' he says. 'I'm not trying to flatter you. I'm being absolutely sincere.'

The food, when it arrives, is not great. The sea bream is not long out of the deep freezer and comes in a heavy-handed butter sauce, and Miranda looks politely appalled at the dried-up pieces of duck that constitute her main course. Unfortunately, like most restaurants I have visited in the Poitou-Charentes, it is a disappointment. The only exception is Le Routier, the French equivalent of a trucker's cafe, on the N10 near Vivonne, where you can eat four courses and drink as much wine as you want for €11.

'If you will excuse me,' says Henri, getting up from the table when the food has been cleared, 'I must visit the little boys' room.'

'Isn't he *darling*?' whispers Miranda, as soon as he is gone. She is on good form today: even more elfin-faced than usual, quick to smile and very tactile, gripping Henri's arm frequently during lunch in order to emphasise a point.

When Desmond asks for the bill, Henri, I notice, looks uncomfortable. He leans over and whispers in my ear, 'I am so sorry. I know that I should pay for you, but…'

'No, no,' I say, embarrassed and reaching in my bag for my wallet. 'There is no reason at all why you should pay for me.'

'What's all this nonsense about the bill?' Desmond's voice booms across the table. 'Give it to me. I'll take care of that.' And in his typically generous style, he has given his credit card to the waitress before anyone can protest.

After lunch we are invited back to Elinor and Desmond's farmhouse, where two of Miranda's neighbours, a couple called Darla and Geoffrey, have been invited to join us for early evening drinks. Behind the wrought-iron gates their dog Royston, a very large Staffordshire bull terrier, performs back-flips and mid-air somersaults at the sight of visitors. According to Desmond, I am one of Royston's favourites. And because I don't think *anyone* has ever seemed so pleased to see me as this big, barrel-shaped dog, I do not complain, even when he stamps his muddy paws on my leopard print shoes and dribbles over the plum satin dress that I am wearing. Henri, however, looks on with an appalled expression. When Royston turns his attention to him and starts sniffing at his trousers, he looks as if he would like to turn and run. 'He's just being friendly,' I say, as I help Desmond to pull the salivating dog off Henri's corduroys.

The plan is to take Royston for a walk before Darla and Geoffrey arrive. Henri is worried about getting mud on his brogues so Elinor provides him with a pair of Desmond's old wellies, while I fetch my walking boots from the car. It takes some persuasion and the combined charm of Desmond and Henri for Miranda to don an old Barbour and join us.

We set out into the cold, late January afternoon, with Royston jumping around with excitement. Today is *not* one of those fabulously crisp January days, when the sun shines and the sky is blue. It's colourless, damp and muddy. We follow the dirt track in front of their house until we are following a path through open fields – a strange little troop trudging across the horizon. In my plum satin dress, waterproof jacket and walking boots, I know I look very strange. Miranda, swamped by Desmond's Barbour, her feathered headpiece bobbing on her head, looks even odder as she trots along with Henri at the rear. Elinor, by contrast, does the outdoors perfectly: she has thrown a waxed green jacket over her jeans and riding boots and a cowboy hat over her long blonde hair. Tall and lean, she cuts a striking figure striding through the countryside. 'Darling,' says Desmond, as he unleashes the dogs to run across the fields. 'You look fabulous in that hat, you know. It really suits you.'

'Thank you, darling,' she replies. 'It was a present from Miranda. She does have a knack of choosing perfect gifts.'

Desmond and Elinor have been married for nearly twenty years, and yet their marriage is still so strong, so overtly affectionate. I'm fascinated by their relationship and would love to ask them the secret of how, after all those years, there still seems to be a strong physical attraction between them.

Desmond is not so shy when it comes to enquiring about my love life. 'So what's going on with *him*?' he asks, when we have walked sufficiently ahead of the others as to be out of earshot. I turn around to check they can't hear and see that Elinor and Miranda are laughing at something Henri has said. He has been the great success of lunch, working his unique brand of nerdy Gallic charm on both Miranda and Elinor.

'Absolutely nothing,' I say.

'Does he know that? I don't think so. Do you know what *his* intentions are?'

'Desmond,' I say. 'I don't. I just thought he might enjoy coming to lunch.'

We walk on in silence for a bit and then Desmond asks, 'So you *are* interested in him then?'

'Desmond! Miranda seems on very good form today.'

'Yes,' says Desmond. 'She is. And she looked so stylish at lunch today, I thought. She always makes such an effort.'

'I love that about her too.'

'But between you and me, that husband of hers didn't treat her very well, you know.'

'Yes, I heard.'

'Miranda's... a little insecure. She can be... how shall I put this... very up and down sometimes. And I must warn you in advance about these friends of hers, Darla and Geoffrey. I don't like them very much, but it's Miranda's birthday and she insisted that we invite them.'

'Oh,' I say. 'What's wrong with them?'

'They're a little… odd. And I don't think they're very good for her. He's a psychiatrist. She was once a florist or something but she and Miranda are always falling out.'

'Desmond!' Miranda's voice shouts from behind us. 'That's enough walking now. I forbid you to go a step further. Turn around *s'il te plait*!'

Desmond chuckles at the sight of the exotic, plumed creature tripping towards us and immediately does as he is told.

It's nice to get back into the warm farmhouse. Elinor and Desmond have spent a lot of time in India and it shows in their decor. Elinor has hung sari fabrics in rich purples, reds and pinks on the walls of the sitting room and has even draped red fabric over the lampshades, which gives the light a soft, rosy glow. Together with the velvet sofas, the ambience feels louche and decadent, inspired, it seems, by an opium den. I take a seat on one of the velvet sofas either side of the fire. Miranda immediately starts an assault on a bottle of Sauvignon Blanc.

Henri takes the glass of Bailey's liqueur that Desmond has poured for him and sits down next to me. He does not look pleased when Royston comes trotting into the room, climbs onto the sofa and wedges his huge bulk between us. I look at Miranda sitting between Desmond and Elinor on the opposite sofa and think how lucky she is to have them as close friends. A woman of less generous spirit than Elinor might resent Miranda's constant presence. But Elinor seems very relaxed about it. In fact, she appears to be enormously fond of Miranda. I figure she is probably secure enough in her own allure not to view her as a threat.

As Desmond forewarned, Darla and Geoffrey are quite an odd couple. He is bearded, bespectacled and very serious;

while she is flirtatious, slightly outrageous and direct to the point of rudeness.

'Sozzled again?' she says, by way of a greeting to Miranda.

I can see immediately why she and Miranda are friends. But I can't see why Darla and Geoffrey are married – and neither, it seems, can they. Darla makes constant reference to the fact that she would like to divorce her husband, but given the weakness of sterling against the euro – they live off the rental income from a flat in Reading – they can't afford to at the moment. Geoffrey takes his wife's constant jibes about their marriage with admirable stoicism. At least I think he does. He is very taciturn and it's difficult to gauge any reaction in his whiskery face. If he speaks at all, it is in the shortest of spurts.

Darla, meanwhile, speaks in a laconic American drawl – she lived in the States for many years – and when she says something outrageous, it is difficult to tell whether she is joking or not, such is the deadpan delivery. 'I'm on the hunt for a younger man,' she declares shortly after we are introduced. Then, looking Henri up and down, she says, 'You'll do.'

'Hey! Not so fast there,' says Miranda, waving her arms wildly and spilling some wine on the velvet sofa. 'I saw him first. And it's *my* birthday so I get first dibs on the men.'

Geoffrey stares, Desmond chuckles and Elinor leaves the room. I am sure I detect a weary expression on her face.

'Golly, my goodness!' says Henri, who endearingly favours the sort of exclamations that pepper Enid Blyton books. 'This is very unusual, to have two ladies fighting over me.'

'So do you have a girlfriend?' asks Darla, after establishing that Henri and I are not a couple, 'because I'm quite serious about looking for a younger man.'

'No,' he says, making a strange sucking noise with his teeth and looking stressed. 'I don't.'

'Why not?' demands Miranda.

'Gosh,' says Henri, 'I do not know the answer to that.'

'Now, Miranda, I'm sorry to say that we're too broke to buy you a birthday gift,' says Darla, with startling honesty. 'We're really on our uppers at the moment. Geoffrey will be passing the hat round in a little while. All charitable contributions gratefully accepted.'

'Passing the hat?' whispers Henri, lightly touching my knee on the sofa.

'I'll explain later,' I say, pulling my knee away.

I give Miranda her present – a full gamut of anti-ageing products, which includes face, décolleté and eye wrinkle-prevention creams (all sent to me by a well-known beauty brand). Miranda is delighted, clapping her hands together like a child, as she tears away the wrapping paper.

'Oh, *mon Dieu*, how wonderful!' she declares. 'Something for all my wrinkles. Now *écoute!* I've been meaning to ask you: I've run out of that marvellous Chanel foundation you gave me. I don't suppose you have any more? Perhaps I could come over for a rummage in those big plastic crates of yours?'

'Er... I'm not sure I have any foundation at the moment,' I say, a little taken aback by the request, given that I have just handed over about £150 worth of beauty products.

'Storage crates?' says Darla, looking at me with renewed interested.

'Yes,' says Miranda. 'This darling girl is a beauty journalist and you should see all the free products she has stashed away in her spare room.'

'I wouldn't mind a rummage myself,' says Darla.

'Maybe we can both drop by next week on our way to Lidl?' says Miranda, looking hopeful. 'We could bring a bottle of wine and have a girls' night in and play around with your beauty products. I could do with a new bottle of perfume as well, if you have any.'

'Well actually, I've just given a lot of stuff to Médecins Sans Frontières, so my crates are fairly empty at the moment,' I say, feeling really miffed. I like Miranda a lot but I'm unimpressed by this display of naked acquisitiveness, fuelled perhaps by all the Sauvignon Blanc that she has drunk.

I'm even more shocked by her reaction to Elinor and Desmond's gifts. 'Chocolates!' she exclaims with a brittle smile, her voice sounding hollow. 'And a pot plant. How sweet of you.' Then, when Elinor and Desmond disappear into the kitchen to fetch the canapés, she turns to Darla and says, with a spitefulness that takes me by surprise, 'What the dickens am I supposed to do with these?'

'What?'

'Elinor knows I don't eat chocolates. As for the pot plant, look at it! It's half-dead and only fit for the bin. They might as well have given me a nasal hair trimmer for all the use that is.'

Henri looks as embarrassed as I am at this unexpected display of churlishness. Much as I find Miranda entertaining, I am shocked on Desmond and Elinor's behalf. After all, they have shown her nothing but kindness, even hosting her birthday celebration.

'Honestly, I always put so much effort into the presents that I buy her,' Miranda continues. 'And I've bought *her* lots.'

'Well if you don't want the chocolates I'll have them,' says Darla.

'Be my guest,' says Miranda. 'I saw them on offer in Lidl last week, two for one.'

She says this just as Elinor returns and I can tell by the expression on her face that she has heard the last comment. But she chooses to ignore it, setting the canapés down on the table.

'Don't you think you've had enough to drink, Miranda?' says Geoffrey suddenly.

'No, I don't, thank you very much,' says Miranda. 'And what's it got to do with you anyway?'

'You're pissed,' says Geoffrey.

'How dare you!' says Miranda, her feathery hairpiece bobbing dangerously. 'How dare you lecture me? You should look at your marriage before you start telling other people how to live their lives.'

'I'm merely pointing out that you've drunk too much,' says Geoffrey, 'and might regret it in the morning.'

'Regret? How about the fact your wife can't stand you?' Miranda continues. 'She's always talking about putting rat poison in your coffee. And if I was married to you, I would too!'

'Miranda, please,' says Elinor.

'It's OK,' says Darla. 'What she's saying is true.'

I shift uncomfortably in my seat, embarrassed that Henri is being forced to witness such an extraordinary display of Brits behaving badly. But with admirable aplomb he manages to engage Elinor in a lengthy conversation about her home-made vegetarian samosas, ignoring the stand-off between Miranda and Geoffrey. Thankfully, Desmond returns and says something quietly to Miranda which manages to defuse the situation. But a little while later, Geoffrey gets up to go.

'If you want to stay, you can,' he says to Darla, 'but I'm off.'

'Oh great, so I either come with you now or get to walk eight kilometres home in the dark,' she replies.

'You can't go,' says Miranda. 'It's my birthday. Why are you people all so bloody boring?'

Desmond laughs, and not for the first time I wonder at the indulgence he shows towards Miranda.

'Darling, could I have a brandy please?' says Elinor, when Darla and Geoffrey have gone.

'Of course, darling.'

Elinor, who rarely drinks alcohol, downs it in several gulps and then gets up and disappears into the kitchen. She is gone for a long time, during which Miranda regales us all with tales of Darla and Geoffrey's rather strange marriage. When Elinor returns, I notice that her eyes are red and puffy. It looks like she has been crying.

'I'm going to bed,' she says.

'Darling, are you OK?' asks Desmond, getting up from the sofa.

'Yes. Please don't make a fuss.'

'What's wrong with you people?' says Miranda. 'None of you know how to have a good time.'

Elinor stops dead in the doorway and stares at Miranda coldly. 'You,' she says, 'should be ashamed of yourself.' And with that she walks calmly out of the room.

'I think we'd better be going too,' I say, getting up. 'Desmond, thanks for a lovely time. Miranda, can we offer you a lift home?' (It seems to me that the least I can do for Desmond and Elinor is to offer to take Miranda off their hands.)

'No thank you, darling,' she replies, to my amazement. 'I'll probably stay here tonight.'

It is dark outside. Desmond gets a torch in order to see us out to the car. The temperature has dropped while we've been sitting in Desmond and Elinor's cosy den, and the darkness is so opaque that our frosted breath is the only thing visible on the night air. 'Look at that,' says Desmond, escorting us across the gravel courtyard, seemingly unruffled by the day's denouement. He points up to a navy sky, dotted with stars – a sky that Van Gogh could have painted. 'Look! You can see Orion. And the North Star.'

'My goodness!' says Henri. 'Magnificent.'

Somewhere overhead, an owl hoots.

Henri thanks Desmond profusely for his hospitality and I manoeuvre the car around, trying to avoid hitting a woodpile. As we drive along the narrow winding road that leads out of the hamlet, Henri is strangely silent – possibly stunned by his close encounter with *les Anglais*. I switch my headlights to full beam, so dense is the darkness around us, and am forced to brake when a cat runs in front of us from a dilapidated barn. And then Henri leans forward in the passenger seat and touches my knee.

'I never thought this could happen to me again,' he says.

'What?' I ask, feeling uneasy. 'I'm sorry about today. It was all a little... strange.'

'Oh, I *really* enjoyed it,' he says, with real enthusiasm. 'But, tell me, do I have a chance at all?' He clutches his hands together and tilts his head skywards as if in prayer.

'How do you mean?'

'Do you have a boyfriend?'

'No,' I say, wishing immediately that I'd said yes.

As I drive along the narrow road, with its hairpin bends, I can see his glasses gleaming in the darkness, his teeth flashing in a wide smile. 'Oh, thanks to God for that,' he says, clasping his hands in apparent joy. 'The thing is, I am in love with you.'

'But you hardly know me,' I say, horrified. I know that Frenchmen don't hang around when it comes to love – Eric certainly moved with speed, both in pursuing and leaving me – but there is something unbalanced in Henri's declaration.

'Maybe this is a little too quick for you but it was love at first sight for me – a *coup de foudre*,' he says, his voice quavering. 'When I first saw you at the Liberty Bookshop at my poetry reading, I knew you had been sent to rescue me from my darkness...'

'Darkness?' I ask, feeling doubly alarmed and wondering if the day has any more unpleasant surprises to throw at me.

'The thing is... I have had so much darkness... so much pain in my life. You are like a beacon of hope,' he says. 'Never did I think this could happen – that I could fall in love again.'

'Look, this is...'

'I don't even mind if you sleep with other men. It can be an open relationship.'

'An open relationship? Why on earth would you want that?'

'I love you and I want you to be free. So I don't mind if you sleep with other men, so long as there is room in your life for me.'

I think of my recurring dream – the one in which I'm travelling down a dark, deserted country road alone. Now, here I am in real life facing an even more alarming scenario: I'm travelling along a dark, deserted country road with a deranged passenger on board.

'I don't know what to say.'

'Say that you will give me a chance.'

'Tell me something about your last girlfriend.'

'We split up five months ago. But it is very painful for me to speak of it.'

'So why did the relationship finish?' I ask, relieved that he did at least have one.

'I cannot tell you. It was an open relationship anyway. She saw lots of other men. But please, I do not want to talk about her. You will think badly of me…'

This does not sound very good. And I have to drive 20 kilometres back to Mathilde's village with him in my passenger seat. I grip the steering wheel and try to appear calm.

'Look, I hardly know you,' I say. 'And you hardly know me.'

'But I want you more than anything,' he replies. 'Already, in the short time I have known you, you have lit up my life. I do not have much luck with women generally,' he says. 'I do not have a lot of confidence in that respect. But with you it is different…'

'But, really you don't know me. And you… I know hardly anything about you.'

'Well, what do you want to know? Tell me!'

'What was your last girlfriend like?'

'I don't want to talk about her. Believe me. I love you,' he declares, before reiterating his willingness to share me with another man. I put my foot down in the darkness, determined to get him home as quickly as possible. I'm relieved when we finally arrive in Mathilde's village.

'Will you be OK here?' I say, stopping in front of the dark churchyard, desperate to get him out of my car. It is less than 50 yards to Mathilde's house, but he is not happy with this.

'It is better if you drop me outside the door,' he says. 'Otherwise it is too dark for me to see to get my key in the door.' And so, even though it means I'll have to perform a twenty-point turn to manoeuvre the car around in a narrow, unlit lane, I deposit him outside the door. Even then, he instructs me to wait until he is safely in the house, shoving a letter into my hand before he gets out of the car. With difficulty, I manage to turn the car around in the darkness without hitting a stone wall, and drive home through the dense black countryside alone. Back in Villiers I bolt the door and the shutters and reluctantly read the letter that he handed me. Entitled 'Starlight', it is an opaque declaration of love, hinting at past hurt. It ends with the following verse:

'you are a message
starlight
the musical silence one calls love
us together
born
one'

The phone starts to ring. For a second, I allow myself to hope that it is Jon Wakeman, who I am still waiting to hear from about that game of Risk. But it is Desmond. 'I just wanted to check that you got home safely,' he says.

'Yes, thanks. It's very nice of you to check.'

'Did he try it on?'

'No, he didn't.'

'Well, I'm surprised. But very relieved. I don't think he's the man for you.'

'No. Is Elinor OK?'

'Yes, she's fine thanks. She's in bed. But Miranda is still awake and showing no signs of flagging.'

Since Desmond makes no reference to Miranda's bad behaviour, which strikes me as very odd, I don't either. I go upstairs to bed feeling depressed. It's been a very strange day. I feel bad for Henri and the darkness he hinted at or whatever pain he has suffered. But is there a reason, I wonder, why I only seem to attract unstable, unhinged people? Why the divorced and the emotionally unbalanced seek me out? There certainly seem to be a lot of damaged people lurking in the French countryside.

Chapter 12

Pink Cocktails in Paris

'HAPPINESS DOES NOT lie in another pair of shoes,' I tell myself, as I stand mesmerised by the window of the Roger Vivier boutique on the Rue Faubourg St Honoré in Paris. *Happiness does not lie in another pair of shoes*. But the silver, buckled shoes are winking at me seductively from their perch in the sugar-pink window and it's hard to ignore their siren call.

In my head, I run through the reasons why I should not buy them:

1. They cost as much as a new bathroom suite.

2. I haven't earned any money for months and my credit cards are reaching tipping point.

3. I need another pair of shoes like a cashmere store needs a plague of moths.

4. A pair of silver shoes with spindle-thin heels is as much use in the French countryside as a pair of wellingtons with perforated soles.

HAPPINESS DOES NOT LIE IN ANOTHER PAIR OF SHOES. Ten minutes later I leave the shop clutching a stiff, glossy carrier bag containing the silver shoes. The belief that I can spend my way to happiness has triumphed yet again.

Back at the hotel, I pour myself a glass of champagne from the well-stocked private bar and add some expensive bath oil to the boat-sized tub in the master bedroom. Next door in the sitting room (a word that does not do justice to the vast, elegant space) Diptyque candles release a seductive scent of jasmine and rose (a pleasant change from floor varnish and paint) and soft music is playing on the high-tech sound system. I am living a life of mind-boggling luxury – albeit just for two nights – at the Hôtel Plaza Athenée in Paris.

The hotel, which is situated on the Avenue Montaigne, the most exclusive shopping street in Paris, is a favourite of the Sultan of Brunei, Russian billionaires and top models. I am here to write a travel piece for a British newspaper and, such is the clout of the newspaper in question, I have been given the newly decorated €6,600 Eiffel penthouse suite, the best suite in the hotel. After months of roughing it in rural France I cannot believe my luck. Only three people have stayed in this suite so far and, unbelievably, I am one of them. Decorated in a modern art deco style – all dark woods and powdery blues – it is more like a hip Parisian apartment or private club than a hotel room. It has a separate lounge and dining area, two enormous bedrooms and huge wraparound window, from which the Eiffel Tower appears close enough to reach out and touch. And for just ten minutes every evening, the famous landmark is transformed into a glittering tower of light, thanks to 20,000 strobe bulbs. It is like having my own private light show cum art installation just outside the window.

It is February, a week before the couture shows in Paris and there is a definite buzz in the air. Patrolled as it is by *mesdames* in mink bomber jackets and their miniature dogs, the air on the Avenue Montaigne is scented with puffs of expensive Guerlain or Caron perfume. It looks, feels and smells expensive. And with so many top models and fashion editors in town for the shows, the glamour quotient has been upped. Earlier today, I spotted top fashion photographer Patrick Demarchelier taking pictures of a well-known model striding down the Avenue, while outside the Dior boutique paparazzi on mopeds lay in wait, fat lenses at the ready, for a well-known American actress. In my former life as fashion editor of a well-known newspaper, I'd have felt obliged to wait with the photographers in the hope of a story. Today I kept walking and it felt good.

As I lay out an embroidered black dress on the bed, I think how nice it is *not* to be surrounded by unpacked boxes, plastic crates and cans of paint. For months my daily uniform has consisted of jeans and a tatty old pair of Ugg boots spattered in battleship-grey paint, as I spend my days sanding and varnishing floors and painting skirting boards. So, as always, I am really looking forward to an opportunity to dress up. I climb into the bathtub – so big you almost need a ladder – and lie back in the scented water, soaking up the luxury around me: the smooth marble floor, the clouds of white towels, the walk-in sauna and steam room and the shower big enough to accommodate a football team. Even from the bathtub I have a superb view of the Eiffel Tower by pressing a button that turns the window from opaque to clear.

It's all in sharp contrast to my dingy bathroom in Villiers, which has no bath or shower cubicle, just a grimy old shower tray with fungus growing in the grout. Taking a shower is, by necessity, a very precise ritual that involves holding the hand-held attachment as close as possible to the body in order to avoid flooding the bathroom. And just to add a frisson of excitement, because the shower tray empties very slowly, I have approximately three minutes before it starts to overflow. No matter how often I scrub it down with bleach, it's the sort of bathroom where you emerge feeling less clean than when you went in.

I am leading a very schizophrenic life. I write about luxury goods from very unluxurious surroundings. At home in Villiers it still feels like I am camping out. I don't even have a wardrobe or a chest of drawers but am forced to pile up clothes on a chair, whereas here, in the Plaza Athenée, I have a whole wall of walnut closets. I have been living on bread and cheese and coffee for what seems like forever, but suddenly delicious, gourmet food is only a telephone call away. This morning I had a cooked breakfast of scrambled eggs and smoked salmon under the dazzling chandeliers of the Alain Ducasse restaurant downstairs, while yesterday, for lunch with the hotel's *directrice* of communications, I had a delicious mushroom risotto. And just in case I get hungry before dinner, a plate of hors d'oeuvres has been delivered (without my asking) and left on the glass dining table, along with a basket of fresh fruit and a box of chocolates by the famous Parisian *pâtissier* Pierre Hermé.

Ever since I moved to France, life has been a series of goals and decisions — from the colour of the paint for the spare room, to the make of fridge and the height of the kitchen sink. When you are in an unfinished house, there is always some small achievement to look forward to, even if it is just putting up a light fitting. Concentrating on small steps to improve everyday life has helped focus my mind somewhere other than on Eric, though thoughts of him are never, if I'm truthful, very far away. Part of the reason for this, I think, is that I have not found anyone to replace him, and for at least a year after he left I still believed that he would come back to me.

As I climb out of the enormous bath, it occurs to me that anyone suffering from sadness at the break up of a relationship should ditch their creature comforts and rough it a little. The desire for hot water, a bed, a bathtub and cooking facilities, I have discovered, takes precedence over yearning for lost love. Wonderful though it is to be living in such opulence and sleeping in 400-thread-count sheets, my short stay at the Plaza Athenée also serves to underline the threadbare nature of my emotional life. The point of a huge bathtub with a view of the Eiffel Tower, subdued lighting and a big bed with layers of starched white linen is to share it with someone else.

The phone rings. It is Olivier and his boyfriend Christian, to tell me they are waiting in the bar downstairs. By a stroke of luck they happen to be in Paris on a buying trip for their Notting Hill boutique and so I have arranged to meet them for drinks and dinner. At least I will have *someone* to show this amazing hotel suite to. I quickly get dressed, take my private lift to the ground floor and walk through the hotel's amber-scented corridors to the bar, where I find them sitting in a highly prized alcove table.

The bar at the Plaza Athenée, with its traditional oak panelling, ice-blue Murano chandeliers and a bar modelled on a giant iceberg, is quite simply *the* place to be seen in Paris, *coup de champagne* in hand, come cocktail hour. The clientele consists of a mixture of louche but powerful-looking men puffing cigars, chic Parisians, some mega-rich Russians and a sprinkling of top models. Olivier spots a well-known footballer sitting in one corner, and a famous French actress huddled up with a younger man in another.

'Wow,' says Christian. 'I can't believe you are staying here.'

'Me neither.'

Over champagne we discuss the latest shops and places to go in Paris. Then the barman sends over a selection of avant-garde cocktails for us to try including a pina colada ice lolly served on a bed of startling pink ice. It is absolutely and immediately lethal. A few licks and I am giggling helplessly.

'So how's the house going?' asks Christian. 'And more importantly have you met a man yet?'

'The house is getting there slowly,' I say. In fact, I had ticked another room off the 'to-do' list – the *petit salon*. It was a monster job to tint the floorboards dark chestnut and apply three coats of satin-finish varnish single-handedly, but it meant that I could retrieve my sofas from storage at the Liberty Bookshop and finally have another room to live in other than my bedroom.

'And yes, I've met several men, but they've all been a little unbalanced.' I tell them about Victor the estate agent and Henri the poet, who in the aftermath of Miranda's birthday bombarded me with emails and phone calls. He even phoned Elinor to request copies of pictures that she had taken of me over lunch. Thankfully, she thought to ask my permission first. And then shortly after Christmas, I received a letter from him, written in near perfect English.

Dear K,

I hope you received my emails and best wishes card. I also want to apologise. I've been quick with you, almost brutal. I hope you don't take me for a lunatic or a mad man. I'm

sorry I shocked you by proposing so fast. Are you angry?
I have no news of you. Could you please write? Life away
from you tastes [sic] so dull. Anyway, I won't bother you
again by reasserting the truthfulness of my feelings; Hamlet
will do it so much better than I:

'Doubt thou the stars are fire.

Doubt thou that the son doth move;

Doubt truth to be a liar;

But never doubt I love.'

And if I should sound excessive, then remember:

To be wise and love

Exceeds man's might.' [Troilus and Cressida]

Love,

Henri.

Shortly afterwards, I mentioned what had happened to
Mathilde. 'I am so sorry, but Henri is very immature as far as
women are concerned,' she said, before promising to have a
word with him. And after that, fortunately, he stopped phoning
and emailing.

'It was a relief,' I say. 'I was worried he might turn into a
stalker.'

'He still might,' says Christian.

'Are you ex-directory?' asks Olivier.

'No.'

'Well, in that case he can find your address very easily. If he
goes to *Les Pages Blanches* and types in your name and area,
he will get your full address and even a map of how to get
there.'

'Oh really?' I say. 'You can find someone's address in *Les
Pages Blanches*?'

'Yes,' says Olivier. 'Even if you only have a rough idea where they live.'

I put down my ice-lolly cocktail, the significance of this piece of information hitting me like a lightning rod.

Later, we head for dinner in the Marais, and afterwards take a taxi back to the Plaza Athenée, past the illuminated fountains of the Place du Concorde and the glittering trees threaded with white lights on the Champs-Elysées. Olivier and Christian come up to my suite for a nightcap. They stop dead in their tracks when I open the door. 'OH. MY. GOD,' says Christian, taking in the looming shape of the Eiffel Tower, the vast expanse of walnut floor and the huge white L-shaped sofa.

It's fun giving them the tour, my high heels clacking on the parquet corridors as we go from room to room (six in total, including bathrooms). Christian is blown away by the bar. He stands behind the walnut counter top, with its selection of wine and champagne glasses, and does a very camp impersonation of Tom Cruise in *Cocktail*.

Olivier sticks his head in the fridge. There are three different types of pink champagne alone. 'Let's open one,' says Olivier. 'My treat. It's a shame to stay in this room and not drink champagne.' He calls room service to request a bucket of ice, while Christian figures out how to play the music system. The three of us then dance around the vast space with its amazing view of the Paris skyline until nearly 1.00 a.m. But after Christian and Olivier have gone, I survey the enormous sitting room and wonder what to do with myself. The bottle of champagne, I notice, is still half-full and it seems like a waste, so I pour myself another glass.

I've had a wonderful evening, eaten fabulous food in fabulous surroundings with two friends that I love dearly and now here

I am about to sleep in five-star luxury. Life doesn't get much better than this, does it? Well… actually it does. I try to push thoughts of Eric out of my head, but two of those thoughts are very persistent: the first is that I wish he was here; the second is that, if I wanted to, I could find out if Eric is in France. The truth is that I have no idea as to his whereabouts. He could still be in London, or he could be working as a marine biologist in Scotland for all I know, or fighting coastal erosion in New Zealand. I look at the keyboard that connects to the huge flat-screen TV. I know it's a bad idea, that *nothing good will come from this*. It's the sort of thing that a stalker would do. But I'm not a stalker. I'm a perfectly sane individual (or as sane as I've ever been). And surely most people in my situation wouldn't be able to resist?

'*Nothing good will come of this*,' I say, draining my glass of champagne and kicking off my silver shoes. 'Nothing good at all.'

And so I reach for the keyboard that controls the huge plasma screen, click onto the Internet and download *Les Pages Blanches*. Guilt-ridden, I type in Eric's name and I take a guess that he is living on the Île de Ré. Just typing in the words 'Île de Ré' causes me pain like a punch in the solar plexus – writing up the perfume article caused me similar pain – as it all comes flooding back. I feel sick with a horrible mix of nostalgia and excitement (although the combination of frozen pina coladas, red wine and pink champagne could also have something to do with it), as I watch the information unfold on the enormous flat-screen TV. A telephone number for Eric Paul Arnault comes up immediately, along with an address, a map of how to find it and even an aerial view. And so, in the early hours of a cold Saturday morning in February, in a luxury hotel in Paris,

I discover that Eric is living in La Flotte, a little port on the Île de Ré. I discover from the map that he lives just one road back from the sea. After all this time, I finally know where he is.

I wait until I am back in Villiers to phone. I'm not sure what I hope to achieve; certainly not a conversation with him. I am not ready for that. I phone out of curiosity more than anything. In less than three rings a female voice answers. She is French and sounds young – perhaps in her twenties – and slightly breathless.

'Can I speak to Eric please?' I ask (in French).

'I'm sorry. He's not here at the moment. Can I take a message?'

I resist the temptation to ask where he is and when he will be back. Instead, I say, 'No it's fine. I will call back later, thank you.'

From this short exchange I have learnt a lot. She sounded upbeat, happy, unbothered by another woman phoning to ask for Eric – in other words, secure. Secondly, I know that Eric is living with a French woman. This gives me some solace as it means he did not leave me for Suzanne Dance, the American woman whose emails I found. Or if he did, he is not still with her. Thirdly, I now know that Eric is living less than 100 kilometres away from me. I did not know this when I bought my house, but thanks to a strange twist of fate, I am now living just over an hour's drive from where he lives.

I hang up, feeling very alone. I wish I could talk it through with Dave. But Dave is in Hong Kong and even if he was here, he wouldn't want to talk to me. On the floor next to my desk lies the carrier bag containing my new silver shoes. Now, rather than winking at me flirtatiously, those shoes have become a form of recrimination. A pair of shoes cannot keep you warm at night. They cannot tell you that they love you, stroke your hair when you are ill or bring you coffee in bed on a Sunday morning. *Happiness really does not lie in a new pair of shoes.*

Chapter 13

Progress

BY MID-MARCH – after another mammoth session with methylated spirits and *vitrificateur* – the kitchen floor is finished. Although the kitchen lacks shelving and storage and most of my culinary equipment is still packed away in boxes in the spare room, at least I have a fridge and a sink and (hurrah!) an oven with a gas bottle. This particular hurdle was overcome with the help of Claudette's husband who came to Intermarché with me to collect it and Dylan who gave me a lesson in how to connect it without blowing myself up (although there was a delay of a few days between buying the gas bottle and connecting it, since on getting it home I realised, annoyingly, the necessary *'adapteur'* to connect it to the oven had to be bought separately). But the fact I'm able to cook hot meals and have got three rooms into a habitable condition means that I can now concentrate a little more on pitching ideas for articles, which has taken a back seat to floor-polishing of late.

Life at Maison Coquelicot is really looking up. I notice that little green shoots – which Claudette identifies as hyacinths – have appeared among the mass of weeds in the stone flowerbed. I am thrilled by their unexpected appearance and take it as the cue to tackle the courtyard. With spring on its way (early thanks to the shifting seasons), it would be nice to look out of the window and see flowers growing in terracotta pots rather than a rubble mountain.

Desmond kindly volunteers both himself and Miranda for the job. 'Miranda?' I say. 'Are you sure?'

Not only am I worried that it will be awkward after the events of her birthday, but nearly every time I have seen Miranda, she has been dressed in sequins and high heels with full *maquillage*. And given her bird-like frame, I can't quite see her shovelling rubble.

'Don't worry, she's a good little worker,' says Desmond. 'She's helping me to build a garden fence. And in return, I'm going to mend her roof. We help each other out all the time.'

Miranda arrives with Desmond on the designated day, dressed in tracksuit bottoms, rubber boots and a little woolly hat. I hardly recognise her without the usual war paint, but thankfully she is in an upbeat rather than antagonistic mood. Surprisingly, she makes no mention of her birthday and she doesn't seem at all embarrassed (which makes me think she probably doesn't remember much of it). 'Don't worry, darling girl,' she declares as she walks through the door. 'I'm very agile, you know, and quite a good little grafter.' She is as good as her word. Donning a pair of heavy rubber gloves, she gets stuck into the rubble straight away, sorting plastics, woods and metals into separate piles – the French are very organised about recycling and different materials have to be disposed of separately at the tip. Using spades, we shovel the different piles into Desmond's trailer and ferry them to the *déchetterie*. It's hard physical work and it takes an entire morning and several trips to the tip to clear the rubbish, but there is a huge sense of accomplishment when the job is finished.

'Have you got a broom?' asks Miranda, when we return to the house. 'I'll sweep the yard.'

'And we might as well get this table up while we're here,' says Desmond, referring to the enormous Laura Ashley oak dining table, currently lying against a wall in the *petit salon*, too heavy to move unaided. We unwrap it from its protective plastic and assemble it on its side, screwing the legs into the enormous tabletop using Allen keys. Then between the three of us we turn the heavy oak table upright and manoeuvre it into position. We add the two oak benches and then Desmond and Miranda sit down at the new table, while I make coffee.

'Oh, isn't this house just *darling*,' says Miranda. 'This table just seems so... *friendly*. It's made a huge difference to your kitchen. Aren't you just thrilled skinny with it?'

I nod enthusiastically. The table is a major step forward. It means that I can now invite friends over for dinner and start repaying some of the many meals that I owe. To thank Miranda and Desmond for their help, I offer to buy them lunch in the Café du Commerce, but Desmond declines. 'You don't need to buy us lunch,' says Desmond. 'We're your friends and happy to help out. That's what friends are for. And anyway, I promised Miranda that I'd drive her into Poitiers to visit Lidl. Her favourite shop.' He winks. Miranda beams. And I wonder again why Elinor is so relaxed about her husband spending so much time with another woman – particularly a woman whom she herself appears to have fallen out with. I am curious to know if they managed to kiss and make up after the angry scene on Miranda's birthday, but neither Miranda nor Desmond make any mention of it, so it doesn't seem right to enquire.

One Thursday morning towards the end of March, I spot Jon Wakeman looking at tomato plants at the village *foire*. I haven't seen him since I bumped into him in the *boulangerie* on Christmas Eve and he gave me the money that I needed to pay for my *bûche de Noël*. He never did call as promised, so to save him the embarrassment of excuses, I walk past pretending not to see him. But he catches up with me as I am buying some hyacinths.

'Hello,' he says.

'Oh hi,' I say, pretending to be surprised. 'I haven't seen you for a while. I still owe you three euros.' I fumble in my bag for my wallet to repay him but he waves his arm to stop me.

'Don't worry about that,' he says. He tells me that he has been in the UK for work and is back for a couple of months to work on the B&B. After some small talk about a rotting beam in one of his barns, he says, 'What are you doing tomorrow night?'

'Nothing that I know of.'

'Do you fancy a drink in the bar in St Secondin?'

'OK,' I say, trying not to sound enthusiastic. The bar in St Secondin, not far from Villiers, is one of the few in the area that is still French-owned and the liveliest for miles around. (In other words, it stays open after 7.00 p.m.)

'I'm actually meeting one of your neighbours there to discuss a little business deal but I would be free around seven.'

'One of my neighbours?'

'Yes, Dave Cole. I think he lives in the same village as you, doesn't he?'

'Dave is back from Hong Kong already?' I say, trying not to sound too alarmed. I wasn't even aware that they knew each other, but I suppose I know most ex-pat *Anglais* within a 30 kilometre radius of my village, so there's no reason why they shouldn't too. I'm intrigued as to what kind of business deal they might be discussing, and wonder if Jon knows about Dave's recent financial troubles.

'Yeah, I think he's back for a few days' holiday,' says Jon.

'Actually, thinking about it, I did promise to drop by and visit some friends tomorrow evening,' I lie, for I really do not want to bump into Dave with Jon around. 'What about the following evening?'

And so the deal is done. I give him my phone number and he promises to pick me up on Saturday evening. And then I rush off in case he changes his mind.

Having lived in a top-floor flat in London for many years, gardening does not figure highly on my list of personal accomplishments. In fact, until I moved to France, I was blissfully unaware of the seasonal nature of flowers. While I had noticed that daffodils and hyacinths, for example, normally appeared around Easter time, that was about the extent of my horticultural knowledge. And so, on Saturday morning I go to Jardiland, the garden centre in Poitiers, and buy myself an instant garden: two deep blue hydrangeas, two jasmine plants, a purple hibiscus and half a dozen velvety red rose bushes – all of them in full bloom. I also splash out on a wrought-iron table – an essential part of *la vie française* – which will be delivered the week after next. I have never been remotely interested in garden centres before, but now I have outdoor space, I am smitten. I could happily have spent a day in there meandering among gnarled olive trees in tubs, rose bushes, geraniums and rows and rows of unfamiliar flowers – all as colourful as a make-up artist's palette. When I get home I don't bother to plant my purchases. I just drop them into terracotta pots or, in the case of the hydrangeas, place them, in their plastic tubs, on top of the earth in the stone flowerbed. It's the lazy girl's approach to gardening, but it works. The sight of those big, blousy hydrangeas through the kitchen window and the bolt of intense blue and purple in the courtyard becomes a small but significant daily pleasure.

Having planted my instant garden, I spend the rest of the afternoon tidying up the house ready for Jon Wakeman's visit and deciding what to wear. The phone rings when I am painting my toenails pink.

'Hi, it's Jon.'

'Oh hi there,' I say. 'How are you?'

'Fine thanks. Did you get the message I left earlier?'

'No,' I say. 'I was in Poitiers at a garden centre.'

'Well the thing is, I can't make tonight, I'm really sorry. I did leave a message earlier but I wanted to make sure that you got it.'

'Oh?' I wait for some excuse, like 'A major pipe has burst, flooding my property', 'I am extremely ill' or 'I am really sorry but I forgot I was already doing something', but none is forthcoming. Instead he says, 'I guess I'll see you around.'

'Yeah, see you around,' I say, surprised at how disappointed and angry I feel. I spend the rest of the afternoon wondering what made him change his mind. And I can't help thinking that Dave just might have had something to do with it.

The first day of spring arrives – a day, in my view, not to be celebrated if you are single. At least in the autumn you can hide away with a good book and a bottle of Bordeaux. Not so in the spring, when you are confronted with loved-up couples at every turn. And so, having woken up to pigeons cooing and hordes of birds singing brightly somewhere outside my window, I drag myself around to the Café du Commerce to jolt myself awake with *une petite noisette*.

The sun is shining and the sky is a pretty hyacinth blue, but it's still a little chilly to sit at a table outside. Instead, I slip into the cafe, nodding the customary *'Bonjour, Messieurs'* to the oldish men in flat caps already drinking pastis – even though it's breakfast time. As I take a seat on the red faux leather banquette, I spot Jon Wakeman sitting on his own, reading a French Sunday newspaper and drinking an espresso. It's an awkward situation since it's just over a week since he abruptly cancelled our 'date'. He nods hello and looks worried that I might join him. 'I'm afraid I can't stop,' he says, getting up. 'My girlfriend is arriving today and I have to go and pick her up from the airport.'

'You have a girlfriend?' I say, incredulous.

'Yes,' he says.

'See you around,' I say.

I drink my espresso alone, trying to make sense of this revelation. He certainly kept his girlfriend under wraps, never mentioning her once. Perhaps it is someone he has only just met. Either way, it is not good news. I walk back across the square in the sunshine and, to cheer myself up, stop at the bakery for a baguette and a fix of René Matout in his baker's whites. As usual on a Sunday morning, the bakery is the epicentre of all activity in Villiers. People dash in and out clutching multiple baguettes; some drawing up at speed in their cars and leaving the engine running while they run in to buy bread. I can see

René in the back room, his large bear-like frame standing next to one of the giant steel bread-making machines, talking and laughing with someone out of sight.

I am trying to decide between the glistening chocolate *bombe* quivering behind the glass and a rather prim looking *religieuse* filled with violet-flavoured confectioners' custard when I catch a glimpse of the man the baker is talking to. An extraordinarily handsome guy of Latin American extraction, with a schlock of dark hair and astonishing cheekbones, appears framed in the doorway. Tanned and wearing jeans and a black T-shirt (tight enough to reveal a very buff body underneath), he is carrying a large silver tray of choux buns on his shoulder. Wow! The new baker has hired some hot new help in the kitchen, thereby lowering the average age in Villiers by several decades! Things are really looking up.

Yet, despite the excitement of the baker's new assistant, my spirits are low as I walk back down Rue St Benoit towards Maison Coquelicot. It seems that almost everyone in the world is part of a couple – apart from me (and possibly Dave). And I'm convinced that René Matout and his assistant probably have gorgeous lovers stashed away somewhere. Back home I make myself another coffee, drag a wicker chair from IKEA outside and eat the chocolate *bombe* in my courtyard, surrounded by my potted hydrangeas and hibiscus. And the reality of my situation slowly sinks in. There is a blue sky above me and invisible birds are singing somewhere beyond the high stone walls. I am living a life that many people dream of: sipping coffee in a beautiful courtyard in France on a Sunday morning, surrounded by sunshine and flowers. It is time to start enjoying my new life. It is time to start looking outwards at the life going on around me, to get moving. The need to burn some excess calories is another motivation: unloved is one thing; fat and unloved is not a good look.

Since moving to France, most of my energies have gone into beautifying the house and I have not paid much attention to my own exterior. Whereas in London I had mirrored closets at every turn, here I don't have a single mirror. I think I must be suffering from the opposite of an eating disorder, because in my mind I feel as thin as a willow but the truth is that I've been eating an awful lot of René Matout's brioches and tarts and my clothes are starting to feel noticeably tighter.

When you first move to France, as most ex-pats will tell you, you lose weight. The stress of moving, the physical labour and the lack of cooking facilities meant that, in my case, the kilos dropped off like the buttons on a cheap cardigan – even when my diet consisted mostly of sporadic snacks of bread and Brie. But as soon as you are comfortably installed with functioning oven and fridge and have found your way to the local market, the weight starts to pile back on faster than you can say foie gras.

It doesn't help that much of the social life in rural France revolves around eating enormous meals in other people's houses (when I lived in London, dinner was often liquid and by Laurent Perrier). In London, where my work required attendance at fashion and beauty launches, mostly populated by women in their twenties and as lean as crispbread, a few extra kilos would have spelled both career and personal disaster. Here the winter was so long and cold, I could even argue that the extra insulation helped to cut down on the fuel bills. To begin with, a few extra kilos do not bother me. But they do seem to bother my French friend Mathilde. Although she is in her late forties, Mathilde is as thin as a slice of cucumber and, like many Frenchwomen, blessed with good ankles, not to mention steely self-abstinence. She seems to have taken it upon herself to railroad me onto a *régime* – or at the very least count calories on my behalf.

During the Wednesday afternoon 'Entente Cordiale' Anglo-French conversation group at the Liberty Bookshop recently, a stout Yorkshirewoman called Shirley, who had also been eating too many of the new baker's macaroons, announced that she was about to go on a diet. 'Good idea,' cried Mathilde, suddenly animated. 'Maybe you and *Ka-renne* could do it together. You could have a weight loss competition.' The hints continued to flow like cold rosé on a warm summer evening. Wandering around the local supermarket with Mathilde, she stopped and pointed to a brand of mineral water called Comtrex. 'This is what French women drink when they have gained some pounds,' she said archly. 'It is full of magnesium and minerals that help weight loss. Maybe you should try it?' Another time, while having lunch with her and Sebastian, she looked at me knowingly when I declined some cucumber and yogurt salad. 'Don't worry,' she said. 'I know you are on a *régime* but this is not at all fatty.'

I can't be too cross with Mathilde, as I know that she has my best interests at heart. But even *Madame Figaro* appears to be in on the conspiracy. Every Saturday I open the magazine to find it full of bottoms as smooth as a beach pebble and the latest potions and pills to keep it that way. So I capitulate: if I am to subscribe fully to the French lifestyle, I am going to have to join what *Madame Figaro* calls *'la lutte contre les capitons et les kilos'* – the struggle against cellulite and kilos.

But, and I know this sounds like a lame excuse, exercise is not easy in rural France. In London my day began with a brisk twenty-minute walk to buy a cappuccino. Here I am just twenty paces from the village square and (very dangerously) the *boulangerie*. The nearest gym is 25 kilometres away in Poitiers. Even if I was inclined to go (which I am not), going to the gym just seems so… un-French. I certainly never envisaged myself in gym kit when planning My New Life in France. Nor is running or *le jogging* an option. As (almost) the only *Anglaise* in the village, I'm aware that my behaviour is being monitored closely. Were I to start running circuits around the village square it would no doubt give my neighbours greater cause for mirth than when I asked an artisan to send me a postman (*un facteur*) instead of a bill (*une facture*).

The truth is that you *never* see a French woman jogging, wearing trainers or looking pink from exertion. Yet they must be doing something other than apply cellulite gel. I press Mathilde on the subject of her exercise regime – I am convinced that she is doing thousands of stomach crunches and rear leg-lifts in private but considers it un-chic to admit it – and she tells me that French women like to walk a lot.

And so, on Sunday afternoon on the first day of spring, I put on my trainers and start to walk. I tell myself that I will just walk to the next village of St Maurice, which is about half a mile away. I walk downhill from Villiers towards the old village with its hotchpotch of old houses with mismatched terracotta-tiled roofs, the peeling paint of the blue-grey shutters visible in the spring sunshine and an explosion of orange-pink geraniums on doorsteps and windowsills. The smell of woodsmoke and damp earth has been replaced by a fresh greenness – notes of green shoots and sap combined with a hint of white florals, most noticeably jasmine. Crossing the little stone bridge, I arrive at the twelfth-century church which has lain on my doorstep, unexplored, for a full seven months.

Inside, it is far more beautiful than I imagined. Rather than cool and dark, it is cool and light – all creamy stone and marble, the pale decor serving to intensify the colours of the high, arched stained-glass windows. This would be a beautiful place to get married, I think to myself as I leave the cool interior of the church and walk uphill through the narrow, cobbled main street of St Maurice. I walk past houses with distressed wooden doors, past the *mairie* with French flags fluttering above the entrance, and past the iron gates of the enormous chateau that dominates the village. It's just after lunchtime and there is not a soul around. The stillness of a Sunday afternoon in France is very soothing.

Rounding the chateau, I turn into a narrow country lane and keep walking. I have no idea where I am going but it doesn't matter. Within minutes, I am in beautiful, open countryside, surrounded by lush green and golden fields as far as the eye can see. I pass the occasional field of sheep but there is absolutely no one else around but me. I walk and walk, enjoying the lemony-pale spring sunshine and grass verges dotted with poppies and bluebells. The longer I walk, the happier I feel. How could I not have known that such beauty lay on my doorstep?

I have been walking for several hours and I have no idea where I am or how far I am away from home. I come to a wooden bridge at the end of a narrow footpath. To my left is an old, ramshackle cottage with pale green shutters and wisteria climbing up the walls. In the garden, over a low stone wall, I catch sight of a familiar face: René Matout lying on a blanket on the grass, next to another man. To my surprise, I also recognise the face (and body) of the man sharing the blanket with him. It is the good-looking Latin guy that I saw in the back room this morning. And as the truth gradually dawns, I wonder how I didn't notice this before: René Matout is gay and the Latin guy his lover. It takes me a moment to take on board this fact. My 'gaydar' (usually spot on after decades in the fashion industry) has failed badly in rural France.

René and his lover look shy, almost embarrassed to see me. I smile, as if to let them know that I am in on their secret and that I'm not at all surprised to two men lying snugly together in a garden in the countryside. Despite the discovery that René is never going to be my husband, as hoped for by Claudette, I am genuinely happy for them. They have found happiness together in a quiet rural village rather than gay Paree, or the bright lights of another metropolis.

'What a surprise!' I say to René, when he notices me over the wall. 'I thought you lived above the *boulangerie.*'

'No, we live here,' he says, sitting up and pointing at the cottage behind them, their secluded love nest.

'*C'est très jolie,*' I say (my stock phrase for many situations in France).

'Yes, Pascale and I, we're very happy here,' says René, smiling. I'm not sure what to say next, so I tell René that I think I'm lost.

'No, you are not lost,' says Pascale with a lazy smile. 'Just keep going on this road. It will take you to the village.'

By the time I reach Villiers, I have been walking for over two hours and the effect on my mood is astonishing. The discovery of all this beauty on my doorstep – the potential of all the roads and narrow country lanes that I passed and have yet to explore – leaves me feeling almost euphoric. Suddenly, new possibilities have opened up. I don't even care that Jon Wakeman has a girlfriend.

Chapter 14

The Antiques Dealer of Angouleme

I HAVE COME to accept that I have no chance of finding myself a hot Frenchman in Villiers. The average male is sixty-five-plus and more often than not dressed in blue overalls, a flat cap and wellington boots. That's quite a style challenge, even for a former fashion editor. I have come to accept that I am not going to meet anyone for a while and must concentrate on getting the house finished. And that, of course, is when I meet someone.

One Sunday afternoon at the end of April, I visit a *brocante*, or antiques fair, looking for an old gilded mirror to hang over the fireplace. There is an entrance fee of ten euros, which might explain why I am the only customer there. It is cool and dark inside the local *salle des fêtes*, or village hall, and I immediately spot a potential mirror near the door. But on closer inspection, the frame is over-restored and the price inflated. When I turn around, I find a very attractive man looking at me intently. In his late thirties, he has dark hair, olive skin and eyes the colour of coffee beans.

'Do you like it?' he asks.

'It's pretty,' I say, 'But the gold frame, looks... a little too yellow... too new.'

'Then would you like to buy a carpet?'

He indicates behind him, to a wall of oriental carpets, but his smile suggests that he is not seriously trying to sell me a carpet.

'No, thank you. I don't need a carpet at the moment.'

'Are you English?' he asks.

'Yes.'

'You live here?'

'Yes.'

'In this village?'

'Yes.'

'What are you looking for?'

'A mirror.'

'You won't find anything good here,' he says.

'Oh.'

'*Ecoute!* What's your name?'

I tell him. He holds out his hand. 'Pleased to meet you, *Karenne*. He pronounces the 'r' in my name with a real flourish. I am Christophe. Now, listen! Write your telephone number down here and when I see a good mirror I can tell you.' He is already handing me a pencil and paper. 'Tell me, what sort of thing are you looking for?'

'Similar to that mirror in size. Nineteenth-century or earlier, gold frame, but pale gold... Not too yellow. And not too restored.'

'I know exactly,' he says. 'I have an English client with a chateau near here and he is always looking for mirrors. Mirrors and chests of drawers as he has many rooms to fill. So now I will also look for one for you.'

'It's very nice of you. Thank you.'

'In fact, since I am often here visiting my client, maybe we could have a little aperitif together one evening?'

'OK,' I say, thinking it could be useful to have a friend in the antiques trade.

'Are you married?' he asks.

'That's a very direct question.'

'*Are* you?'

'No,' I say.

'Listen,' he says. 'What are you doing on Thursday?'

'I don't know yet.'

'What about if we meet for an aperitif?'

'You live where exactly?' I ask.

'Angouleme.'

'Angouleme?' It is at least 100 kilometres away. 'That seems like a long way to come for an aperitif.'

'Yes, but I am coming back anyway to deliver a chest of drawers to my English client, so it is not a problem. Do you have a boyfriend?'

'No.'

'Perfect, so we are both single. I will take you out for an aperitif on Thursday and we can discuss your mirror.'

'OK,' I say, trying to sound nonchalant. 'Thursday. Maybe. Give me a call first.' I continue browsing around the fair – all the while aware that he is watching me – since I'm also looking for an old wrought-iron *boulanger*'s stand or bread rack to use as a bookcase. I return home empty-handed but thrilled to have bagged a potential date. Pouring myself a celebration glass of rosé that evening, I realise there is a lot of truth in the old adage that you never know when you might meet someone.

He calls later that evening. *'Ka-renne,'* he says, 'It is Christophe.'

'Hi,' I say, trying not to sound too excited.

'Thursday is OK?'

'Yes, I think so.'

'What time?'

'Seven o'clock?'

'Impeccable. I will call you when I get there.'

He calls shortly before lunchtime on Tuesday. I'm in the middle of painting a kitchen cupboard. *'Ka-renne?'* The voice at the other end of the phone is low, sexy and slightly urgent. I brace myself for the cancellation of my first and only date in over eighteen months.

'Yes?'

'It's Christophe. I am here.'

'You're here? Where exactly?'

'At the cafe in front of the *mairie.*'

'What?'

'Yes, I had to deliver the chest of drawers to a client north of Poitiers. I found myself near your area with the rest of the afternoon free and thought why not drop by?'

I look at my watch. Christophe is two days and seven hours early. I am wearing jeans with holes in the knees and my hair is dirty. I also need to wait in until 2.00 p.m. for the delivery of my garden table from Jardiland.

'You don't sound pleased that I am here?'

'Yes... yes, I am pleased. It's just that I'm in the middle of something at the moment... but I will try and get there as quickly as possible.'

Galvanised into action, I cast aside the paintbrush and run upstairs to wash my hair. While I'm in the shower, the doorbell rings and my wrought-iron table (in a very pretty French blue) is delivered from Jardiland. I rush downstairs, hair still wet, and as the delivery men manoeuvre it into place in the courtyard, I think of the al fresco breakfasts that I will eat there in the spring sunshine; all the glasses of chilled rosé that will be consumed here on hot summer evenings with friends. The table represents another giant leap forward at Maison Coquelicot. Admiring it through the kitchen window, I notice that more green shoots have appeared in the stone flowerbed. It's so exciting that in among all the weeds which I still haven't got round to removing – and without me doing anything at all – something beautiful seems to be growing.

It takes me less than twenty minutes to dry my hair and swap my decorating clothes for a summery dress printed with poppies and a scarlet cardigan. I find Christophe sitting outside the Café du Commerce in the early spring sunshine, sipping a glass of orange juice. I also notice Gérard standing outside the wine shop on the other side of the square and looking in our direction. After Dave, my supposed 'husband', and Jonathan, my pretend SAS boyfriend, he is probably intrigued by the speedy pace of my love life. (If only he knew the truth!) 'Ah, *Ka-renne*,' says Christophe, standing up to greet me. As I wonder whether to kiss him on the cheeks or not, I experience that cringy 'first date' feeling. It is so long since I've been in this situation, and I never imagined I would be at the age of thirty-eight. But he solves the dilemma by planting a kiss on each cheek. Christophe is much better looking than I remember and is dressed well (in jeans, a navy shirt and a green waxed jacket). Here at last is boyfriend material that won't need restyling. He looks masculine, tanned, intelligent and – this is definitely a first for me – *wealthy*. He asks what I would like to drink and orders me an Evian, summoning the waiter in a polite but assertive way that I find very attractive.

'So how are you?' I ask.

'*Impeccable*,' he replies. 'And you?'

'Not bad.'

'That's a very pretty dress you are wearing,' he says, revealing himself as a man of good taste, since the dress is vintage Marni, a quirky Italian fashion label much loved by fashion insiders.

I ask him about his trip and we discuss his client's chateau for a while and how the English proprietor is doing a good job of the renovation. He tells me that he has lots of British clients with big chateaux to fill, who spend thousands of euros buying job lots of paintings and antique chests of drawers.

'It takes a lot of furniture to fill a chateau,' says Christophe.

'I'll bear it in mind if I ever think of buying one,' I say.

He smiles and draws on his cigarette. 'So what are you doing here in Villiers?'

'Renovating a house. But I'm also a fashion journalist.'

'And you live on your own? Without a boyfriend?'

'Well, unless he was hiding under the bed, I couldn't see one when I got up this morning.'

Christophe looks puzzled and I figure he has misunderstood my humour.

'A joke,' I say. 'I don't have a boyfriend.'

'*Why* don't you have a boyfriend?' he persists.

'I don't know,' I shrug. 'I just haven't found one yet.'

He asks me how long I have lived here and why I chose this village. I tell him the abbreviated version: that I was visiting a friend one weekend, saw the house and bought it the same day.

'That's a very brave thing to do on your own,' he says, fixing me with his dark, intense eyes. 'It takes real courage to move to a foreign country alone.'

'I never really thought of it like that,' I say. 'It seemed to me like an opportunity. Plus I had had enough of city life – the noise, the pollution, the people. I wanted to live in the countryside and go for lots of walks.' (I don't tell him that I'd reached the point where making a major change in my life was less scary a thought than carrying on with more of the same, or that only very recently did I actually start exploring said countryside.)

His eyes light up. 'You like walking?' he says. 'I *love* walking. And the countryside. I am at that stage of my life, *Ka-renne*, where I also want to be in the countryside.'

'So you must do a lot of travelling with your job?' I say. 'There are so many antique fairs in France.'

He nods. 'Mostly I sell antique chests of drawers and small paintings. I buy a lot at Drouot, the auction house in Paris, and then sell to my English clients for double the price. It's normal. At *brocantes* dealers always buy at half the price.'

I imagine accompanying him to antique fairs all over France, him negotiating massive discounts on my behalf. Here is boyfriend material with added benefits! 'Wow, I would love to go to an auction at Drouot,' I say.

'Well, the next time I'm in Paris, why not come with me?'

'Excellent,' I say, wondering if it's too soon to ask if he has managed to find me a nineteenth-century mirror.

'You know, I could tell straight away that you had good taste,' he says, stubbing out his cigarette.

'Really?' I say, trying not to look too flattered. 'How?'

'The mirror you were looking at. You said to me, maybe the gold is too yellow, maybe the frame is too new... You were right. It was not good quality.'

'No?'

'The frame *was* too yellow. It *was* new. The glass was old but the frame, it had been replaced.'

There is silence for a few minutes and then he says, 'I have not stopped thinking about you since Sunday.'

'You haven't?'

He leans forward and looks at me intently. 'As soon as you walked into the *brocante*, I knew I had to see you again. It was like a lightning strike. You understand? You were the most attractive woman there.'

I was the *only* woman there, but rather than point this out I blush, not sure what to say. There is something very full-on about his seduction technique, but this, I know from previous experience with Eric, is the French way.

'It's such a beautiful day,' I say. 'Would you like to go for a walk?'

'What, now?'

'Yes. I know a really good walk near here.'

'OK,' he says. 'Let's go.'

He stands up to pay for the drinks and I notice for the first time that he is shorter than me, but I'm prepared to overlook this, as he has so much else going for him. We walk down the hill out of Villiers and turn right towards St Maurice, past the twelfth-century church, across the stone bridge, through the narrow streets of the village, and then uphill again towards the old chateau. Around us, everything seems to be coming to life in the spring sunshine: the fields are no longer a dull brown, but have turned a vibrant green, while bluebells and snowdrops and small yellow flowers (whose name I don't know) intermingle with green grass in the hedgerows. The sun is not yet operating at full volume, but the blue sky hints at the promise of the coming months. I am about to experience France in all its beauty.

'So what's it like living in Angouleme?' I ask, as we walk past the high stone walls of the chateau. He lights a cigarette. 'I live with my parents at the moment.'

'With your parents?'

'Yes, but I am looking to buy an apartment.'

'Where?'

'I don't know, yet I would like to be near the sea. With my job, I travel all over France, so it doesn't matter where I am based.'

'Yes, like me,' I say. 'We are in the same situation. I'd also love to live by the sea eventually.'

'Have you ever been to Provence?' he asks, suddenly. 'To St Tropez?'

'No. But I've always wanted to go. Why?'

'I have a holiday apartment just outside St Tropez, overlooking the sea. I will take you there in the summer, if you'd like to go.'

Christophe is sounding better by the minute. 'So you've never been married?' I ask, as we head onto a dirt track that leads to open country.

'I had a girlfriend, until last year,' he says, looking suddenly pained.

'So did you live with your girlfriend in Angouleme before you split up?'

'No. We were living in Paris.'

'What made you leave Paris?'

'I had had enough. It was too noisy. Too much traffic. That's partly why we split up. I wanted to move to Angouleme and she wanted to stay in Paris. But that's not the whole story.' He stops dead and looks at me intently. 'Listen,' he says. 'I am serious. I am at that stage in life where I don't want to live in a city. I want to settle down, lead a quieter life. I am looking for a serious relationship.'

We walk along in silence as I digest this tantalising piece of information.

'How old was she, your last girlfriend?'

'Twenty eight. Now, I want someone my age. Someone who is also serious about settling down. How old are you?'

'Thirty-eight,' I say. 'And you?'

'Thirty-eight too.' He looks around at the vast expanse of silvery-green meadow on our right and breathes in deeply. 'Ah, *impeccable*,' he says and I am not sure if he is talking about the meadow or me.

When we arrive back in Villiers, the clock above the *mairie* shows that it is nearly 5.00 p.m. I'm already committed to going to Elinor and Desmond's for dinner, but I invite Christophe back for a drink in my courtyard anyway.

'*Avec plaisir,*' he replies.

Back at the house we sit at the blue table sipping Evian, surrounded by my recently acquired hydrangeas and jasmine plants.

'This is perfect,' he says. 'This little courtyard is very private. In France, we say that the life lived in secret is the best life.' He looks me straight in the eye as he says this. 'So, can I take you out to dinner?'

'That would be very nice,' I say. 'But this evening I am already going out for dinner with friends.'

'Then when?'

'What about Thursday, as originally arranged?'

'*Impeccable*,' he says.

Later that night, I lie in bed and I cannot sleep for excitement. Could it be that I have finally found a man to fill the gap in my life left by Eric? It's very early days yet but the signs, for once, look very good indeed. Christophe has a lot going for him. First, unlike nearly all my previous boyfriends – most of whom were too poor even to buy me a coffee – he is not on his uppers. Secondly, he, like me, is a free spirit, unfettered by the chains of a nine-to-five job. Thirdly, he is attractive and intelligent. Fourthly, he might be able to get me a good deal on a mirror and – if I'm really lucky – a pair of bedside tables.

He calls me several times before our dinner on Thursday night to tell me how much he is looking forward to seeing me. This, I tell myself, is how it should be: no playing games, or waiting around for a phone call. Good things happen fast. I count down the hours until Thursday evening. In the intervening time, I indulge in a little self-renovation (nothing major – just painting my toenails and applying a little fake tan to my legs), as I am worried that I am starting to look a little too *rustique*. As Miranda is always telling me, it is important to maintain standards, even when living *la vie rurale*. Unfortunately, the John Frieda salon is no longer a cab ride away, so I can't get my highlights done and I'm not sure that the local hairdresser would be able to recreate the complicated three-step process that turns my hair a convincing caramel-blonde.

On Thursday evening, the doorbell rings at almost exactly the agreed time of 6.30 p.m.

'*J'arrive*,' I shout, sticking my head out over the geraniums on the bedroom windowsill. Below I can see Christophe clutching a bunch of orange and yellow gerberas – well, it's the thought that counts – and a bottle of champagne. I also spot my neighbour Claudette, sweeping the pavement and eyeing my house curiously.

'Flowers and champagne. That's very nice,' I say, as I open the door.

'And these also,' he says, handing me two bottles of red wine (how much does he think I am capable of drinking?). 'They need to go in the fridge.' As he moves towards me to kiss my cheeks I detect a sharp, citrus masculine cologne that has been applied with a light hand, so as to only be noticeable close up. 'It was very strange. The man in the wine shop asked me a lot of questions. Almost like an interrogation.'

'Really?' I smile as I think of Gérard attempting to extract information.

'He wanted to know what I was doing here. He asked me who I was visiting.'

'It's a small village,' I say.

Outside, I can see Claudette. She is beating a rug against the wall, while looking directly into my *petit salon*. Other neighbours have also come outside to sweep their doorstep, or bring their rubbish out, in order to catch a glimpse of the unexpected goings on at 7 Rue St Benoit. A stranger parading around the village with flowers and champagne has aroused a great deal of interest.

'Yes, for sure, it is a small village mentality,' he says, nodding towards the window. 'And your neighbours seem like the curious type.'

He asks if there is a local restaurant where we can go for dinner.

'Well, there's Le Vieux Chateau, which is fairly expensive and the food is normally... OK. Or there's the crêperie, but it's very basic...'

'No, not the crêperie,' he says decisively, shaking his head, which I am pleased about. I like a man who makes a decision and who prefers a real restaurant over a crêperie.

At Christophe's suggestion we drink the red wine chilled as an aperitif (although chilled red wine, to my mind, is a bit like wearing a bobble hat with a ballgown – plain wrong, even in high summer). We sit in the courtyard under a blue sky. It's the perfect spring evening, full of the promise of the summer to come.

'It's big, your *rose trémière*,' Christophe says, pointing to the giant green stalk of my hollyhock, which started pushing up out of the ground a few weeks ago and which, to my excitement, is already well over a metre tall. 'So what have you been up to since Tuesday?' he asks.

I tell him that I have been painting kitchen cupboards and pitching feature ideas to my editors in London. Christophe listens intently, his black-olive eyes boring into me. I look at his strong handsome face, his smooth, tanned skin and the merest glimpse of bare chest from his open neck shirt, and wonder at the machinations of fate. If I hadn't decided on impulse to go to the antiques fair that Sunday afternoon, I wouldn't be sitting here with him now.

Later, as we walk down the hill towards Le Vieux Chateau, I'm tempted to broach the subject of this evening's sleeping arrangements but I can't think of a way of doing it elegantly. Clearly, he is not planning to drive back to Angouleme, having arrived with several days' worth of alcohol, but the spare room at Maison Coquelicot is not yet finished. I tell myself that he can always get a room at Le Vieux Chateau.

We are given a table next to the buffet which is already laid out for breakfast; the overhead lighting is so bright that the nuclear reactor at Lussac must be struggling to keep up. Four glum-looking people are sitting in silence at a neighbouring table. Romantic it isn't. There is as much ambiance as a dentist's waiting room, but unfortunately this seems to be the norm for restaurants in my patch of the Poitou-Charentes. The waiter asks what we would like as an aperitif.

'*Deux coups de champagne, s'il vous plaît,*' replies Christophe, without hesitation. I actually feel queasy at the prospect of chasing half a bottle of cold red wine down with a glass of champagne, but appreciate the gesture.

The menu is dispiriting and very heavy. For starters there is a choice of foie gras, fish soup, cabbage leaf stuffed with pork (a Poitevin delicacy) or oysters. I choose the stuffed cabbage leaf, which turns out to be as unappealing as it sounds. Christophe orders the oysters, along with a bottle of Sancerre, and offers me an oyster from his plate. 'No thank you,' I reply, as the waiter pours the pale lemony-coloured Sancerre. 'I like oysters but they don't like me.' He throws his head back and laughs a deep, sexy laugh.

'So, *Ka-renne,*' says Christophe, taking my hand across the table as our starters are removed. 'I still cannot believe my luck that you are on your own. Are you sure you don't have a boyfriend or a husband?' For a second, I wonder what Gérard in the wine shop – who is still convinced that I am married to Dave – might have told him.

'I told you. I haven't had time to organise a boyfriend yet,' I say. 'I've only just got round to sorting out hot water and an oven.'

'Ha! You have your priorities right,' he says, speaking in low, conspiratorial tones. 'Heating and food. Now maybe it is time to find yourself a lover.'

The main courses arrive. I wish I could describe a sensual feast but, as with many meals I have had in the Poitou countryside, it is... *challenging*. My main course, a *salade du périgord*, a salad containing duck gizzards, arrives with a minimal of greenery – one, maybe two, lettuce leaves sodden with dressing – and a fatty deluge of animal bits. I am no faint-heart when it comes to animal innards but this is a little *de trop*. I leave the nicotine-coloured fatty bits piled up on the side of my plate.

I pick up my wine glass to take a sip of the icy Sancerre, suffused with the aromas of lemon, white flowers and straw, and he raises his glass to his lips at the same time. The cool, flinty taste of the wine cleans the palate and the lingering taste of the fatty red meat that I have just ingested. I tell him a story about my niece, who once asked my brother, 'Why doesn't Auntie Karen have a husband?' My brother replied, 'Because Aunt Karen is too expensive.' My antique dealer throws back his head and laughs his deep, sexy laugh. Neither of us says anything for a moment.

'But listen! *Ka-renne*, there is something that I want to discuss with you,' he says, reaching for my hand again. 'I *am* looking for a long-term relationship and I don't want to play any games, but I need someone who understands my job, who accepts that I'm away a lot, without getting jealous. This is very important.'

'Don't worry.' I say. 'I'm not the jealous type.' Fleetingly, I think of Eric and how it never even occurred to me that he would cheat on me. Perhaps I *should* have been more of the jealous type and I might have spotted his infidelity sooner.

'No, *Ka-renne.*' he says. 'I am not saying that you are the jealous type. It's just that for some women it is difficult to accept. My last girlfriend was very jealous. *Christophe, where are you? Christophe, what are you doing? Christophe, who are you with?*' He sweeps his hand in front of him, in a gesture of finality. 'Either you trust someone or you don't.'

'I agree. But surely, she must have realised that as an antiques dealer, it's part of your job to travel to fairs and to meet clients?'

'No. She couldn't accept that at all.'

'So were you very upset when you split up with your girlfriend?'

'No. She cheated on me.' He stops dead and looks directly at me. 'I came home and found her in bed with another man in the middle of the afternoon.'

'You did?'

'Yes. I was leaving Paris to go to an antique fair in the south and I realised that I had left my phone behind, so I came home. It was not even twenty minutes later and I found them in bed together. In the middle of the afternoon.'

'Unbelievable,' I say, shaking my head in sympathy.

'I've been very let down by women,' he says. 'Now, I'm looking for someone who wants a serious relationship. I'm not interested in one-night stands.'

'Nor me,' I say. And once again, I think of the big elephant in the room, which is the question of where Christophe is going to sleep.

'The thing is,' says Christophe. 'You know very quickly if someone is right for you. And there is no point, at our age, in playing silly games.'

I nod in agreement. Christophe, I notice, has hardly touched his fatty steak, which he described as being 'as tough as old boots'. We both pass on dessert. Christophe orders an espresso and the bill, and when it arrives he refuses point blank to let me contribute. 'I am a Frenchman,' he says, handing over his credit card to the waiter. And that is the end of the matter.

There is a thin sliver of new moon in the sky as we leave the restaurant and walk back up the hill towards the village. Christophe notices that I am shivering and gives me his jacket. 'I have really enjoyed this evening,' he murmurs, taking hold of my hand.

'Me too,' I say, and feel a surge of happiness. Although I have ingested a lot of fatty calories for not much pleasure, I have enjoyed Christophe's company. Here at last is a man who knows how to treat a woman. And it's so nice to feel *wanted* again. But I'm not going to invite him in, as I've already decided that I want to be in this for the long haul.

'The champagne should be nice and cold by now,' says Christophe, as we approach Rue St Benoit. This, of course, is the moment to raise the subject of where he plans to spend the night, the moment to thank him for a lovely evening and say that I look forward to seeing him again. I fumble for my keys outside the door, playing for time. '*Don't invite him in,*' I chant to myself. 'It's not a good idea. *Don't invite him in.*' But, as Christophe said, there is no point in playing silly games. I turn the key in the lock and turn to face him. 'Would you like to come in for a glass of champagne?'

Chapter 15

The Long, Graceful Goodbye

TWO WEEKS LATER, I have not heard anything from Christophe, since the evening that we went out to dinner and I invited him in – for more than a glass of champagne as it turned out. I remember the evening only through an alcohol-induced haze, but the following morning, he thanked me for a fabulous evening and said we must do it again soon. I was certain that he would call, but after two weeks of silence, the signs don't look good, which is depressing as I had high hopes for him.

One weekend in May, Mathilde and Sebastian invite me to join them in Marans, a small port near La Rochelle, where Sebastian keeps the yacht that he is restoring. Mathilde is rather vague as to where the yacht is moored but I quickly establish that it's not in water. Instead, I get the impression (I don't know why) that it is in a field. 'You can stay on the boat with us, although I must warn you that it is not very luxurious,' says Mathilde. 'It will just be the three of us as Albert is at his father's this weekend.'

'That's OK, I'll bring my tent,' I say, 'and pitch it next to the boat. I'm really good at camping.'

'I'm not sure it will be possible for you to pitch a tent,' says Mathilde, enigmatically.

I arrange to meet Mathilde and Sebastian in the *port de plaisance*, or yachting port, at 10.30 a.m. on Sunday morning. I arrive nearly two hours late – due to following signs to Marens, an additional 100 kilometres away, rather than Marans – and when I try to call Sebastian his mobile is switched off. Hopefully, I tell myself, they will have found a nice cafe overlooking the port in which to sit and wait. But it is not quite the vibrant port that I imagined. Instead, I find a deserted lock with just a harbour master's office and a few modest-looking boats. There isn't a single cafe in sight. And standing on the quayside in the rain is Mathilde, dressed in wide sailor trousers and a nautical stripe top. (It is, unlike my hastily cobbled together outfit of narrow skirt and high-heeled boots, entirely appropriate to the setting.)

I am hit by an enormous wave of guilt but Mathilde is entirely without recrimination. '*Ka-renne*, I am so glad you are here,' she says, opening the passenger door and getting into my car. 'We were starting to worry about you. We couldn't call you because Sebastian's mobile is dead.' She tells me that the yacht is ten minutes' drive away. 'But we are going to be roughing it a little bit. There is no toilet and no water or light. But Sebastian has the key to the *capitainerie*, so we can use the shower and toilet there tomorrow morning.'

'Great,' I say, trying to sound enthusiastic.

'Any news from your antique dealer?' asks Mathilde.

I shake my head. 'It looks like I won't be getting that mirror, after all. Or the bedside tables,' I say.

'*Tant pis!* Maybe he has lost your number,' suggests Mathilde. 'Perhaps *you* should call him?'

'I don't think so,' I say, trying to be stoical but feeling terrible about it all. 'And I don't even have his number. He never gave it to me.'

'And anyway, you are right, it is not a good idea for you to call him,' says Mathilde. 'That is not how things are done.' French women, I know, expect men to chase them with the same determination as a *chasseur* after wild boar, which is exactly what Christophe was doing, until, encouraged by a large quantity of alcohol, I acted against my better instincts.

Sebastian's yacht is not in a rural green field, as I imagined, but in *le dépôt sec*, an industrial boatyard, with locked gates that require an access code. Mathilde struggles to remember the four digits – 'we will have a problem otherwise' – and eventually the gates open. We drive into a very bleak work-yard, muddy and full of potholes and home to a dozen boats and yachts in various states of disrepair. Sebastian's yacht is perched in a corner, next to a rusty and rather sinister looking barge, and is accessed by a 15-foot ladder with a 'Welcome' mat at the bottom.

He waves from the deck above us. 'Bonjour, *Ka-renne*,' he says, with a twinkly-eyed grin.

'I think you will have to come down and hold the ladder for us,' says Mathilde. 'It is a little dangerous, no?'

'Of course,' says Sebastian, his lanky frame descending the ladder forwards and with some aplomb. I feel ridiculous as I nervously climb the wobbly ladder in the rain in my high-heeled boots. As I reach the top I panic slightly, as there is nothing to hold onto and the deck is very narrow, wet and slippery. 'You must be careful, huh?' shouts Sebastian. 'The deck is not sound. In fact, it is in danger of collapse. Try to jump across to the hatch.'

Somehow I manage to do as he says and climb inside the hatch without incurring any injury, either to myself or the yacht. *The Otter of Bembridge* was made in 1959 – one of the last wooden-hull yachts to be made on the Isle of Wight (or 'Weet' as Sebastian pronounces it). There are mushrooms growing along the windowsill, holes in the polished mahogany woodwork and plyboard covering the rear windows, but it is obvious that it was once a very handsome boat – and will be once again when Sebastian has finished restoring it.

'You see, it is a gentleman's yacht,' says Sebastian with pride. 'A Woodnutt.'

'A Woodnutt?' I repeat mystified.

'That's the name of the boatyard that made it,' says Mathilde.

'It's lovely,' I say, admiring the banquettes, which are upholstered in plush red corduroy. Sebastian tells me that he did this himself using a 'sanger'. I look at him blankly, until I realise he means a Singer, as in sewing machine.

'We thought you could sleep here with your sleeping bag,' says Mathilde, pointing to the banquette next to the small plywood dining table. 'We will sleep in the other cabin.'

'Great!' I say, clocking the various cavities and recesses that could possibly harbour rodents.

I think of the nearest bathroom, at least 2 kilometres away. Anyone unlucky enough to want to go to the loo in the middle of the night will need to negotiate their way across the unsound deck and down that wobbly ladder in pitch darkness, since it transpires that Mathilde and Sebastian have forgotten to bring a torch or candles. They'll also need to remember the code to open the gates and then drive ten minutes to the harbour master's office, before repeating the process in reverse, climbing back up the wobbly ladder in the darkness, unaided.

'But don't worry,' says Mathilde, perhaps noticing the look on my face. 'If it's too much for you, Sebastian has made the back of his van very comfortable, so you can sleep in there.'

I push the sleeping arrangements to the back of my mind as Sebastian opens a bottle of red wine and Mathilde serves up a three-course lunch: salad followed by warm roast chicken and vegetables with strawberries and *fromage blanc* for dessert. She produces all this from a tiny galley kitchen, with no running water and just a camp stove. We sit down at the table and eat from proper plates with proper cutlery and with proper condiments. She has even prepared a salad dressing. It seems to be the test of a true French woman that they can rustle up a decent three course meal *anywhere*.

'So we were thinking of going for a little drive,' says Mathilde, after lunch. 'Sebastian has a brother, Jean-Jacques, who lives near here.'

'But I thought they hadn't spoken in a long time?' I say.

'Yes, that's true. But Sebastian thinks that he would like to pay him a visit today. Don't ask me why.' She shrugs to indicate that she is as surprised by the project as I am.

'Does Jean-Jacques know we are coming?'

'No, it is a complete surprise.'

'And where does Jean-Jacques live?' I ask.

'La Rochelle.'

'*La Rochelle?*' I can't believe that I will have to go there again so soon after meeting the perfumer. (When the article appeared, with three pages of photographs of the Île de Ré, it was even more painful to look at having learnt that Eric is living there.) 'Yes. Don't worry, it is not far. About twenty minutes away from here.'

I briefly contemplate jumping in my car and driving at top speed in the opposite direction. But I survived La Rochelle a few months back; I can do it again, just so long as we don't have to cross the bridge to the Île de Ré. And anyway, who am I to stand in the way of a reconciliation between Sebastian and his brother?

It's raining more forcefully as we climb back down the ladder, making the rungs even more slippery. 'Look,' says Mathilde, opening the rear doors of Sebastian's small two-seater van, when we are all safely at the bottom. 'You could be very comfortable in here. There is very good insulation, as you can see.'

It's true that the floors, ceiling and walls are lined with aluminium foil – rather ominously there is a bucket in the corner – but I can't see any other creature comforts. Mathilde insists that I sit in the front of the van with Sebastian, while she hops gamely into the back.

'Are you sure, Mathilde?' I say. 'I could always take my car and follow you.'

'No, I am fine,' she says, as Sebastian slams the door closed behind her. 'You are too feminine to sit in the back. I am at least wearing trousers.' She lowers her voice to a whisper. 'And anyway, it is good for me. It makes me look young and *sportive* in front of Sebastian.'

There are no seats in the rear of the van, so Mathilde is forced to sit on the floor for the entire journey. She props her head between the driver and passenger seats like a small child. As we drive towards La Rochelle, we pass a sign to the bridge to the Île de Ré and she asks me if I have ever visited the salt marshes there, as salt from the island is very famous.

'Yes,' I say.

'What kind of salt do you use?' asks Mathilde.

'Um, I think it comes in a blue and white box. Why? What do you use?'

'Well, it depends,' she says. 'I have four kinds of salt: big crystals for cooking, *sel de Bayonne* for meat dishes, *fleurs de Ré* for food once it has been cooked and then another salt for the table.'

'You have *four* different kinds of salt?'

'Yes, it's normal,' says Sebastian.

The conversation shifts to oysters, the Île de Ré's other speciality. I say again that I like oysters but oysters don't like me (a joke I have made many times since living in France, always with great success). Sebastian roars with laughter. Not all oysters, it seems, are equal. The ones to go for, he says, are size 3 'special'. The word 'special' means that they have been turned many times. He explains that size 1 oysters are the biggest and oldest (eight years old) and the most likely to make you ill as they have had longer to absorb toxins, size 2 are seven years old and size 3 are six years old and so on. Mathilde and I listen with wide eyes as Sebastian also tells us about a type of potato unique to the island. Cultivated using a special algae, they apparently cost up to €100 a kilo. 'I suppose if you are rich enough to live on the Île de Ré, that's nothing,' says Mathilde drily.

'Maybe we could visit the Île de Ré tomorrow?' says Sebastian.

'*Bonne idée*,' says Mathilde. I say nothing as we drive past the turn-off for the magnificent bridge and the place in the world that has the capacity to cause me the most pain.

It is pouring with rain and the sky is the colour of graphite when we arrive in La Rochelle. Sebastian wants to walk around, so he parks the car in the harbourfront car park and we do a circuit of the harbour in the rain, Sebastian stopping to admire the different boats. After walking long enough to ensure that my boots are squelching with water and my hair is as wet as if I'd just stepped out of the shower, we all climb back into the van and Sebastian announces that we will go to visit his brother now. It takes a good half-hour of driving around to find Jean-Jacques' house. Although Sebastian has been here before, it was a long time ago and he is trying to find it from memory. We follow a narrow road up to higher ground and finally stop in front of a modern white building, with huge glass windows. Perched as it is on a cliff top, it has a direct view of the Île de Ré and the silver-grey Atlantic shimmering menacingly in the distance.

Mathilde and I wait in the van while Sebastian goes to knock on the door. 'It used to be a holiday colony,' explains Mathilde. By 'colony' I assume she means holiday village. 'Sebastian's brother is an architect and he has converted the main reception building into a house.' Mathilde seems nervous but excited. It transpires that she has never met any members of Sebastian's family before – despite being with him for nearly six years.

'All I know is that Jean-Jacques is very quiet and does not say very much,' she says. After a while Sebastian returns to the van. 'OK,' he says. *'On y va.'*

Jean-Jacques, like Sebastian, is tall with long grey hair, worn in a ponytail. Although his skin is slightly more weather-beaten, due to living on the coast, it's immediately obvious that they are brothers. The welcome is friendly but not effusive and Jean-Jacques does not seem at all surprised to receive a visit from his brother after all this time. We enter the house through a workshop filled with industrial-looking machinery. Sebastian explains that it belongs to Jean-Jacques' girlfriend Camille, an artist who specialises in metal sculptures. We follow Jean-Jacques up a staircase and into a large, modern kitchen, one wall of which is entirely glass with a stunning view of an expanse of sea below.

'I hope we are not interrupting anything,' says Sebastian, although it is blatantly obvious that we are. Five very attractive, elegantly dressed individuals, all French and in their thirties, are perched on stools at a high table in the centre of the kitchen. Since it is nearly 6.00 p.m., it's not clear if they are finishing a long, leisurely lunch or are about to start dinner.

'Not at all,' says a slender woman in wide black trousers and a black-and-white stripy top – everyone, it seems, has adopted the maritime dress code – getting up (or rather down) from the table. This is Camille. After introductions and some small talk, she asks if we would like to see the house. Mathilde says that this would be *'super bon'!* We follow Camille through the kitchen and into a large central space, with high ceilings and rooms leading directly off it. The interior walls are made of metal frames with glass panel windows, so it is obvious that it was once office space. Camille shows us the bathroom, the utility room, Sebastian's office and the bedroom. Through the large glass panels, I can see five immaculately dressed children, aged between about three and eleven, sitting in a neat line on the bed. Heads propped up against the grandiose curved wooden headboard, legs stretched out in front of them, they are watching cartoons on a small TV screen placed on a shelf above the bed.

'They are having their own little party,' says Camille.

'*Bonjour, les enfants,*' says Mathilde, sticking her head around the door, and she is rewarded with a polite chorus of '*Bonjour, Madame.*'

We move on to the sitting room, which leads off the kitchen. It's filled with uncomfortable looking modern furniture, liberally interspersed with Camille's artworks. Mathilde admires the fluid, organic sculptures and politely asks lots of questions about her work, before we rejoin the other, frankly terrifying, guests in the kitchen. In London I was used to mingling with Sunday supplement types, but since living in Villiers, I've become a country bumpkin and I'm certain that my conversational skills are not up to this gathering.

Isabelle, dressed in pristine white jeans and a floral chiffon top, and her husband Gilles are friendly enough. They are neighbours of Camille and Jean-Jacques and own a marketing consultancy business in La Rochelle. They are the parents of two of the little girls, in the room next door. But it is the other couple, parents of the remaining three children, that I find intriguing. Arnaud – I do not catch his profession – is bespectacled, intense and very French-looking. He does not smile at all. Nor does he speak very much, but when he does it is in short, rapid-fire sentences, which make everyone laugh. I wish I could understand what he's saying as it is obviously very dry and funny.

His wife Lila is mesmerising: she is French-Cambodian with long dark hair and beautiful, smooth skin in a shade that the French call *café au lait*. Dressed in jeans and a white, see-through tunic which is almost incandescent against the brownness of her skin, she exudes inner peace and serenity. Her husband, on the other hand, is constantly on the move, jumping up regularly to police the children at even the slightest hint of noise or movement from the bedroom.

In an ungainly fashion, I manage to hoik myself onto the stool next to Mathilde. It seems like an age before we are offered any refreshment but eventually Jean-Jacques produces a bottle of champagne from the large American-style fridge. As predicted, he is very taciturn. A gentle, benign presence, he seems happy to fade into the background while his brother holds court, talking about his yacht. Everyone is very polite and interested, asking what kind of boat it is, when it will be seaworthy and so on. But Camille also likes to talk a lot, and for a while the conversation ping-pongs rapidly between the two of them, leaving little scope for anyone else to speak. 'Oof. I think I chose the wrong brother,' Camille says at one point and everyone laughs.

The fast-flowing conversation does not let up even for a second. I understand hardly any of it, which is very humbling as up until this point I'd considered my French to be pretty good. Here, I feel like I am watching from the sidelines of a very fast relay race – all short, conversational sprints and someone expertly picking up the baton when another member of the team has come to the end of their run. I desperately want to understand what they are saying – especially when the conversation moves on to a discussion of the Île de Ré. There is, it seems, no escaping that place. It follows me around like a sad memory.

'Are you able to follow?' asks Mathilde at one point, which is the cue for everyone to suddenly notice the silent presence at the table.

'Not everything,' I say, with supreme understatement.

'Me neither,' says Arnaud, in his intense, quick-fire style, and everyone laughs. Except me.

In rural France just being English is usually enough to impart curiosity value and catapult you to the centre of the conversation. But not here. At this wealthy, erudite gathering, being an *Anglaise* is no big deal. The onus is on me to keep up and no attempt is made to include me in the conversation; no allowances are made for the language gap. The exception is Jean-Jacques, who does not speak at all for the first half-hour. And when he does, to my surprise, it is to me: 'So how long have you been living in France?' he asks in a slow, thoughtful tone. Finally, a sentence I understand.

'Since last August,' I reply. 'About nine months.'

'And do you work here?'

'She writes for English newspapers,' says Sebastian, depriving me of a rare opportunity to speak.

'As a fashion journalist,' adds Mathilde.

This news is greeted with polite silence. And I am even more aware of my muddy boots and wild-looking hair. Thankfully, the conversation quickly moves on.

Arnaud suddenly jumps to his feet again and rushes into the bedroom to chastise the children about something. When he returns, he stands behind his beautiful wife and starts to massage her back and shoulders, in a slow, sensuous rhythm. This continues for an unseemly amount of time. It makes me – and probably everyone else at the table – feel like a voyeur, even though we have no choice but to watch this astonishing display of affection. It's particularly awkward for me as they are directly in my sight line. Each time Arnaud gets up to correct the children (which is often) he has a grope of his wife on his return. At one point, his hand hovers near the neckline of her loose-fitting white top and for a second it looks like he is going to slip his hand down it. The continuous display of sexual tension – the subtext is that he cannot wait to get her home – is very disconcerting, the more so since Arnaud looks so stern and serious and lawyerly. At one point, as the caressing reaches a crescendo and she throws her head back in apparent ecstasy, I am tempted to shout, *'Prenez une chambre!'*

In a brief interlude when her husband isn't lustfully running his hands over her body, I ask Lila how she knows Jean-Jacques and Camille.

'I used to work for Jean-Jacques,' she says. 'And now we are almost neighbours.'

'You live in La Rochelle?'

'No we live in Poitiers but we have a holiday home on the Île de Ré, which is not very far from here.'

'How fabulous,' I say, feeling a familiar stab of pain, and thinking *how totally annoying.* This must be the reason why they were talking about the Île de Ré earlier. 'I've heard that it's very difficult to buy a house there.'

'No,' she says, shrugging her beautiful shoulders with extreme nonchalance, as though talking about buying a new pair of shoes. 'It was very easy.'

I am not so much green with jealousy as the colour of chlorophyll. The Île de Ré seems to have become the most fashionable spot in France (and in terms of real estate, the most expensive). It's galling to accept that it is infinitely more fashionable and picturesque than Villiers – the difference between Stoke and St Ives, Primark and Prada. I feel like an outsider and a failure, surrounded by these attractive, successful couples with their beautiful children and holiday homes on the Île de Ré. Perched on an uncomfortable stool in their midst, it pains to me to think how close I came to having all this too. Instead, I am planning to spend the night in the back of a van in the middle of a boatyard, which for a thirty-something woman is just plain wrong. I sit in silence – not a natural state of affairs for me – and since I can't join in with the adults, I try to converse with the children. The two little boys, who are like miniature versions of their bespectacled father, are now standing next to me, politely waiting for a pause in the conversation.

'How old are you?' I ask one of them.

'I am nine years old, Madame,' he replies with disarming politeness. 'And he is seven.' The two boys wait in silence until they are spoken to, and then ask their mother if they might please have a glass of water. As they're doing so, their little sister – dark skin, almond eyes and without doubt the cutest child I have ever seen – comes rushing into the kitchen and says something that makes everyone laugh. Except her father.

'What did she say?' I ask Mathilde.

'She is asking Sebastian to keep his voice down as it's very loud and they cannot hear the TV,' she explains. Most people would be putty in the hands of this little girl in her pink daisy-print dress and navy cardigan. But Arnaud responds with a very loud 'Shhh' and a fearsome expression on his face. This, I think to myself, is why French children are so well behaved. He jumps up from the table, grabs the toddler by the hand and leads her back to the bedroom.

'*Alors*, you will stay and dine with us?' asks Camille, eventually. This, I realise, is a coded message, for it has an immediate effect. Everyone stands up to leave. I for one am pleased, since we have now been drinking champagne for over two hours and in that time no one has asked to use the bathroom. (This is one of the unspoken rules of French etiquette – I am not sure why it is – but you never, *ever* ask to use the loo when visiting friends.) Camille persists with a 'Yes, yes, but of course you must stay and eat with us,' but everyone is already getting down from the table. The adorable toddler suddenly appears in a bright-yellow fisherman style coat and matching hat but even though we are all now standing, the rapid-fire conversation continues.

'Would it be OK to ask to use the loo?' I whisper to Mathilde.

'Can you wait?' she asks. 'I am in the same situation.'

I stand silent in the kitchen for another ten minutes, caught in a conversational crossfire, before slowly we all start to edge towards the door. No one wants to be the first across the threshold. It's a scene I have witnessed many times at French gatherings, where it's important to give the impression that you are tearing yourself away under duress. A typical exit procedure might go like this: first you announce your intention to leave and ten minutes later you might stand up. You remain here for a minimum of five minutes, preferably ten, before slowly edging out of the room and advancing towards the door as reluctantly as possible. Throughout this process, you must maintain a lively discourse with your hosts. Then comes the check-kissing, followed by some more conversation on the doorstep. Only then can you make your getaway. Having watched my French friends do it many times, I have realised that there is a real art to this – the subtle dance of the long, graceful goodbye.

And so it is chez Jean-Jacques. It takes an age, but we are finally out of the door, kisses and thanks conveyed. I feel for Mathilde as she suffers the indignity of climbing into the back of Sebastian's ancient van, watched by the chic little crowd on the doorstep. As I open the passenger door, I commit one final solecism by bidding everyone a cheerful *'Bonne soirée'*.

'We say *Au revoir*,' says Camille. *'Bonne soirée* is for shopkeepers.'

'What a lucky woman to have a husband as affectionate as that,' says Mathilde, as we pull away, and Sebastian and I know immediately whom she is referring to. 'Even after three children!'

'What does he do in Poitiers?' I ask.

'He's a lawyer,' says Mathilde.

'And I suppose his wife doesn't work?'

'Oh yes, she does. She is an architect. A very successful one,' says Sebastian.

'And did you hear what she was saying about their two boys?' asks Mathilde.

'Tell me!' I say.

'They are both extremely gifted – of a much higher intelligence than is usual for their age.'

I should have known that even their problems would be of the 'too-perfect' kind.

'You should try and meet up with them in Poitiers,' says Mathilde. 'I think it would be good for you to have some friends like that, no? Especially if they have a holiday home on the Île de Ré!'

She asks Sebastian if we can stop by some trees *'pour faire pi pi'*. Instead of asking why on earth we didn't visit the bathroom before we left his brother's house, Sebastian says, 'Ah yes, very good idea', and pulls over at the side of the road, so that Mathilde and I can creep into the bushes. It seems like a suitably humiliating end to the day. Only the day is not over yet.

As we are leaving La Rochelle, we pass a quay where a fishing boat has just come in. And in the few seconds it takes to pass by, I witness a scene so painful that it would have been less hurtful if someone had thrust a knife into my solar plexus. A member of the crew, a man with long hair and a golden tan, lithe-looking in jeans and navy Wellington boots, has just hopped onto the quay. He kisses a girl with very dark hair, who is leaning on the bonnet of a black Golf, waiting for him. The girl is in her early thirties, petite and she looks very French. The man with the long hair is Eric, I am sure of it, and I am gutted. I never was brave enough to dial his number again after finding it in *Les Pages Blanches* but I want to shout out to Sebastian to stop the van, to run over and speak to Eric, like nothing has happened, like several years have not passed. But Sebastian drives on unaware and I sit in the passenger seat, silently devastated.

I am silent for the remainder of the journey back to Marans. Sebastian seems to be in very good spirits having made contact with his brother. I think of Eric and his girlfriend, wrapped in each other's arms. I think of the witty lawyer and his lovely wife going back to their lovely home on the Île de Ré with their three lovely children. I think of Christophe, the antique dealer, who seemed so promising but who hasn't called. I think of Jon Wakeman and his girlfriend, and of Dave enjoying the sunshine (and probably much more) in Hong Kong. And I think of the dark boatyard and the lonely, uncomfortable night that lies ahead, sleeping in the back of Sebastian's aluminium-lined van – like a chicken fillet that's just been popped in the oven. And I feel very depressed. (To think that my friends in London are jealous of my 'perfect' life here.)

'So perhaps we will bump into them if we go to the Île de Ré tomorrow,' says Mathilde. And then noticing my face she adds: 'Oh, maybe you are not so keen on the idea?' Mathilde does not know that the island and I have a history. I have no intention of crossing the bridge to the Île de Ré tomorrow but I wait until we arrive back in the boatyard (doubly sinister in the darkness) to tell them. 'Mathilde, I am so sorry,' I say. 'I hope that you will forgive me but I'm going home.'

'But it is dark and Villiers is almost a two-hour drive from here.'

'I know, but I'm going back this evening.'

'Well, at least stay for some dinner with us before you go.'

'I think its best if I leave now. It's already late.'

'As you wish, *Ka-renne*,' she says. Her face looks pained and I can see that I have offended her. She turns to climb up the ladder to the boat without saying goodbye properly. Sebastian is quiet as he accompanies me to the gate and taps in the code to let me out. I know I have offended them with my abrupt departure, which breaks all the rules of French etiquette. We have not even swapped the mandatory kisses on the cheeks, let alone performed the delicate dance of the long, graceful goodbye.

I drive away from Marans, my heart heavy. There are no road signs to indicate the way back to Poitiers and I drive for 30 kilometres before I realise I'm going in completely the wrong direction. Somehow, it feels like a metaphor for my life. I am alone, lost in France, late on a Sunday evening. As I drive down dark country lanes feeling sad and lonely, I realise that this situation feels very familiar. It is my recurring nightmare – the dream in which I am driving along a dark road, with no idea where I am going.

The following day, a Bank Holiday in France, I wake up grateful to be in my own bed in Villiers rather than the back of Sebastian's van. The sun is shining, birds are singing outside my window and, when I go to the *boulangerie*, René Matout gives me a big grin. He has become much friendlier now that I know his 'secret' (and he's probably relieved that I've finally stopped flirting with him). Back at home, I make a pot of strong Arabica coffee to go with my croissant and freshly baked *pain tradition* and I am sitting in the courtyard admiring my hydrangeas when the phone rings. I run upstairs to the bedroom and, breathless, manage to pick it up just before the answering service kicks in. It is Christophe.

'Eh *Ka-renne*, I am so sorry not to have called.'

'It's been over two weeks,' I say. 'That's a long time not to hear anything.'

'I know. I'm so sorry. I lost my mobile phone and it had your number in it.'

'So how did you eventually find my number?' I ask.

'Oh, I got my phone back. I'd left it in a restaurant.'

'I thought you had forgotten me,' I say.

'*Pas du tout, Ka-renne*,' he says. 'Not at all.'

'So what have you been up to?'

'I've been very busy.'

'Where have you been?'

'In Paris. In fact that's where I am now.'

'Really? But I thought it was a Bank Holiday in France today?'

'Yes, well I'm very busy with clients.'

'On a Bank Holiday?'

'Listen, *Ka-renne*. How about you come with me to an antiques fair in Clermont-Ferrand the weekend after next?'

'But Clermont-Ferrand is at least a five-hour drive away from here.'

'Come on, I am going to be all alone there this time.'

I freeze at these words.

'All alone there *this time*? But I thought you were alone *all* of the time.'

'Listen, I can drive up and see you on Thursday and we can spend the day together.'

'No, it's not possible. I have to work on Thursday.'

'Oh, *Ka-renne*!' he says. 'When am I going to see you?'

'What are you doing this weekend?'

There is a pause. 'I don't know yet.'

'Well what about next week?'

'I'm busy with clients.'

'What did you mean by all alone in Clermont-Ferrand?'

'Eh, come on, *Ka-renne*. I told you not to be jealous.'

'Look, I need to think about this. Leave me your phone number and I'll call you back.'

There is a long pause at the other end of the phone.

'No. It's not possible to give you my number.'

'Not possible?'

'Yes, my phone is for clients only.'

'Well give me your parents' number in Angouleme.'

He pretends not to understand my French.

'Comment? What are you saying?'

'I'm saying it's very suspicious that you won't give me your telephone number.'

'Listen! What about next Thursday?'

'Why won't you give me your phone number?'

'Nah, *Ka-renne*, listen to me...'

'Then maybe I can come and visit your parents in Angouleme?'

Silence.

'No, *Ka-renne*. It's too soon.'

'Too soon for what? You can just introduce me as a friend. It's not a big deal.'

I can feel him squirming on the other end of the phone.

'No, it's not possible.'

'So where are you going to be this weekend?'

'I am going to Toulouse,' he says.

'I thought you said you didn't know what you were doing.'

'It's likely that I am going to Toulouse.'

'Well, I will come and meet you there.'

'It's difficult as I'm seeing clients.'

'Well, don't worry. I can entertain myself and see you in the evening.'

'It's not possible.'

'Why not?'

Another pause. 'My brother is coming with me.'

'Well it would be nice to meet your brother.'

'It's a little complicated.'

'Look, if you are not prepared to give me your phone number, then I'm afraid it's over.'

'No, I can't.'

'Right, well goodbye then.'

He pleads with me for a while and then, just as I am about to hang up, he says, 'Look, I can't because… I have a wife and two children…'

'You have a wife and two children?'

'Yes.'

For once my French doesn't fail me. I call him something unprintable (of which I'm not proud) and hang up the phone. How did I not pick up on this earlier? I think back to the stories he told me: how he was very seriously looking for a girlfriend; how badly he had been deceived by women; and how jealousy ruined his last relationship. I guess I wasn't the first person that he picked up at an antique fair. How could my judgement be so flawed?

The phone immediately starts ringing again and I know it's him. I head round to the Liberty Bookshop for a coffee but this is no refuge. As soon as I step through the door I see them: Jon and Dave sitting at a corner table with a woman that I guess must be Jon's girlfriend. She is attractive in a low-key way: long brown hair, no make-up and wire rimmed glasses that give her a serious, intellectual air. Jon looks over and gives me a curt nod and I see his girlfriend looking over at me. Dave pretends not to notice me. He seems to have a spooky habit of pitching up at the absolute low points in my life. I can't stay here, feeling like an outsider and a loser. Instead, I buy a bar of chocolate from Dylan and leave immediately.

Back at home, I go up to my bedroom and check the phone messages. Christophe has called five times. I sit down on my bed, the sunlight streaming in through the windows, highlighting the dust on the wooden floorboards. The light bounces off the silver Roger Vivier shoes that I bought in Paris a few months ago, creating twinkling shadows on the walls. It feels as if they are taunting me. I might have impeccable judgement when it comes to accessories and the cut of a pair of trousers, but in terms of potential boyfriends my judgement is flawed. There has to be a reason why I am attracting the wrong kind of suitor – the deceitful and the borderline deranged.

I look at the silver shoes, and the rail crammed with expensive designer clothes. These are the clothes that I worked so hard to get – the symbols of weekends spent at the office, evenings working late and miserable trips abroad with psychotic photographers. While other people were getting themselves a husband and a life, I was out buying shoes. And this is what I have to show for it – a rail full of clothes that I no longer wear and pile of shoeboxes the size of Kilimanjaro. The reality is that I have no need for most of these things. There aren't enough days in the year to carry all the handbags that I own.

And, chic cocktail parties in La Rochelle aside, where in rural France am I going to wear a transparent red chiffon dress or a pair of black Manolos with straps that cover the foot like a cobweb? Suddenly, I can't stand the sight of these clothes and accessories. Rather than symbols of success, they seem to represent all that is wrong about my life.

I run down to the kitchen, find some giant bin bags and start to discard the items that I have been clinging on to for years. As Dylan in the bookshop is always telling me, you have to remove things from your life to let new stuff in. Well, that's what I am doing. These clothes represent my past: the red velvet Prada wedges that I was wearing when I met Eric; the Gucci beaded satin trousers that I wore to Le Caprice for his thirtieth birthday; the rosebud print Marni skirt that I am wearing in my favourite photograph of the two of us on the steps of Sacré Coeur. It all goes into the bin bags, along with a zebra print Prada handbag, the Lanvin cocktail dress in fuchsia satin that I've never worn and the navy YSL suit that cost a month's salary. I even throw in my prized Bottega Veneta navy cashmere coat – a source of great (but short-lived) happiness when I found it discounted in an outlet village near New York. These clothes represent my old life and root me in the past. I don't need them anymore.

I don't look back. I stuff shoes, handbags and clothes into the bin bags like so many sad memories. Anything that doesn't fit my life now is dispatched with a ruthlessness that surprises me. By the time I've finished, there are less than a dozen pieces hanging on the rail – a couple of pairs of jeans, a few printed cotton skirts and (for special occasions) a sundress. I also hold onto my favourite Joseph hippy coat, trimmed in astrakhan, because it is warm and will be useful in the French winter.

It feels like I am starting over. The following morning I take the three bin bags to the local *dépôt-vente*, or second-hand shop, with instructions to give the proceeds to Médecins Sans Frontières.

Chapter 16

Summer

IT IS JUNE and the courtyard is in full bloom. The French have a word for this: *'épanouie'*. But it doesn't just apply to flowers. It can also be used to describe the blossoming of a person. Admittedly, I have cheated as far as the courtyard is concerned, shipping in the plants from Jardiland rather than trying to grow them myself. But my jasmine and Provençal lavender plants are thriving in their terracotta pots, gently scenting the courtyard in the early evening, while the scarlet rosebushes, purple hibiscus and orange-pink geraniums are a joy to behold through the kitchen window. The taste police probably wouldn't approve of the clashing colours – I've read enough gardening magazines to know that white and green is the good-taste colour scheme *du jour* – but to my untrained, novice gardener eyes, the courtyard is beautiful. I eat my breakfast there in the morning to the sound of birds singing, and in the evening I sit in my secret garden with a glass of chilled rosé, inhaling the scent of jasmine, lavender and often the barbecue smoke from my neighbours' courtyard on the other side of the high stone wall.

I am never short of company. In fact, I have made more genuine friends in the short time I have lived here than I did in almost two decades of living in London. Mathilde and Sebastian, who fortunately are still speaking to me after my brusque exit from the boatyard in Marans, call by several times a week with surplus celery, tomatoes or herbs from their garden, while Lola and Dylan sometimes swing by for a glass of wine after closing the bookshop for the day. Claudette pops in all the time, often with a little gift from her allotment overlooking the chateau. 'Naturally *bio* [organic], eh?' she jokes, as she hands over a lettuce or a bulb of purple-hued garlic. But it is Desmond and Miranda who are my most frequent (and most entertaining) guests. They often drop in announced, usually on their way back from a shopping trip to Poitiers, full of energy and infectious good humour. The three of us will sit around the wrought-iron table and chat for hours in the warm evening sun, with an aperitif turning into a bottle of wine or two and usually a simple meal of risotto and salad. I have stopped feeling guilty about Elinor, having asked her once, very directly, if she minded Desmond spending so much time with Miranda. 'Darling, if it keeps him out my way and gives me peace and quiet for my yoga, I'm happy for him to spend as much time as he likes with her,' she replied.

'This garden is so beautiful,' says Miranda, as we sit in the courtyard late one evening, candles flickering all around us. 'You must be so happy here.'

'Yes,' I reply. 'I am.'

Despite the fact that I am nearly forty and on my own, my life feels that it too is in a state of *'épanouie'*. This is partly because I have decided to scoop up all the sad feelings I have been travelling around with for so long and pack them away, like old clothes. Rather than wait for happiness to drop down out of the sky, I have decided that I am going to find it in small ways. I find pleasure in the simple, daily rituals of French life: waking up to the peal of church bells and birds singing above the high stone walls; throwing open the shutters first thing to the sight of sunshine and geraniums; walking up to the bakery on the square to buy freshly baked croissants. And then, after a day working at my computer, the early evening ritual of watering the roses and the potted herbs – basil, sage, chives and rosemary – in the courtyard signifies that it's time to relax. My favourite ritual of all, however, is hanging out the washing. Having lived in a top-floor flat with no outside space for most of my last ten years in London, being able to peg my clothes on a washing line and watch as they sway seductively in a subtle breeze is a real luxury. There is no bottled scent as lovely as that of just-washed cotton sheets hung out to dry in the sun. Finally, I have found pleasures that do not involve a credit card.

The house, meanwhile, is nearly finished: the brown wallpaper has been obliterated, replaced with walls freshly painted in pale, chalky colours from Farrow & Ball; I have a kitchen with a fridge and an oven and a sitting room with sofas to sit on. Even the horrible bathroom has been transformed into a light-filled, pristine white space with a new super-flat shower tray surrounded by watery-green mosaic tiles. And through the recently installed skylight I now see an intense summer blue sky as I take a shower in the morning. Life is definitely looking up. Maison Coquelicot, filled with colour and prints, is unrecognisable from the sad, unloved shell that I bought. The work is not finished yet. In fact, the two items left on the 'to do' list – the installation of a wood-burning stove in the fireplace and the renovation of the exterior – seem like the most significant. But still, I wonder what Madame Mauboussin would make of it now? Despite enquiring of my neighbours, I have managed to find out very little about my spinster predecessor. 'She kept to herself,' is all that Claudette will say when pressed on the matter.

And then, one day in early July, I make a surprising discovery. One of the artisans, Monsieur Fillon, who comes around to give me a *devis*, or quote, for the renovation of the exterior, seems to be eyeing my house with more than a professional interest. I invite him into the kitchen to discuss the work and notice that he seems fascinated by the changes that I have made – to the extent that I offer to show him around upstairs too. As I open the door to the rear bedroom (once covered in pink psychedelic wallpaper) he looks very nostalgic.

'I used to live here,' he says. 'In this room.'

'So did you know Madame Mauboussin?' I ask, intrigued and excited that, at last, someone might be able to shed some light on the former occupant.

'Yes, she is my mother.'

'Madame Mauboussin is your mother?' I ask, incredulous, as I look at the handsome, dark-haired man, who I guess is in his early forties. 'You lived in this house with her?'

'Yes.'

'But I thought Madame Mauboussin never married?'

'She didn't. She was forty-four when she met my father, Alphonse Fillon. He was much younger than her – in his late twenties – so when she became unexpectedly pregnant with me, it was a big scandal,' he replies. 'The neighbours were greatly occupied by the news.'

Yessssss! Good for you, Madame Mauboussin, I think to myself.

'When they found out that I was on my way, they were going to get married, but then he died in a road accident – a collision with a tractor,' Monsieur Fillon continues. 'My mother was just four months pregnant at the time.'

'Oh my goodness,' I say. This is sad news, but not as sad as the script that in my head I had written for Madame Mauboussin, living here in a brown-wallpapered house on her own. It also explains why Claudette was reluctant to talk about her scandalous former neighbour.

'And then my wife and I lived here with her for five years after we got married,' Monsieur Fillon continues. 'In exactly this room. It had bright pink wallpaper.'

'I know,' I say with a smile, overjoyed to have all my received ideas about the house and its former occupants overturned.

'In fact, two of our children were conceived here,' continues Monsieur Fillon, confirming my theory that the house had once been full of love and life.

'And how is your mother now?'

'She is in good spirits. She was always very independent but now she is in need of medical care, which is why she moved to the nursing home. But my family and I, we visit her there often.'

Monsieur Fillon, given his connection to the house, is clearly the man for the job, and so, after receiving his meticulously detailed *devis*, I accept immediately and he returns towards the end of August to carry out the work. The transformation is amazing. In less than a week, the stonework has been spruced up and restored and the ugly grey pebbledash facade replaced with smooth lime plaster. Monsieur Fillon and his team also paint the dull brown shutters a pretty blue-grey and, with red geraniums in full flower on the windowsill, Maison Coquelicot is once again in full bloom, or *épanouie*. It's as if the grande dame has had her old, flaky, over-made-up layers exfoliated and is ready to present her best face to the world again.

With the house almost finished – but for the installation of the wood-burner – I throw myself into French country pursuits: the cooking, the gardening and the cycling. I learn how to cook paella, grow tomatoes and take a cutting from a plant. I promise myself that when I lead a more organised existence, I will get a dog. And life starts to develop a slow, easy rhythm: on Wednesday I go to the Entente Cordiale conversation group in the Liberty Bookshop to improve my French; early evenings I go for long bike rides with Lola; on Saturday mornings, I drive into Poitiers, where I stock up on organic vegetables at Le Pois Tout Vert before stopping off at Jardiland to buy a new plant for the courtyard. Sometimes I drive into the centre of Poitiers and look around the market that takes place in the shadow of Notre Dame Cathedral every Saturday morning, and afterwards I will arrange to meet Sebastian and Mathilde for a *café crème* in the Café des Beaux Arts. And it is there, one Saturday morning in July, that I receive another big surprise, which turns my perceptions on their head. I am sitting in the sunshine outside, flicking through the latest miracle creams in *Madame Figaro* magazine while waiting for Sebastian and Mathilde, when suddenly I spot the bespectacled lawyer from the Île de Ré – the one with the beautiful wife and children and seemingly perfect life – walking across the square. He did say that they lived in Poitiers, but this is the first time that I have spotted him and his wife. Except that... the woman he is with... the woman he is holding hands with... is not his beautiful wife. Behind my sunglasses, I squint in the sunlight to make sure I am not imagining it, but it is definitely him. And now he is stopping to kiss the woman in broad daylight. *He is having an affair.* I avert my eyes, shocked at this realisation. To think I was jealous of their perfect life. Nothing, it occurs to me, is quite what it seems and you never know what is really going on in other people's lives.

As for me, I have reached a state of equilibrium, living in sync with the seasons and increasing my knowledge of nature. Admittedly, I've started from a low base point but I now know that (global warming aside) blue hyacinths appear in my stone flowerbed in February and bluebells appear in the surrounding countryside in May, closely followed by poppies, while my favourite flower, *rose trémières* or hollyhocks, are in full bloom in June.

I can now also match most vegetables to a season. In Marks and Spencer on Kensington High Street, strawberries and green string beans – indeed any fruit and vegetable you could possibly want – were available all year round, air-freighted in from Kenya or Peru. At Le Pois Tout Vert, the organic shop in Poitiers, I learn to live with what is available that week. The seasons are also reflected in the gifts that friends give me from their gardens. I drop by Elinor and Desmond's house to walk Royston, and leave with four perfect-looking green peppers from their garden and three carrier bags full of small, bitter black grapes – an eighteenth-century variety, which Elinor assures me makes excellent grape juice. I spend an afternoon washing and de-stalking them. The grapes are small and fiddly and roll everywhere as I try to stuff them into the juicer. Soon there is purple grape juice splashed up the Farrow & Ball Pointing white walls and squashed into the new oak floor.

'What have you been doing?' says Lola, when she calls by one evening to go for a bike ride. 'It looks like a scene from a Hitchcock movie in here.' And all for two jugs of gunky purple juice, already fermenting in the fridge. Factoring in the time spent juicing them and the incidental damage to clothing and decor, the home-produced grape juice has proved more expensive than a bottle of Chateau d'Yquem. But this is the sort of thing that you do in the summer in rural France. In late July and August many of my French friends devote entire days to making jam or turning the surplus from their garden into gratins and *cassoulets* to stow in the freezer for winter. Since moving here, I too seem to spend a very large proportion of my time in the kitchen. In the French countryside, a degree of self-sufficiency is essential, since if the fridge is empty after 7.00 p.m., there is no corner shop to fall back upon. No more instant lasagnes or bags of pre-washed salad from M&S for me; instead, almost everything I eat is made from scratch.

As a lifelong urban dweller, it is blackberrying that provides one of the biggest thrills of my new rural life. In August I cycle into the surrounding countryside with Lola, where we discover narrow lanes brimming with blackberry bushes. We nickname a particularly abundant stretch 'Blackberry Alley'. We go back the next evening, armed with plastic tubs, to pick the shiny black fruits. I acquire bramble cuts and nettle stings and almost sustain an ankle injury jumping across a ditch. But by the end of the evening, we have buckets of a fruit that is free, naturally organic and just a ten-minute bike ride away. 'I can't believe you have never been blackberrying before,' says Lola, amazed. 'I had you down as a real country girl.' This feels like a huge compliment, if completely erroneous, as I grew up in a suburb of Liverpool.

The next day I discover how easy it is to make an apple and blackberry crumble. High on the aroma of caramelised sugar, I make three in rapid succession, making inroads into the blackberry mountain. I give one to Claudette, put one in the freezer and save one for Sunday lunch. To celebrate the first anniversary of My New Life in France, I have invited Claudette and her husband Michel, along with Mathilde and Sebastian, to experience traditional English cuisine in my little courtyard garden. Their expectations, I suspect, are low. But I am planning to do my bit to turn around my host nation's uncharitable view of British cuisine.

The secret, I have decided, is not to try and compete on the same playing field. That means nothing fancy, stuffed or traditionally French. Instead, I dig out an old copy of Delia Smith. Now Delia might have been eclipsed by trendier chefs in the UK, but her cottage pie with leek and cheese topping proves to be big hit with my French friends. Even Mathilde, who normally eats only a tablespoon of anything, asks for seconds. The blackberry and apple crumble is an even bigger hit.

'*Bravo, chef!*' declares Mathilde, at the end of the meal. And then, surveying the latest work on the house, she adds, 'You know *Ka-renne*, she has not bad taste for *une Anglaise*.' Praise indeed!

'This house,' says Claudette, 'has a very happy feeling.'

Sitting in the warm, shaded courtyard with my friends, as lunch morphs into early evening, I feel a deep sense of belonging. Later, as Claudette stands up to leave, I wonder how I didn't notice her shoes – a pair of eye-catching silver Roger Viviers, which she must have bought from the local *dépôt-vente* where I offloaded my surplus designer clothes. Designed for evening, they look charmingly eccentric worn with Claudette's grandmotherly floral dress.

And so in small pleasures, the company of my new friends and the beauty of the French countryside, I achieve a state of equilibrium. The summer months pass all too quickly but, during the long hot days and drawn-out evenings, my love affair with the French countryside – and my happiness – grows. But then, just when I am least expecting it, the past jumps out and ambushes me again. One Monday morning in late August, I log onto Eric's old email account in order to make some changes to the credit card used for billing – for he is still the master name on the account and for some reason the service provider cannot change that – and discover an email entitled 'holiday pictures' from one Rob Bolton. I know I shouldn't probe any further and I know it's wrong to read other people's emails but I do – shamefully, without even a moment's thought. Clicking open the email, I find the following:

Hey Eric!
Hope all is cool with you. Back in the US now and wanted to say thanks for all the great pizza. We had a great time on Ré and really enjoyed eating at your restaurant. I am attaching a couple of pictures of La Flotte. You might recognise the pink sun hat that my mother is wearing as belonging to your wife.
Keep in touch!
Rob.

I know I shouldn't but I download the pictures. The first shows a woman in her fifties, sitting on a seawall, with a red and white lighthouse visible behind her. The second features a man standing outside a restaurant wearing a long white apron. His hair looks short but it's hard to tell – it could just be tied back – and he looks like he has gained a little weight, but it is unmistakably Eric. The expression on his face is a mixture of reluctance and bemusement. Obviously, he has deliberately given his over-enthusiastic customer his old email address.

And, so, sitting in front of my computer, I discover that:

1. Eric owns a pizza restaurant on the Île de Ré.

2. Eric has possibly been eating too much of his own pizza. (And he is no longer the boy with the long, golden hair, frozen in my mind from all those summers ago; nor is he the man I saw jumping off a fishing boat in La Rochelle back in May.)

3. Eric is married.

The last discovery is painful but the pain, like having your legs waxed, is sharp and swift rather than lingering. I always knew that I would have to face this moment. But now that it has finally arrived, it feels like resolution of sorts. I study the photograph for an age and then, I can't stop myself: I run up to the spare room and dig out a box of photos of us together, including my favourite picture of the two of us holding hands on the steps of Sacré Coeur in Montmartre, Paris – me in a long Marni rosebud print skirt with sunglasses on my head; him in a white shirt and jeans.

'*Coucou!* Anyone at home?'

Just as I am about to embark on another sad trip down memory lane, Miranda calls in through the sitting room window. I can see Desmond standing outside in the bright sunshine with her. They had mentioned that they might pop in en route to Castorama, the DIY store in Poitiers.

'What's the matter?' says Desmond, as I open the door. 'Why the glum face? Aren't you pleased to see us?'

'No, no… it's not that.'

'Who's this?' says Miranda immediately spotting the photograph of Eric that I have left lying on the sofa. 'Gosh, isn't he handsome?'

'Miranda, that's *so* not what I want to hear,' I say, quietly. 'That's my ex-boyfriend and I just discovered that he's married.'

'Oh!' says Desmond, uncharacteristically stuck for something to say.

Miranda does not miss a beat. 'I think, my darling girl, that it's time you found a new one.'

Chapter 17

Pie Night

THE AUBERGE DE Bléssy is decorated with multicoloured fairy lights and makes a romantic spectacle in the foggy darkness. It looks like a scene from a movie and although the event I am about to attend is inauspiciously known as 'Pie Night', it feels like there's magic in the air. This, I think to myself, would be a perfect place to meet someone, although there's not much chance of that at a gathering of (mostly) retired ex-pats. I've come along partly out of curiosity but mostly because I promised Miranda, who was strangely insistent that I come. Tempting though it was to stay at home with a bottle of red wine and a good book, I've driven 20 kilometres on a cold October evening to eat pie and chips and watch an outfit called the Blue River Band.

The bar is warm and welcoming, with a wood-burning stove blazing in the stone fireplace. Amazingly for a British-run bar in rural France, there are even some genuine French people present: four elderly men playing a card game at a table in a corner. I pay my seven-euro entrance fee to Ernest, the English owner, and head for the back room, where I can hear the Blue River Band playing an old Eric Clapton number. The band consists of a husband and wife hippy duo, who have lived through the Woodstock era, and a weather-beaten old roué with more lines than a map of France. I am wearing my black hippy coat, trimmed in shaggy astrakhan, which, without having planned it, fits perfectly into the late 1960s/early 1970s groove. Everyone is seated at long trestle tables. I spot Miranda, dressed in black sequins and with glitter in her hair, sitting at a table with Darla and her husband Geoffrey, the rather odd couple that I met at Miranda's birthday. So they haven't got divorced yet then, I think to myself. Jon Wakeman is sitting with them.

'Darling girl,' Miranda cries over the music as I arrive. 'You made it. I'm thrilled skinny.'

Jon is tapping his hand on the table in time with the music. Based on previous encounters, I am preparing to be cold-shouldered but to my surprise, he flashes me a *very* friendly smile.

'You know Karen?' Miranda shouts at him. He nods and pulls out the chair next to him for me to sit down. His long hair looks madder than I remember, sticking out in all directions. I want to be cold with him, given that he stood me up so rudely a few months ago, but it's difficult.

'How's the house going?' he shouts.

'Yeah, not bad. How's the B&B?'

'It's coming along… slowly,' he says. 'I've had to go back to the UK to earn some money.'

'How long are you out for?'

'Only for a few days unfortunately. Then back again at the end of November until the end of January. Would you like a drink?'

Has Monsieur Wakeman undergone some kind of personality makeover? I wonder, as he heads off to the bar. I'm certainly intrigued as to what's caused this sudden turnaround. Miranda waves at me excitedly. 'Isn't he *adorable*,' she says. 'Look at his hair – all over the place. Apparently, he cut it himself this evening. He's just so lovely... and guess what?'

'What?'

'He might be single soon. It sounds like things aren't going well with his girlfriend.'

'How do you know that?'

'Apparently, she doesn't want to come and live here. She's an accident and emergency doctor. He says that she's got to make a decision soon or it's over...'

'Really?'

'Yes, he wants to get the B&B finished as soon as possible and move out here full time. But she's dragging her feet.'

'He told you all this?'

'Yes, he's quite philosophical about it,' said Miranda, her eyes twinkling with excitement. 'If she doesn't come out soon, it's going to be curtains for her.'

Am I imagining it or is Miranda trying to set me up with Jon? It would explain why she was so keen for me to come along this evening.

'How long have they been going out?' I ask.

'Seven years apparently, but it hasn't been right for the past year, which is why he never mentioned her. The only thing is, darling girl, for some reason he thought you were married.'

'He did?'

'Yes, apparently the man who runs the wine shop in Villiers told him that not only did you have a husband who was away most of the time but that you also had a lover in the SAS, fighting in Afghanistan.'

'What?' I say, wide-eyed.

'But don't worry. I've put him straight on all of that.'

'Shh, look, he's coming back.'

'So, darling girl, have you seen Elinor or Desmond recently?'

'Not for ages. They both seem very busy at the moment.'

'Are they? Doing what?' asks Miranda.

'I don't know. I invited them along tonight but they said they were already busy.'

'Oh,' says Miranda. 'Probably a good job you didn't. Strictly *entre nous*, Elinor and I have had a bit of a fall-out.'

'A fall-out?' I think back to the showdown on Miranda's birthday but having seen them together since, figured that they had kissed and made up. 'Nothing too serious, I hope?'

'Darling girl, let's not go there.'

By the time Jon returns with the drinks, I have been accosted by the man on my right – a former fireman from Wales, who wants to know what I am doing out here, how long I've been here, where I live, etc. He introduces me to his wife, a thin woman with a grey bob, bottle-thick glasses and a startled expression on her face. It's hard to hear above the noise of the band but when I try to speak to her she just stares at me, like a startled rabbit. I yell louder but get the same blank gaze. Jon comes to my rescue.

'You're wasting your time.'

'Sorry?'

'I saw you trying to talk to her but she's too drunk to speak.'

'How can you tell?' I ask.

'I just can,' he says with a wink.

The steak and kidney pie is dished up and bottles of HP sauce are distributed. I watch as people around me enthusiastically pump it over the sludge on their plates. It is very strange to be sitting in a bar called the Auberge in the middle of a quiet French village, surrounded by British people, either tucking into glutinous pie or singing drunkenly and morosely along to Led Zeppelin's 'Stairway to Heaven'. I feel sorry for the one French couple sitting in our midst who must have stumbled in here by mistake, perhaps foolishly imagining that the bar was still under French ownership. Now, here they are, stoically eating the food in silence, and looking like they've just survived a road accident as they survey the sozzled Brits around them.

'Not so much pie night as pie-eyed night,' observes Jon, as if reading my mind.

This was exactly the sort of scenario I planned to avoid when I first arrived in France, but strangely, I find that I am enjoying myself. Jon nudges me. Miranda, as usual, has elected not to eat and is now swaying along to the music with the drunken woman who was sitting opposite me. She appears to be using Miranda's slight frame to prop herself up. 'Oh dear,' I say. Then I ask one of several questions that I am dying to know the answers to.

'So, what happened with the business venture you were planning with Dave?'

'Business venture is overstating it a little,' he replies. 'Dave was interested in renting one of my barns for storing his microlight but in the end we decided it wasn't a good idea.'

'Oh,' I say. 'Is Dave a good friend of yours?'

'Not really. I just know him in the same way I know lots of people out here.'

Suddenly there is a loud crash. Miranda has been pulled to the floor by her drunken dancing partner. There is a tangle of chairs, and a collective intake of breath. Jon is the first on his feet to check that they are OK. He helps them both up from the floor and gently assists the former fireman's wife back to her seat. Miranda follows, swaying slightly in her high heels as she returns to the table.

'So, darling boy,' she says to Jon. 'What about this Christmas dinner dance in Anzac in early December? Karen is coming, aren't you?'

The concept of a dinner dance sounds quite alien to me – something that people of an older generation do – and Christmas seems ages away, but Miranda has already signed me up for a ticket, assuring me that it was 'oodles of fun' last year.

'That sounds like an excellent plan,' says Jon. Then, turning to me: 'If you're definitely going, then maybe we could meet up and go together?'

'Yeah, that'd be great,' I reply, still wondering what lies behind this new charm offensive. But the dance is at least six weeks away, which gives him plenty of time to cancel.

It transpires that Darla and her husband Geoffrey – who seem to be getting along better this evening – are also going. 'Look,' says Darla, leaning into the conversation. 'If you can both get yourselves here, you can come with us. Then if you want to have a drink or two, you can crash the night at ours – we've got two sofa beds – and that way, you don't need to worry about driving.'

I haven't done 'crashing' since my student days and I prefer my own bed to someone else's sofa. But maybe I should live a little dangerously. Ex-pat events are hard work without alcohol. So, against my better instincts, I find myself agreeing to the plan. Later, we all stand outside the twinkling bar and say goodbye, our breath white and visible on the freezing night air. Darla is giving Jon directions on how to get to her house. 'Look, it's only half a mile up the road. Why don't you both follow me back now, just to make sure you know where it is.'

'OK,' says Jon.

Shivering in the cold, I realise that I have left my scarf in the bar and run back inside to get it.

Jon is still waiting outside when I return. Everyone else has gone. I follow his car to Darla's. She is waiting in her car outside her house and gets out when we both pull up. After giving Jon her phone number so that he can confirm plans nearer the time, she directs us to a little patch of scrubland at the end of the narrow, bumpy lane, in which to turn around. Jon Wakeman is in front of me, so he goes first, then I follow. It takes me a while as it a tricky manoeuvre to reverse in the opaque darkness, without backing into a ditch. Jon drives off without waiting for me, even though we are both going in the same direction. The darkness is rendered even more opaque by swirling pockets of fog as I drive cross-country through the narrow, winding lanes surrounded by dark, open fields. It's a little scary as I'm not even sure I am going in the right direction. But it's very wintry and strangely atmospheric. I wonder if Jon is thinking the same thing as he drives through the same foggy darkness a few minutes ahead of me. What a shame he did not have the manners to wait.

The big event of November is the installation of my wood-burner. The Godin, made from matt black cast iron, has been standing hopefully in front of the fireplace, waiting to be connected, for months now. I bought it on impulse in August, having spotted it on sale in a DIY store at a huge discount. At the time, I did not even know if the chimney was in good working order, and the fireplace was still all boarded up, but since it is impossible to live in rural France and *not* have a real log fire, I decided to take the risk. More importantly, I wanted to give Maison Coquelicot back its soul. To have a fire roaring in the *petit salon* again, generating warmth on cold winter evenings, seemed like the final symbolic step in bringing the house back to life.

But buying the Godin was the easy bit. The difficulty was finding the right kind of artisan to install it. As usual, when faced with a problem, I went to the local *mairie* for advice. The answer, it transpired, was a plumber. The clerk in the *mairie* obligingly wrote down the number of a local artisan and a company to sweep the chimney. I also discovered that if you have a wood-burner and you don't have your chimney swept once a year, your household insurance will not cover you for fire. So I organised the chimney sweeping and asked Monsieur Lazare, an artisan who specialised in installing wood-burners ,to come and give me a *devis*. It was expensive. The steel tubing that goes up the chimney, I discovered, costs almost as much as the wood-burner itself. But Monsieur Lazare looked like he knew what he was doing and so I hired him to do the job.

The installation day dawns bright and clear but with a gratifying downshift in temperature. Monsieur Lazare, who has already cancelled two previous appointments, and was due to arrive at 9.00 a.m., calls to say he is going to be late. It is 5.00 p.m. when he finally appears. He rushes into the house with a young apprentice in tow, races up to the attic at speed and then hurtles back down to the van as if competing in some physical endurance test – all the time shouting breathless instructions to his apprentice. Between them they unfurl 10 metres of steel tubing from the van and run back into the house and up into the attic with it. While all this is happening, his mobile phone rings at least three times and I can hear him saying, '*Oui, chérie*, I will be there very soon. Very soon.' Something tells me that his mind is not on the job.

His apprentice climbs through the small attic window and onto the roof and drops the silver tubing down the chimney, while Monsieur Lazare shouts frantic instructions from outside. Then there is the sound of a saw and then a drill as he connects the elbow and collar to the wood-burner and metal tubing. Dizzy with the speed of it all, I shut myself away in my bedroom until he shouts upstairs to say the job is done. When I go down to look, the wood-burner is standing several feet in front of the fireplace rather than neatly recessed into it. Worse, there is a gaping hole crudely hewn in the panel behind the wood-burner to accommodate the connecting pipe. Even with my limited knowledge of DIY and fireplaces, I can see that this is a very bad idea as all the warm air will just disappear through this hole and go straight up the chimney. When I query the positioning, Monsieur Lazare flashes me a charming smile and tells me that it is not possible to put the wood-burner inside the fireplace, though I do not understand why. That, surely, is what fireplaces are for? But on the matter of the badly cut hole, Monsieur Lazare smiles disarmingly, says he has a solution, and asks for directions to the nearest DIY store. He rushes off at speed, returning less than ten minutes later with a big silver funnel or 'collar'. It covers the gaping hole around the pipe but it looks ridiculous and causes the wood-burner to stand even further away from the fireplace, so that its front legs are standing on the wooden floor, rather than the tiled hearth. When I point out the potential fire hazard to Monsieur Lazare, he shrugs and agrees that the collar is too big but tells me that it was the only one that they had in stock. With an apologetic smile, he says there is nothing more he can do today and rushes off to meet his *chérie*. I am not sure what to do next but it is hard to be angry as he is so very charming.

Anyone who has lived in rural France for any length of time will tell you that the dark winter months can be difficult and it is easy to feel isolated locked away behind closed shutters. But for me, the winter gloom is punctuated by short work trips to Paris and London and the months pass quickly. Christmas is soon on the doorstep and this year I am planning to do it *properly*. Late one Friday afternoon in December, I head over to Intermarché to buy a tree. It is the first time in my adult life that I have had a full-sized Christmas tree. In London, I had to be content with a knee-high tree, constrained by space and the fact that I lived in a top-floor flat and didn't really fancy hauling a Norwegian pine up three floors. The fact that I am contemplating a Christmas tree really symbolises how much Maison Coquelicot has moved on in the past twelve months. This time last year I was sleeping, eating and working in my bedroom; while the sitting room was a dangerous obstacle course of dusty boxes and bubble-wrapped furniture, to be negotiated en route to the front door. I was in no position to put up a tree or invite friends over for drinks.

But now I have successfully renovated a house in France. Alone! In celebration of that fact, I buy the biggest tree I can find in Intermarché. An assistant helps me wheel it out of the store in a trolley and we manoeuvre it into the back of my car, leaving the hatchback open. On the way home I hit a traffic bump and the tree slides out of the back of the car. I jump out, rescue it (with great difficulty) from the road and stuff it in again, showering copious amounts of pine needles over me and the back seat of the car. At times like this, it would be *so* useful to have a boyfriend. At least at the other end, I only have to drag it in through the front door. Having propped it up in a bucket in a corner of the sitting room, I brave the cold, dusty attic and find the large cardboard box marked 'Christmas decorations'. I seem to have accumulated a lot of baubles over the years. Only last week, on a work trip to Paris, I was unable to resist the hanging glass icicles and cheeky-looking fairies in Le Bon Marché department store.

In the sitting room, I pour myself a large glass of red wine, light some scented candles and spend a happy hour draping the tree in tinsel and slipping the red and gold baubles onto the branches. When I have finished, I switch on the fairy lights and admire the effect. But it is a bitter-sweet experience putting up a Christmas tree alone. On the one hand, the tree seems to symbolise a new chapter in my life, since in the years after Eric left I could not bear the idea of a Christmas tree in the same way that I could not bring myself to listen to music. But at the same time, I feel unbearably sad when I think back to the first festive season that we spent together. Rather than throwing the tree out with the rubbish in the New Year, Eric planted it in the small patch of communal garden. Despite the hard, rocky ground, it flourished until the following Christmas, when he brought it inside and we decorated it all over again.

'The difference between you and me,' I remember him saying, 'is that you always rush to throw things away – especially when they don't work – whereas I like to find a way to hold on to them.' Those were the days when he still worried that I was going to throw *him* away. Who would have guessed that it would be the other way round? But the last Christmas that we spent together, I recall, he did not bother to plant the tree in the garden.

I am rescued from forlorn memories of Christmases past by the phone ringing. To my surprise, it's Jon Wakeman, whom I hadn't even realised was back in France.

'Hi Karen,' he says. 'How's it going?'

'Fine thanks. I've just put up the Christmas tree.'

'That's funny. I've just been doing exactly the same. I hope you don't mind but I got your number from Miranda. I was wondering if you were still on for the Christmas dinner dance in Anzac tomorrow night?'

'Yes,' I say, thrilled that he has remembered. With so many weeks having passed since Miranda first proposed it, I thought he would have forgotten.

'I only got back yesterday,' he says, 'but I spoke to Miranda and she has booked us tickets, and Darla and Geoffrey are expecting us to stay over the night. I was wondering if I could pick you up at around six o'clock?'

'That would be excellent,' I say and give him the directions.

'See you tomorrow then,' he says.

'Really looking forward to it,' I say.

'Me too.'

Chapter 18

A Minx in Anzac

I WAKE UP the following morning feeling hugely excited about tonight's ex-pat event. In the afternoon, I cycle through the bleak, wintry countryside with Lola, who has managed to escape the Liberty Bookshop for a couple of hours. The dull brown landscape is unrecognisable from the lush, yellow and green fields that we cycled through in the summer. Afterwards, Lola comes in for coffee and to rifle through my latest stash of French country-living magazines.

'Oh, it looks like you've had your wood-burner connected,' she says, entering the *petit salon*.

'Don't get me started on that,' I reply. Every time I look at the Godin, rather than experiencing a rosy glow at the thought of warm, cosy evenings to come, I feel hugely irritated at a job badly done.

'Well, at least it's plumbed in now,' says Lola, looking on the bright side as usual. 'Have you tried it out yet?'

'No. I'm waiting for a wood delivery and also I'm not sure it's safe. Though I might be able to find some bits of wood in the garage and I suppose there's no harm in giving it a go...'

In the garage I find a few pieces of pine, which I put in the wood-burner along with screwed-up pieces of newspaper and a couple of firelighters. I throw in a match and Lola and I stand back expectantly. Amazingly, it starts to burn. There is smoke and flames. Not exactly roaring flames, but flames nonetheless. Lola and I stare at the flames, transfixed. Unfortunately, the pine releases a noxious, sickly odour before burning itself out. 'Hm. It's probably been treated with something,' says Lola. 'Still, it's going to be so brilliant when you've got proper logs.'

'Yes,' I say, thinking that I am still several steps away from that all-important, roaring fire. The house hasn't quite got its soul back yet.

After Lola has gone, I take a shower and get dressed in a green knee-length skirt with a big bow at the front and a little black cardigan. For once, I am ready ahead of schedule and chatting to Desmond on the phone – he is considering coming to the dinner dance in Anzac too – when the doorbell rings. I stick my head out of the upstairs window and see Jon standing below in the darkness.

'Be right down,' I shout.

'Possibly see you and Elinor later, then,' I say to Desmond.

'Oh, Elinor won't be coming,' he says. 'Ex-pat dinner dances aren't really her thing. It will probably just be me on my own.'

I rush downstairs to open the door. In the low-lit *salon*, the lights on the Christmas tree are glittering, rose-scented Diptyque candles are burning on the mantelpiece (to remove the sickly chemical smell of the pine I burnt earlier) and two red table lamps cast a soft pink glow over the room. A Buddha

Bar CD is playing softly in the background. I hadn't planned it that way, but it couldn't be more romantic if I'd tried.

'Come on in,' I say, as the cold air rushes into the hallway. 'I'm ready to go. I just need to find my sleeping bag.'

'This is very nice,' he says, his cheeks pink from the cold night air. He pauses for a second and looks around the room. 'But, you know, there's one thing I just don't get.'

'What's that?'

'Well, you've got that lovely marble fireplace there. Why didn't the artisan recess the wood-burner into the surround, rather than standing it in front of it? After all, that's what fireplaces are for.'

'You know, that's very weird,' I say. 'You have just walked in and pinpointed the exact thing that has been preoccupying my thoughts for the past couple of weeks.'

He laughs. 'Well, I guess it's uppermost in my mind as I've just installed mine,' he says.

'You did it yourself?'

'Yeah, it's really easy.'

I think of the money and time I have thrown at the installation of this wood-burner, only to be unhappy with the result, and not for the first time, I think how much easier life would be if I had someone in my life to share the burden of DIY.

'I could probably have installed it for you,' says Jon, as if reading my thoughts.

Now there's an offer. 'OK, found my sleeping bag,' I say, blowing out the candles. 'Shall we go?'

Jon drives fast but competently and during the twenty-minute drive along dark country lanes to Darla's house, I find out more about him. He tells me that he's sold his house in the UK and wants to move out here full-time but his girlfriend isn't so keen. He is still in the process of converting his house in a nearby village into a B&B – targeted at visitors to the racetrack and airfield nearby – and he is also planning to have rare-breed animals on his land. Gloucester Old Spot pigs (whatever they are) seem to loom very large in his future plans. I also learn that he has a four-wheel drive (which he refers to as his 'tank') and a shotgun and comes from a family of gamekeepers in Gloucestershire. I forgive him for the carbon-catastrophic four-wheel drive, as he rarely uses it and at least he could argue that in the country he needs it. And there is, I have to admit, something quite sexy about a man with a gun.

After a few minutes of silence, he says: 'It was very foggy, coming home from the bar that night in Bléssy. I was a bit worried about you.'

'You were?'

'Yeah. After I turned around, I waited for you at the end of Darla's road but I didn't see your lights. I figured you must have gone home a different way in the end.'

'It took me ages to turn around,' I say, pleased at this revelation. So he did wait for me after all.

The dance is in the enormous *salle des fêtes* in Anzac. There is a huge stage at the front and a banner saying 'Joyeux Noël 2002' even though it is 2007. The lighting is retina-searingly bright and very unflattering. Long trestle tables covered in white paper tablecloths have been set out on either side of the room and a dozen or so people are milling around by the bar where several trays of complimentary Kirs are waiting. We hand over our numbered tickets to get our drinks and then claim the trestle table closest to the bar. I have Jon to myself again as Geoffrey and Darla are chatting to friends that they have just bumped into.

'So what made you decide to move to France?' I ask.

He tells me that he loves the countryside and rural pursuits, that he likes camping and climbing mountains. He goes back to the UK to earn money as an IT consultant to do up his B&B. 'But that's enough of me,' he says, after my lengthy cross-interrogation. 'What about you? How do you manage to work from here?'

I tell him that I go back to London once a month for work appointments. 'And sometimes I go up to Paris for fragrance launches or to do shop research,' I say.

'If ever you need a lift to the station or airport just let me know,' he says. 'I'd be very happy to take you.'

'Likewise,' I say. 'Where do you stay when you go back to the UK?'

'It depends,' he says. 'Jennie has still got a flat in Oxford, so I usually stay there. But I travel around quite a bit.'

'Well, I've got a spare room in Villiers, where you can always stay if you need to,' I say.

He looks puzzled. 'Well, that's very kind of you, but why would I need somewhere to stay in Villiers when I already have a house with five spare bedrooms just down the road?'

'I'm so sorry! I think that's what you'd call a blonde moment,' I say, stunned by my own stupidity. He starts to laugh. It's a long time before he stops.

'Well, if ever I find that I've had one drink too many in Villiers and can't get home, I will definitely take you up on the offer,' he says when finally able to speak again.

'That's unlikely. Everything in Villiers closes at seven,' I say. 'Including the bar.'

'The bar in St Secondin stays open later. I haven't forgotten my offer to take you there one evening, if you like.'

'Really?' I say, remembering the rude way that he stood me up. 'But what happened last time? You cancelled at the last minute and didn't even give me a reason.'

'I'm really sorry,' he said. 'It just seemed like a bad idea.'

'So what's changed?' I ask.

He looks embarrassed. 'Well, I was chatting with Gérard in the wine shop and he mentioned that you had a husband and a French lover. And I thought you sounded a bit... dangerous.'

'Dangerous?'

'Yes. You sounded like a bit of a minx to be honest.'

'A minx?' I say, not sure how to respond. 'That sounds rather naughty.'

'Exactly!' he says.

Does this count as flirtation, I wonder, or just friendliness? It's so long since I flirted with anyone, except the gay baker, that my once impeccable intuition is now as blunt as an old baguette.

I remind myself that he has a girlfriend. But still, the evening is panning out far better than I could have imagined.

'Shall I go and steal us some more drinks?' I say.

'Go on then,' he says, with a wink. 'I dare you!'

I sidle up to the bar and grab two more Kirs, avoiding eye contact with the barman. The allocation is one aperitif per ticket but it looks like lots of people haven't turned up to claim theirs, as there are half a dozen trays of them. I hand Jon a Kir with a triumphant flourish.

'Excellent,' he says, with a wink. 'So I *was* right.'

'How do you mean?'

'You are a bit of a minx.'

Around us, the room is slowly filling up with mostly silver-haired people. The average age of our fellow guests is probably sixty-five. 'You do realise that you are the youngest here by several decades,' says Jon suddenly, as if reading my mind again.

'Why? How old are you?' I ask, surprised, since I assumed we were both around the same age.

'A lot older than you.'

'I doubt it. How old?' I say.

'I'm thirty-nine.'

'Well, how old do you think I am?' I ask.

'You can't be more than about twenty-eight,' he says, looking at me intently.

'You are deliberately flattering me.'

'No. I'm not. You're definitely under thirty-five. Maybe I knocked a few years off to be on the safe side, but you definitely don't look any older than thirty.'

'God, I think I love you,' I say.

'Good,' he replies with a smile.

'*Yoo-hoo*! Hello, boys and girls!' shouts Miranda, who has arrived with Desmond. She is wearing a fitted leopard-print jacket with jet beads wound tightly round her neck and she has a sparkly black ornament in her hair. 'How are you, darling boy?' she cries, pouncing on Jon. 'And Karen, don't you look fabulous, darling?' Once again, I think how generous-spirited it is of Elinor to stay at home and let her husband squire another (very glamorous) woman around the Poitou-Charentes.

As Miranda sweeps Jon into her arms, Darla leans over to me. 'If I wasn't married I'd jump on him,' she says. 'In fact, even though I *am* still married, I'm thinking of jumping on him. And anyway, I'm hoping to be divorced soon.' I laugh and not for the first time wonder if she means it. Miranda seems to be thinking along similar lines because she proceeds to monopolise Jon, sitting down next to him for dinner. She's on glittering form and I don't blame him for suddenly forgetting about me. I am sitting opposite them and so have a great view of them laughing and enjoying themselves. It is extremely galling to be nudged out of the picture in this way – and by an older woman.

'May I say, Karen, that you are looking particularly gorgeous tonight?' says Desmond, sitting down next to me. He is wearing a violet shirt and a navy corduroy jacket and is looking pretty sharp himself.

'You always say that. You're just flattering me.'

'No, I really mean it. That colour green really suits you. Your hair looks lovely, your skin glowing and radiant…'

'That would be the two Kirs I've just drunk,' I say with a wink.

The food, a cold buffet consisting of flat slices of reconstituted meat and limp-looking salad, is a disappointment. It is rationed out by a battalion of formidable-looking British women, one of whom grabs the serving tongs from my hands as I serve myself some grated carrots. 'I'll do that,' she says, dropping a minuscule portion on my plate. She adds an equally small portion of mixed-bean salad and some greenery and *voilà* – Christmas dinner, ex-pat style.

When the remnants of the horrible meal have been cleared away, an annoyingly jolly ex-pat takes to the stage and forces us to sing Christmas carols. It's a bit how I imagine life in an old-folk's home to be. Soon he has split the room into two halves, singing alternate verses, in a contest to see who can sing the loudest. This is followed by 'The Twelve Days of Christmas', with each table responsible for a different number. Our table is 'five gold rings' and each time our line comes around we stand up (Miranda's idea) and belt it out. The other tables eye us suspiciously, as if we have been hitting the sherry. There follows a sequence dancing demonstration, involving three elderly couples. And then the disco starts, which is the cue for most people to leave. Desmond, who loves to dance, suddenly perks up. 'Come on,' he says to me. 'Let's dance.'

'Careful, my darling girl,' says Miranda. 'I broke my ankle dancing with him at this very event last year.'

'What's going on with this Jon bloke?' Desmond asks as we dance to Roxy Music's 'Midnight Hour'. 'You like him, don't you?'

'What makes you say that?'

'I saw the two of you together when I arrived.'

'Yes, but it doesn't mean anything.'

'Come off it,' says Desmond, pulling a disbelieving face. 'You do like him. I can tell.'

'Yes, I do. But not like that. It's just that he's really funny. And it's nice to have someone nearer my own age to hang out with. Anyway, he seems to have forgotten about me now. Look, he's dancing with Miranda.'

'Yes, I can see that,' says Desmond, glaring in their direction.

We dance on, through the DJ's endless chat – DJs in rural France, be they French or English, always talk over and between tracks – through Tom Jones, ABBA and the Bee Gees. Most people left immediately after dinner and the Christmas carols and there are only half a dozen of us on the dance floor, but strangely, I am enjoying myself. Over my shoulder I can see Miranda performing the cancan to 'Tears of a Clown'. She looks like she is having a very good time. I dance with Desmond until the slow numbers are played, signalling that the evening is coming to an end. 'Let's go and sit down,' I say, as I detect the start-up notes of a Phil Collins track. I might be in the middle of rural France, where none of my former friends can see me, but I've got to draw the line at dancing to Phil Collins.

Miranda and Jon, however, are still on the dance floor. 'I thought he had a girlfriend?' says Desmond, nodding in their direction. 'Why isn't he with her?'

'She's in the UK.'

'Well, she's a fool,' says Desmond. 'Look at him. If she wants to hold on to him, she should get herself out here as fast as possible.'

I look over to where he is pointing. Miranda is no longer doing the cancan. Instead, she has her arms around Jon's neck and they are swaying along to 'Lady in Red'.

'They're just having fun,' I say. But I have to admit that I feel more than a little miffed at being upstaged by a woman twenty years older than me. And it feels strangely disloyal of her to have made such a beeline for Jon. There was I thinking that she had earmarked him for me!

We collect our coats and follow Darla and Geoffrey across the crunchy gravel outside the *salle des fêtes*. 'How is Miranda getting home?' asks Jon.

'I'm assuming, since they arrived together, that Desmond is giving her a lift,' says Darla, using a credit card to scrape the ice off the window.

But suddenly, I hear Miranda's voice across the car park. 'I'm not getting into that car with you. You're an absolute tosser!' she is shrieking at Desmond.

'Miranda,' he says, his voice firm but calm. 'You're drunk. Get in the car and I'll drive you home.'

'I don't want a lift home from you,' she replies. 'I *hate* you!'

'Oh dear,' says Darla. 'Looks like Miranda has drunk too much again.'

'Fine,' says Desmond. 'Then go with them.' He turns and calls over to us. 'Darla! Miranda is coming with you. Can you make sure she gets home safely?'

I am shocked at the way Miranda – now wobbling across the gravel in her high heels – has spoken to Desmond and by yet another display of petulant behaviour. Jon gets out of the car to hold the door open and she climbs in next to me, so that I am no longer sitting next to Jon.

'Hang on. I think I should go in the middle,' he says, as the car fills with the heady scent of exotic oriental perfume.

'That's better,' he says, sliding in next to me.

'So, darling boy, aren't you just thrilled skinny to be squeezed between us?' says Miranda, putting her hand on his knee.

'I can't believe my luck,' replies Jon.

'I had to get away from Desmond,' says Miranda. 'Sometimes I really hate that man.'

'Hate is a strong word,' drawls Darla. 'And Desmond is pretty good to you.'

'Hmm. Well, it's a two-way street. I've been good to him too,' says Miranda. 'But sometimes, he... he... really makes me mad.'

'What happened?' asks Jon.

'Oh, let's not go there,' says Miranda. '*Mais écoute!* How many people in that room do you think will be getting some nookie tonight?'

'Not many,' mumbles Geoffrey from the passenger seat, breaking his usual silence.

'Exactly what I think,' says Miranda.

Jon chuckles. I sit in silence, intrigued as to what caused the bust-up with Desmond.

The conversation, as we drive through the blacked-out countryside, switches to wood-burners. Miranda has a problem with hers – problems with wood-burners, it seems, being endemic at this time of year – and Jon offers to take a look. As the car pulls up outside her house, he says that he will drop by tomorrow morning.

'Oh would you?' My dear boy, you really are a gem,' she says. She climbs out of the car blowing kisses to everyone. 'Hope to see you again before I'm very much older,' she cries. We wait as Miranda skips up her dark path and opens the front door before giving a cheery final wave.

'I feel so sorry for her,' says Darla, as we drive away. 'It must be freezing in there. Her wood-burner is her only source of heating. And she can't use it. It really is too bad.'

'She seems quite vulnerable,' says Jon.

'Miranda always has that effect on men,' says Darla. 'They all want to look after her. Don't tell me you've fallen for it too.'

'I wonder what caused the argument with Desmond?' I say.

'Oh, probably just the drink talking,' says Darla. 'They're always falling out and then getting back together. I don't think she could survive without him. But I'm surprised Elinor puts up with it.'

'So how well do you know Miranda?' Jon asks Darla.

'Pretty well. Miranda can be very hard work,' says Darla. 'And sometimes it's hard to have sympathy.'

'What do you mean?'

'She's a flirt,' says Geoffrey.

'I realised that,' says Jon, chuckling. 'But very good company.'

'She ought to be careful,' says Darla. 'She flirts with every man she meets. She did it with our local baker Bernard. She invited him to dinner and I watched her do it with my own eyes – and then the next day, he turned up on her doorstep…'

'What happened?' asks Jon.

'She was outraged. I told her, "Miranda, you have no right to be. It's very dangerous flirting like that and then not following through." Poor Bernard was really confused.'

'But she's an attractive woman,' says Jon. 'I can see why he fell for her.'

Back at Darla and Geoffrey's, Darla invites us into the kitchen for a nightcap.

'I think I am ready to turn in,' I say, bored with talking about Miranda. Jon, on the other hand, shows no sign of flagging. Darla leads me through to the sitting room, where there are two pull-out sofa beds. As we make them up with beige flowery sheets, Darla asks if I have met Jon's girlfriend. 'No, but I saw her once in the Liberty Bookshop. She's a bit older than him.'

'Really?' she says. 'Jon likes older women? Maybe that means I stand a chance?'

'I think Miranda got there first.' I say.

After saying goodnight to Darla, I unfurl my sleeping bag and zip myself into it, feeling disappointed that Jon hasn't followed and the evening doesn't look like it's going to end in a cosy conversation *à deux*. I leave the light on for him and try to go to sleep. He does not come to bed for at least another hour, which is annoying since I was hoping for an amusing dissection of the evening. When he finally creeps into the room, I ask him if he would mind getting me a glass of water.

'OK,' he says, and goes back into the kitchen for another fifteen minutes.

'Oh, you're still dressed,' he says, surprised, as I extend a fully clothed arm out of my sleeping bag for the glass of water.

'Easier to make a quick getaway in the morning.'

I wake up at around 6.30 a.m. with a dry mouth and a thumping headache. I am surprised to find that Jon is sitting on the edge of his bed, looking over at me.

'You're awake?'

'I couldn't sleep.'

'Was your bed uncomfortable?'

'No, I was wondering whether or not to jump on you.'

WHAT? 'Jump on me?'

'Yes.' He pauses. 'To stop you snoring.'

'I was snoring?' I say, horrified.

'No, I'm kidding you,' he says. 'I just couldn't sleep.'

'Shall we just get up and go?' I suggest, really keen to get back to my own bed.

'I was hoping you'd say that,' he says. We fold up the sheets and duvets together in silence and make the beds back into sofas.

We creep out of the front door, so as not to wake anyone. It is cold and not yet fully light outside and my head is pounding as we drive back through the grey, misty countryside, which is punctuated with opaque pockets of fog.

'I'd better not tell Jennie that we slept in the same room,' he says suddenly.

'Why not?'

'I just don't think she will like it.'

I feel nauseous and desperate to get home. Unfortunately, there is a diversion in place as we approach the square in Villiers.

'Oh yeah. I forgot. It's the Christmas market today.'

'That's OK. We can go around the back of the chateau,' he says.

As we climb the steep winding road that leads around the chateau, passing old stone cottages and allotments, and with the church spire visible in the distance in the pale blue light, it all seems impossibly romantic. 'We are so lucky to be living here,' I say.

'I know,' says Jon.

I haven't stayed out all night in years – and never in France – so it's a strange sensation as we pull up outside my house. It's not yet 7.30 a.m.

'Thanks a lot for the lift,' I say, realising that he has turned the engine off

He turns and looks at me. 'To be honest, I was hoping I could come in for a coffee.'

'Oh, um… yeah, sorry. Of course. No problem.'

'It's just that I'd quite like to look around the market and it seems a bit silly to drive back to my village and then come back again,' he says. 'And I told Miranda I would go and look at her wood-burner this morning but it seems a little early yet.'

'Oh yes, of course.'

Much as I like Jon's company, I am dismayed. My headache is threatening to turn into a full-blown migraine. All I want to do is remove last night's make-up, brush my teeth and fall into bed for a couple of hours with a glass of water, some ibuprofen and a good book. Now I have to entertain him until the Christmas market opens. As I get out of the car, I can hear shouts and bangs from the square, as the shopkeepers set up their stalls; and there is a frisson of excitement, a real sense of anticipation in the cold December air.

The *petit salon* is warm and smells of rose, thanks to the candles on the mantelpiece. It's also in complete darkness because the shutters are closed. I leave them that way – it's kinder on my head – but switch on the Christmas tree lights and red table lamps to make the room more welcoming. 'The brothel look,' says Jon, with a wry smile. I make him coffee and sort out green tea and two headache tablets for myself. He follows me into the kitchen while I do this, which is a little unnerving. 'I wonder how Miranda is feeling this morning,' he says, with a grin. 'She's quite mad, isn't she?'

'Yeah, she is.'

'She seems like quite a laugh to go out with though.'

'You seem very interested in Miranda.'

'No. I have a girlfriend, who I love.'

Ouch!

'Well, I can see why you might be attracted to Miranda,' I persist. 'An attractive older woman and all that.'

'I'm *not* interested in Miranda in that way.'

'Oh, really?' I say, raising an eyebrow.

'Look, the truth is, I need to increase my social circle if I'm going to live out here full time. Miranda seems like a laugh. And so do you. But that's all.'

'Hmm.' I narrow my eyes.

'Look, I'm really glad that I met you,' he continues. 'You're the only person I know who's close to my own age and it will be fun to go out together.' He looks me directly in the eye and then says very pointedly: 'But I'm not looking for anything other than friendship.'

'That's cool,' I say, feeling very disappointed, though it seems to me that he doth protest too much. Either way, friendship is better than nothing. 'Look, the *boulangerie* will be open now. Let's go and get some croissants. We can look around the market while they're setting it up.'

'Excellent idea.'

I put on my hippy coat and we walk up to the square. The few neighbours that we pass on the way – all clutching baguettes from the *boulangerie* – look at Jon with interest.

Goodness knows what Gérard will make of my latest male friend. In the square, Christmas carols are being played through the antiquated sound system and the *boulangerie* is lit up with red lamps and white fairy lights twinkling in the windows. René Matout has really gone to town with his decorations.

'See, the baker has gone for the brothel look too,' I say, which makes Jon laugh. 'It's very fashionable in Villiers.'

In the half-light of a winter morning, it is as if someone has cast a piece of pale, smoky-blue organza over the village. The air is scented with wood smoke and (outside the *boulangerie*, at least) vanilla, while the temperature is cold enough to turn breath to white vapour. It is how winter should be – and has been for centuries in this little corner of rural France. Underneath the steely sky, the *marchands* are busy setting up their stalls, cracking jokes, laughing and calling out to each other. The Christmas market is as much of a social event as it is about commerce. Every now and again they stop to stamp their feet and rub their hands together against the cold. Outside the *mairie*, a small merry-go-round has been installed overnight. The scene is impossibly romantic. I can't stop thinking that I am in a movie. It's a shame that Jon and I are only going to be friends as this would make a very memorable beginning.

René himself is behind the counter in the *boulangerie*, because of the earliness of the hour. He greets us with a warm grin and disappears into the back, returning with a tray of *pains au chocolat*.

'*Attention!* You must wait five minutes before eating these,' he warns, as he deposits them in paper bags. 'They are very hot.' Clutching the warm paper bags, we do a circuit of the square. With Jon at my side the world seems like a very friendly place. We pass familiar faces, French and English, who stop to say hello and I feel a warm glow inside at the realisation that *I belong here. I am part of this.* 'Ahh *Ka-renne*, come by here,' shouts a familiar voice in heavily accented English. Outside the wine shop Gérard, the owner, has set up a makeshift stand consisting of a wooden wine barrel, with samples for tasting. 'Come, try a little wine,' he shouts, his breath frosty in the cold morning air, his cheeks as red as the fleece Santa Claus hat that he is wearing. No doubt he wants to find out more about the latest man on my arm.

'We're just going to have some breakfast,' I say. 'But we'll be back later.'

Across the square, the Liberty Bookshop is lit up and welcoming in the morning half-light and Jon suggests that we drop by. 'It's only ten to eight. The Libertys don't open until ten o'clock,' I say.

'Come on. I'm sure they won't mind,' he says.

Through the windows, I can see Dylan moving around, getting ready for the busy day ahead. He looks surprised to see us but makes a decent stab at pretending it is normal for Jon and me to arrive on his doorstep together so early in the morning.

'Can we come in for a coffee?' says Jon.

'Yeah, sure,' says Dylan. After he has put the coffee on, he comes over to sit with us, padding across the tiled floor in his goatskin moccasins.

'We just got back from a party near Confolens,' I say. 'That's why we're up so early. We stayed over at a friend's house. On separate sofa beds.'

'Cool,' says Dylan. 'And was it good?'

'What?'

'The party?'

'Um, yeah. It was fun.'

We chat with Dylan for a while, mostly about the day's events, which include a string quartet, a brass band and carol singers, and then we walk back to Maison Coquelicot. Jon is going to look at Miranda's wood-burner, as promised. Since Desmond and Elinor live very close by, I ask him if he would mind stopping to pick up some wood for me. 'Desmond said I could borrow some until my wood is delivered next week,' I say.

'No problem,' he says. 'Does Miranda know how to get there?'

'She practically lives there.'

Once Jon has gone, I decide to crawl under the duvet and read. After all, it is Sunday morning. It feels very cosy and nice to be lying in bed as I hear my neighbours chatting and calling to each other below my bedroom window, on the way to the market. An hour and a half later, the doorbell rings again, and when I throw open the bedroom windows I see that Jon is back. He doesn't look happy. 'Well that was a complete waste of time,' he says, as I open the door, allowing a rush of cold air into the warm house.

'What happened?'

'The shutters were closed. I rang the bell for ages and no one answered the door.'

'She was probably hungover from last night,' I say.

'Yes, well, it was a little weird, because there was another car parked outside.'

'Really?'

'And it looked like Desmond's.'

'Are you sure?'

'Yes. He drives a navy BMW doesn't he?'

'Well, that's one of his cars, yes. How strange,' I say, thinking aloud. 'But it's possible that he's lent it to Miranda. He and Elinor have got quite a few cars between them and I know that Miranda's old Citroën is always breaking down.'

'But that's the car that he was driving last night,' says Jon. 'I saw it in the car park. That's how I recognised it.'

For the first time, it occurs to me that Desmond and Miranda might be having an affair. It seemed too obvious – they spend so much time together and so obviously enjoy each other's company and there is definitely a kind of chemistry between them – but now I realise that this might be some weird kind of double-bluff. And it would certainly explain why I had seen so little of Elinor recently. She probably knows about it and is really upset. But I push the idea out of my mind.

'So I'm afraid I couldn't get your wood, because I didn't know how to get to Desmond and Elinor's without Miranda,' Jon is saying. 'But I've got an idea. Why don't we drive over to my place later? I could show you my house and we could bring back some wood from my barn.'

'OK,' I say, pleased at the idea of seeing his house. 'That sounds good.' Now that my hangover has gone, I can't think of anything nicer than spending the rest of Sunday with Jon.

I open the shutters to let light into the dark sitting room. In the narrow street outside I can see neighbours with baskets full of shopping from the market.

'Shall we go and have a look around the market again, now that it's all set up?' Jon suggests.

'OK,' I say. 'Look, if you don't have anything else planned, why don't you stay for lunch? I could buy some vegetables in the market and we could have sausages and mash.'

'That would be nice.'

The Christmas market is in full swing when we reach the square, and I can see through the windows of the Liberty Bookshop that it is packed, with both French and ex-pat faces that I recognise. Jon and I walk around the outside of the *mairie* first, past a profusion of oyster sellers and *saucisson* producers offering samples of their wares. Most stands sell just one product: a fancy cheese from the alps or Pineau, a sweet grape liqueur from the Charente, bottles of herb-infused olive oil or identical fat, round jars of foie gras. Another stall offers unusual breads, some of them the size of small boulders, a few sliced in half to reveal the dense, snowy-white texture beneath the crust. I try a small square offered by the *marchand* and it is too delicious to resist. I buy one of the boulders and have it cut in two, so that I can give one half to Jon.

We pass a stall selling a colourful patchwork of soaps from Marseilles in a profusion of scents – lavender, vanilla, vervain, rose, sweet pea, jasmine, honeysuckle – and stop at another offering bouquets of mistletoe and holly that have probably been cut from the branch that morning. I buy one of each, and then we stop at another market stall selling willow log-baskets to watch a man quietly weaving more strands of willow into a sturdy round basket.

The square is now filled with the smell of food: the scent of sugar and vanilla from a stand busily selling crêpes and warm, spicy apple juice is superseded by the aroma of fried onions and sausages from a neighbouring *marchand* as we walk around the market.

'Oh look,' says Jon suddenly. 'There's Desmond.' Sure enough, Desmond is walking around the square alone. He is wearing jeans and a leather flying jacket, his camera in his hands. He comes straight over as he spots us and I fling my arms around him, pleased as always to seem him. But he is looking subdued, not his normal ebullient self.

'What brings you over here?' I ask.

'Oh, I just thought I'd get out of Elinor's way for a bit,' he says. Desmond is noticeably cool with Jon. 'Hello,' he says. "What a surprise to see you here. You don't live in Villiers do you?'

Jon explains that no, he doesn't; he's just here for the market. We continue strolling around the market in an uneasy threesome, stopping to look at the life-size nativity scene in front of the *mairie*. Someone has stolen the big doll that was supposed to be baby Jesus and the crib is empty. But Mary and Joseph are still in situ. The stuffed figures look charmingly homespun, but three live donkeys give the scene some authenticity. 'Look,' I say, pointing to an animal with a long shaggy coat, like dreadlocks. 'A Rastafarian donkey.'

'It's actually a very rare breed of donkey,' says Jon, 'called a *baudet du Poitou.*'

'How do you know that?' I ask, impressed that he knows this kind of stuff.

'I'm planning to have one in my garden.'

The donkeys are already at the fence and eating out of Jon's hand.

'I know – you could give them some of these carrots and turnips that I just bought,' I say, offering him the bag of vegetables that I had bought for our lunch. He bites the turnips in half with his teeth before offering them to the donkeys, which strikes me as a very thoughtful gesture.

Desmond, meanwhile, hangs back. I notice that he is taking photographs of the donkeys, from such an angle as to cut Jon out of the shot. I go and stand next to him. 'So did you spend the night with him?' he asks.

'Yes, I did.'

Desmond looks displeased.

'Over at Darla's. On separate sofa beds,' I add. 'Look, can you take a picture of us both with that shaggy donkey?'

'If I must.'

I go to the fence and stand next to Jon. Desmond gets ready to record the moment with his camera. And then, just as I am stroking the *baudet* on the nose, it bites my hand. Hard. Jon is laughing.

'It's not funny. Look, it's left an imprint,' I say.

'Show me,' says Jon, and he takes my hand and examines it.

'I think you'll live,' he says.

'Look, I'll leave you to it, shall I?' says Desmond suddenly. 'I'll see you soon, Karen.' And he leaves without the usual kisses.

Back at Maison Coquelicot, Jon opens the bottle of Madiron that he just bought from Gérard, while I prepare the vegetables.

'I don't think Desmond likes me,' he says, pouring out two glasses of the dense purple-black wine.

'He was probably annoyed that you were dancing with Miranda so much last night,' I say.

'What do you mean? There's nothing going on between me and Miranda.'

'Yeah, but Desmond doesn't know that. He's very protective towards her.'

I light a candle to make things more festive and we eat lunch at the refectory table in the kitchen. Afterwards, he helps me to decorate the fireplace with the holly and mistletoe that I bought in the market, and then we sit on opposite sofas, chatting about life in France and renovating houses in general. With the Christmas lights twinkling, and candles burning, only a roaring fire could improve the setting.

In the late afternoon we drive cross-country with a limpid winter sun casting a pale light over the flat frosty fields. Everything looks much more alive than it did in the dull mist of morning. Jon, I can tell, adores the countryside. Whenever he sees an interesting bird in a field, he slows down to take a better look. I am not at all interested in birds – and I can only just about tell the difference between a sparrow and a cockatoo – but I do a good job of pretending.

He lives in a small village about 12 kilometres away, in a double-fronted stone cottage with blue shutters, surrounded by a stone wall. Behind the house there is a huge barn and a lot of land. I shiver in the cold as he shows me around the various outbuildings, explaining which livestock will live where, and as we roam round his large, wild-looking garden, he points out his walnut and cherry trees and the patch of overgrown land that will be home to the rare breed of pig that he is planning to stock. 'Pigs are brilliant for clearing land,' he explains.

He shows me into a very tidy barn where he keeps wood, and he puts a pile of logs of different sizes in the boot of his car ready to take back to Villiers. Then he gives me the guided tour of his house, starting with the cosy, cluttered kitchen. It is obvious that he is very good at DIY – he has even done the electrical rewiring himself – but he is clearly years, not months, away from opening his B&B. Nearly every room has yet to be stripped of the mandatory brown flowery wallpaper, and redecorated.

Back in the sitting room, he gets down onto his knees to light the enormous wood-burner.

'OK, now watch! This is how you do it,' he says, creating a small, methodical pyre of scrunched-up newspapers and firelighters, with small sticks of wood layered on top. 'You need to have gaps between the pieces of wood. That way the air can circulate.'

The fire gets going almost instantly, which is a relief because the house is freezing. I sit in a chair close to the fire, watching the flames, while he goes into the kitchen to make coffee. Then he sits down next to me with his laptop and shows me photographs of the rare breeds of animal that he plans to have. In addition to spotty pigs, these include strange fluffy black hens, and creamy-beige-coloured cows. While he is explaining the merits of the fluffy black hen, the phone rings. It is a friend in the UK. The conversation that ensues seems to be for my benefit.

'Yeah, went to a dance last night... with three very attractive and entertaining women... one of them is here with me now...' He looks at me and flashes a cheeky grin. 'She's got blonde hair... offered me the use of her spare room... told her that it was very nice but I've got five of my own... no, she hasn't got Sky Sport... otherwise I would have taken her up on the offer straight away.' He winks at me.

While he is talking, my eyes wander around the room. Like the rest of the house, it feels lived-in and friendly. And rather touchingly, he has really gone to town on the festive decorations. His Christmas tree is covered in tinsel of many mismatched colours. It is not a good-taste tree, but a lot of effort has gone into it. There are also ceramic angels suspended from the beams of the ceiling and tinsel draped along the shelves and tacked to the walls.

'Sorry I didn't mention you by name,' he says as he puts the phone down. 'But I figure no names, no pack drill.'

'What?'

'Better not mention any names,' he says. 'And then no one can get into trouble.'

'But we can't get into trouble anyway. We haven't done anything wrong,' I say.

It is dark by the time we arrive back in Villiers. Jon brings in the logs from his car and stacks them by the side of the wood-burner. I try to light the fire, building a little pyre, as he demonstrated earlier. 'No, not that piece of wood yet. It's too big. You have to build it up gradually,' he says, as I try to shove a large log into the wood-burner. 'Here, let me do it. It's probably better if you watch.' And so, practically hopping from foot to foot with excitement, I watch as Jon lights the fire. With his expert touch, it is soon going strong.

Jon doesn't know it but this is a very significant moment. At last Maison Coquelicot has a fire roaring at its heart once again. 'Would you like a glass of wine?' I say.

'No thanks. I've got to get back to call my girlfriend' he says, hovering by the door. 'But thanks again for lunch.'

'Thanks for the logs,' I say.

'Well, I guess I'll see you soon,' he says and heads towards his car in the frosty darkness. I close the front door, turn the lights out – the better to watch the fire – and spend the rest of the evening lying on the sofa, mesmerised by the dancing flames. I feel absurdly happy. Maison Coquelicot has got her fire back; I have real wood, piled up one either side of the fire like in design magazines; and I have spent a full twenty-four hours in Jon's company. I have eaten dinner, breakfast and lunch with him, and been invited back to his house for coffee. He has a girlfriend but he wants to be friends with me. And I can't help thinking that my life is going to be so much better with him in it.

Chapter 19

Christmas Day

I AM OBSESSED. Consumed. Mesmerised. Utterly in love... with my wood-burning stove. Let me count the ways in which I love it: the challenge of getting the flames going; the thrill once it takes; and then the satisfaction of feeding it, poking it and rearranging the logs inside, not to mention watching the myriad different ways that a log can burn. I am starting to worry that I might never leave the house again. In the cold days leading up to Christmas, I even take to working downstairs on the sofa in front of the fire, laptop propped up against my knees. Maison Coquelicot has thawed, dropped the frosty facade and revealed herself to be surprisingly warm-hearted. We are now comfortable with each other. Night after night I stay at home sitting by the fire with a glass of full-bodied red. It feels like I have finally created a home.

It was Mathilde who sorted out my wood-burner problems in the end. Dropping by for a cup of Ricoré, a mix of coffee and chicory beans, she was outraged to find the stove standing on my polished wooden floor rather than the tiled hearth. 'It is a fire hazard,' she declared. 'These artisans, they think they can get away with anything because you are a woman alone. Give me his number. I will call him and get him to come back and do the job properly.'

I am not sure exactly what Mathilde said to Monsieur Lazare, but it worked. Almost immediately he phoned, and asked when I would like him to come back. 'Tomorrow morning?' I suggested, expecting much evasion and procrastination.

'Madame, I will be there at nine a.m.,' he replied. And to my amazement he was. He came with the correct size *collier*, or collar, this time, and, better still, it was black so that it matched the back panel. He did the work with good grace, and when he had finished the wood-burner was no longer standing on wooden floorboards but on the tiled fire surround, as it should have been. Afterwards, I braced myself for Monsieur Lazare to bump up the bill for his extra trouble, but when it arrived a week later it was considerably less than originally projected. Bravo, Mathilde!

Then, a few days ago, I became the proud owner of a woodpile. After waiting in on three separate mornings for Monsieur Tessier, only for him to cancel at the last minute – 'I'm so sorry, Madame, I know it is annoying' – he finally arrived by tractor and deposited two *cordes* of wood at the entrance to my garage. A *'corde'*, incidentally, is a cubic metre of wood – that's a lot of logs. Even with Claudette and her husband helping, it took nearly two hours to transfer them all to the back of the garage and pile them up neatly. Despite ruining my favourite cashmere cardigan and a pair of suede boots in the process – no, I don't know what I was thinking of either – it was deeply satisfying to look at the mountain of neatly stacked logs. I was going to relish the rituals of self-sufficiency involved in bringing them in. And for €140 I had enough wood to heat the house for the winter.

But, as the French would say, I still wasn't quite out of the *auberge* yet. To begin with, I could not get the logs to burn. The optimum arrangement, as Jon taught me, was four little scrunched-up pieces of newspaper with a firelighter in the middle, and several small sticks of wood arranged in a precarious pyramid on top so that the air could circulate underneath. This would get the fire going sufficiently to put the first log on top. *In theory.* The reality was that I spent a lot of time on my knees relighting smouldering sticks of wood and shoving vast quantities of scrunched-up newspapers and noxious paraffin firelighters into the wood-burner. Given the trouble that I go to to avoid toxins in everyday life – buying paraben-free beauty products, organic food and even environmentally friendly detergent – it was ironic to be releasing a toxic *mélange* of chemicals into my sitting room on a nightly basis.

For there are certain unattractive truths about log fires that only become apparent when you have one. The first is the amount of paraphernalia involved. In magazine pictures, log fires are invariably shown with a neat, symmetrical, very photogenic stack of logs on either side. What you don't see is all the other stuff that's required; the giant matches, boxes of firelighters, piles of old newspapers and three different sizes of logs as well as the kindling (very messy and unphotogenic), needed to get the thing going. You also need a large dustpan and brush on standby and a pair of fire tongs for poking the fire and moving the burning logs around. A log fire, let me tell you, is *very* hard work. And that's *before* you get to clean out the ashes on a daily basis, sweeping up the dust – which gets everywhere – and scrubbing off the soot from the glass frontage. On the bright side, at least I won't be developing bingo wings any time soon. My lungs, however, are definitely feeling the strain. In the few days that the wood-burner has been up and running, I have developed a sore throat, a dry cough and a permanent headache. I have also noticed that the longer the stove burns the more it releases a very sickly, toxic smell. And then I spot the scorch marks on the panels above the fire surround and realise why: the white gloss paint (with which Alain, my decorator, had painted the entire sitting room, including the fireplace) is hot and tacky to the touch and is releasing a warm soup of toxic, volatile vapours into the sitting room.

Since renovating the house I have discovered that one step forward nearly always means two steps back. I *so* wanted the wood-burner to be working in time for Christmas Day, as I have invited Miranda, Elinor and Desmond for lunch – having checked beforehand that Miranda and Elinor are back on speaking terms – and I want them to be able to eat it without incurring lung damage. The only solution is to remove the gloss paint and replace it with paint that can withstand high temperatures. I call Pluriservices in Civray, an organisation of unemployed artisans who are available for hire by the hour.

Astonishingly, given that it is so close to Christmas, they agree to dispatch *un bricoleur* (handyman) the following day. I am glad to hear it is Gwen, a French guy who previously put up some shelves for me, and who speaks English with a Brummie accent having lived in Birmingham for eight years. He disconnects the wood-burner and then applies paint stripper to the painted panel and slowly the white gloss disappears. He then sprays on matt black, fireproof paint made to withstand temperatures of

up to 600 degrees. *Et voilà.* Hopefully, that should be the end
of my wood-burner woes. I have also discovered some 'natural'
firelighters made from wood chippings. They do not smell as
toxic as the paraffin kind, but unfortunately they are not as
effective either. It takes about half a box and a week's supply of
newspapers to produce just a few modest flames.

'Your logs are too big,' says Jon when he drops by
unannounced.

'How can they be? I've got three different sizes *and*
kindling.'

'Well, you need some smaller ones to get it going. You have
to build it up *gradually.*'

The following evening, he arrives with a box of finely
chopped wood and a mini-axe, thoughtfully gift-wrapped and
tied with ribbon.

'I really appreciate the gesture,' I say, choosing my words
carefully. 'And it is a *very* thoughtful present. But I don't think
I can have an axe in the house.'

'Why?' says Jon, looking puzzled.

I tell him that I think it is too unlucky/scary to have an axe
lying around but the (devious) truth is that I have absolutely
no intention of chopping up logs as I am hoping that he will
do it for me.

'Well, have a good Christmas,' says Jon, as he leaves, taking
his axe with him. He is going to Bordeaux tomorrow to pick
Jennie up from the airport.

Since this is the first Christmas I have hosted in my new home,
I want it to be perfect. I drive 40 kilometres to the turkey farm in
order to pick up the black turkey I have ordered. (Black turkeys,
apparently, taste better.) In London, I used to buy a turkey from
Lidgates, the organic, stratospherically expensive butcher in

Holland Park. This year's turkey is also organic, but bought directly from the farm it costs less than a third of the price.

I am worried that I will see turkeys running around the farmyard, or worse, be made to choose one and have it killed before my eyes. Fortunately, the turkey is handed over in a plastic bag. I have already asked Miranda about innards and such, since she bought her turkey here last year. 'Don't worry,' she says. 'That will all have been dealt with and its head will have been chopped off.' Welcome news, as I am very squeamish about poultry. I don't even like looking at the pale, goose-pimpled turkey flesh, let alone putting my hand inside to stuff one or remove giblets.

And so, on Christmas Eve, wood-burner installed, Christmas lights twinkling and turkey in the fridge – along with organic vegetables, mince pies, chocolates and Christmas pudding ferried back from the UK on the Eurostar on a recent visit – I am all set. I have even decorated the front door with the holly from the Christmas market and hung up mistletoe above all available door frames. *Et voilà.* With all the accoutrements of a traditional rustic Christmas in place, I pour myself a large, congratulatory glass of red wine and am about to flick through Delia's Christmas cookbook – she might not be fashionable but she's big on organisation – when the phone rings. It's Miranda. 'Hello, darling girl. Are we all set for tomorrow?'

'I think so.'

'You've got the turkey?'

'It's in the fridge.'

'You mean you haven't taken it out of the fridge yet?'

'No. Should I have?'

'Yes, it's supposed to stand in the baking tray overnight. Didn't you know that?'

'No. I didn't.'

After I put the phone down, I take the bird out of the fridge, but as I unwrap it I receive a nasty shock – in the form of a pair of beady eyes, a hairy neck and a beak. *Merde!* The bird still has its head attached! Feeling ill, I shove it back in the plastic bag and call Miranda.

'The turkey's head is still attached.'

'Good grief! It hasn't been chopped off?'

'No.'

'But I bought my turkey there last year and all that was dealt with.'

'Well my turkey still has its head attached.'

'Darling girl, you're going to have to be brave and chop it off. Have you got a meat cleaver?'

'No. And even if I did, I'm far too squeamish to do it'

'I know! What about Jon? His father was a gamekeeper. He'll know what to do. Shall I give him a call?'

'Would you?' I say, wanting to give Miranda a hug. 'That's a really good idea.'

'Leave it to me. I'll be back in touch before you're very much older.'

Five minutes later the phone rings again. It is Jon.

'Hi,' he says. 'I hear you've got a problem. Do you want me to come over and sort it out?'

Yes. PLEASE! YES!

'No, don't be silly. I don't want to put you to any trouble.'

'I don't mind.'

I think to myself, Please come over now! but find myself saying instead, 'I'm sure you've got better things to do on Christmas Eve than drive 12 kilometres to chop a turkey's head off.'

'We're just at home. I could come over now.'

'No, honestly, it's fine. But perhaps you could tell me how to do it.' He starts to describe what I already know: sawing through it with a sharp knife, et cetera. All I can think is, IDIOT! You should have let him come and do that for you!

'Well, have a nice Christmas then,' he says.

'You too.'

I toy briefly with the idea of calling Dylan, who is only around the corner, and asking him to do it, but he's a strict vegetarian, so it would be inappropriate. Instead, I pour myself another glass of wine and decide to get up early tomorrow and deal with the problem then.

At 10.30 a.m. I am woken from a deep sleep by a phone call. It's Elinor. 'Just checking you were up and slaving away in the kitchen,' she says cheerily.

'Oh yes, I certainly am,' I say, trying to hide a voice still heavy with sleep and give the impression that I have been up chopping vegetables for hours.

'Good. We'll see you round about one o'clock then. We're picking Miranda up en route.'

Merde! The turkey with its spooky beak and eyes is waiting for me downstairs in the kitchen. And *merde* again, for according to Delia's Christmas schedule, it should be in the oven by now. I've got two and a half hours to have a shower, get dressed, lay the table and prepare Christmas lunch from scratch. If only I'd done what Delia had suggested and peeled the potatoes and parsnips last night.

Do the thing that you least want to do. Now! Repeating one of the many motivational mantras taught to me by Dylan, I go down to the kitchen to confront the task in hand. Gingerly, I peel back the plastic bag and recoil instantly at the dead eyes staring at me. I run back upstairs and pick up the phone. Jon answers after just a few rings.

'JonhappyChristmasisKarenIhopeI'mnotinterruptinganythin g.' The words come out in breathless rush. There is silence on the other end of the phone.

'It's just that... you know last night, you offered to come over and chop my turkey's head off?'

'Yes.'

'Well, I was wondering if you would like to come over for a Christmas drink this morning and do it?'

There is a pause. 'I suppose I could.'

'Are you sure? I really don't want to put you out or anything.'

'No, it's OK. But we're just in the middle of something at the moment.'

Merde! Merde! Merde! I put the phone down feeling like an idiot. Spurred on by an adrenalin rush of embarrassment, I go down to the kitchen, find a carving knife, don thick rubber gloves and, with grim determination, hack the turkey's head off. It's pink and long and snake-like, with a hard bone in the middle. I fling it in the bin, rush upstairs and phone Jon again. This time, his girlfriend answers. She doesn't bother with any niceties such as 'Happy Christmas' or even 'Hi'. Instead, she just says: 'I'll get Jon for you.'

'It's OK,' I say, breathless. 'I'm just calling to say: problem dealt with. I just did it myself.'

There is silence on the other end of the phone.

'But why don't you come over for a drink anyway?' I say.

I'm confident that they won't. I figure his girlfriend won't even pass on the message. But not long after I have put the turkey in the oven, and just as I am about to start grappling with the vegetables, the doorbell rings. Jon and his girlfriend are standing on the doorstep. 'We thought we'd see how you were getting on,' he says. 'It sounded like you needed help.' Jennie hovers behind him, looking like she has been dragged along under duress. She is wearing jeans and what looks like a man's oversized grey sweater. 'So where is this turkey then?' she asks, after Jon has introduced us. 'You need to turn it over,' she says crisply when I opened the oven door to show them. 'And you should put some foil around it, so that the steam can help it to cook. Here, I'll do it.'

Her manner is brisk and efficient. I can only watch in awe. 'The reason why the head was left on,' she says, 'is that the French like to use it as a decorative table piece.'

'Oh, how horrible,' I say.

'You haven't peeled the vegetables?' she says, surveying the disarray in the kitchen. 'Most people do that the night before.'

'Not yet,' I say, hugely annoyed with myself. By now the log fire should be lit, the potatoes should be in the oven and the table should be laid with festive candles and Christmas crackers. Instead it is covered with potato peelings and prawn shells.

'Do you want me to light the fire?' asks Jon.

'That would be *so* brilliant,' I say.

It's all very awkward. 'Well, now that everything is under control,' I say (when it blatantly isn't), 'I think it's time for a glass of champagne.' In my experience, there are few situations that cannot be improved by opening a bottle of glacially cold pink Laurent Perrier. Unfortunately, this isn't one of them.

'It's a bit early for alcohol, isn't it?' says Jennie, accepting the glass reluctantly.

'It is Christmas,' says Jon, getting up from his knees, the fire now going. I switch on the Christmas tree lights to add a little more atmosphere to the room. They sit in stiff silence, side by side on the sofa, and there seems to be little chemistry between them – at least none is evident from their body language. I bring the parsnips and carrots into the sitting room in a bowl, so that I can chat to them as I peel. But it is not easy doing both at the same time and I am really glad when the doorbell rings again. Elinor, Desmond and Miranda sweep in, in a wave of cheery greetings, perfume and party clothes. Miranda is dressed, as always, as if for a cocktail party in a fitted purple satin cocktail dress and a sparkly hairband, while Elinor is wearing plum-coloured velvet, a colourful embroidered shawl and lashings of jet beads around her neck. They have both made quite an effort.

'Darling boy! What a lovely surprise,' says Miranda, as she walks into the room and sees Jon. Desmond looks taken aback and more than a bit displeased.

I take their coats, sort everyone out with a glass of champagne and leave them to chat while I get down to serious business in the kitchen. Miranda and Elinor, seated side by side on the sofa, are on sparkling form. I can hear Elinor giving a humorous account of the terrible food at a 'ladies do lunch' event that they both recently attended in one of the local, British-owned *auberges*. It is followed by peals of laughter. 'Anything I can do to help?' asks Jon, following me into the kitchen.

'No, no, it's all under control,' I say.

'Is it?' he says with an arched eyebrow. 'Are you sure?'

'Yeah, almost. You can hand around those olives if you like.'

Jon goes back into the sitting room and Desmond appears. 'Well, this is a surprise,' he says. 'What's that Jon Wakeman doing here? And with his girlfriend too, I see.'

'I invited them for a drink.'

'Yes, I noticed. They're drinking all the champagne. That means far less for us.'

'They're hardly drinking anything,' I say.

'Are they staying for lunch?'

'I don't think so. I think they are going to their neighbours'.'

'Good.'

Why, I wonder, does Desmond dislike Jon so much?

'Here,' I say. 'If you want something to do, you can open this.' I hand him the bottle of Chateau d'Yquem that I was given earlier in the year at the launch of an anti-ageing cream made from d'Yquem's famous grapes. The sweet, golden wine is very expensive and said to go particularly well with seafood and white meat, so I am serving oysters, langoustines and giant prawns for the first course in order to show the wine off to its best advantage.

'I hope you are not pouring this while *he* is still here,' says Desmond. 'I'm sure he won't appreciate it.'

Miranda appears with an empty bottle of champagne. 'Isn't this marvellous? It's such a nice surprise to find Jon here too. Isn't he adorable?'

'He's not to be trusted, that man, I'm telling you,' says Desmond.

'Oh do shut up. You're just jealous,' says Miranda.

I send Desmond back into the sitting room with Miranda to top up everyone's glasses. I open the oven to check on the turkey and then try and turn it over using oven gloves, sending hot fat splashing everywhere. 'All under control, darling?' asks Elinor. Standing at the kitchen door, she can tell from my stressed pink face that it isn't.

'OK, what can I do to help?' she asks, rolling up her sleeves. I set her to work, assembling the seafood platter. She clears up the potato peelings first and is heading towards the bin when I remember the nasty surprise (particularly for a vegetarian) lurking within. 'Give those to me,' I say, but it is too late. She has seen the turkey's face peering out from the top of the rubbish pile.

'Good god,' she says, an appalled expression on her face. 'What's *that*?'

'I'm so sorry. You weren't meant to see that,' I say, hastily covering the beak and hairy neck with a plastic bag.

'Oh, goodness. I feel quite ill,' she says, clutching the edge of the table. 'I'd better sit down.'

Jon reappears and I tell him what happened. 'Where is it?' he says, laughing. I point to the bin. He deftly uses a plastic bag to dispose of the neck and head in the bin outside. After washing his hands, he hovers by the fridge as I start to lay the table.

'Why don't you stay and join us for Christmas lunch?' I say.

He looks very tempted. 'I'd like to,' he says, 'but we promised our neighbours that we would have Christmas lunch with them.' He pauses. 'Though it looks like it's going to be a lot more fun here.'

Jennie appears in the doorway. 'Sweetness, I think it's time we were going,' she says, her voice brittle.

Desmond is immediately more relaxed once they have gone. 'You know, I'm not sure I like this Jon Wakeman,' he says.

'Oh stop it,' says Miranda. 'You don't even know him. You just feel threatened because there is another man around for a change and it threatens your position as leader of the pack.'

'I'm beginning to think that you fancy him,' says Desmond.

'Don't be so ridiculous,' says Miranda. 'He's just really good fun. And very helpful. He promised to have a look at my wood-burner.'

'I thought I told you *I* would do that,' says Desmond.

'Yes, you did,' says Miranda. 'Several months ago. And I'm still waiting.'

'He seems perfectly nice to me,' says Elinor.

'I don't think he's trustworthy,' says Desmond.

Disagreements over Jon aside, Christmas Day with my adopted family passes in a convivial blur. We pull crackers and wear the paper hats, and Miranda has bought party poppers that shower brightly coloured curls of paper over the table. The turkey, which only Miranda and I are eating since Desmond and Elinor have brought their own nut roast, is delicious, as is the Chateau d'Yquem. After the Christmas pudding and chocolates, we exchange gifts. I receive a cheese knife from Miranda, who knows I like kitchen gadgets (something I have in common with Dave) and an amaryllis from Desmond and Elinor. Miranda's gifts seem especially thoughtful: she has bought Desmond a chocolate brown corduroy jacket. He tries it on for size (it fits perfectly), pronounces himself thoroughly pleased with it and gives her a hug, saying, 'You have such great taste, Miranda, you really do.'

Elinor also expresses delight at the scented candle that Miranda has bought for her – beautifully wrapped in gold paper with a flourish of red ribbon. 'A sensual blend of sandalwood and aphrodisiac blend of ylang ylang, guaranteed to delight the senses,' she reads from the box. 'How lovely. I will burn this in my yoga class.'

'Do be careful, darling,' says Miranda. 'I don't want Florence Coppinger coming over all frisky during downward dog.' (Florence Coppinger being a silver-haired lady in her seventies, permanently on the hunt for a man since her husband died last year.)

'And this is for you,' says Elinor, handing Miranda a little package that turns out to be a hair slide with a black feathery plume attached.

'Oh, isn't it darling!' says Miranda, jumping up and kissing them both, like a small child.

Over lunch, I wonder again about the dynamics of their relationship. If there is any tension between the three of them I cannot see it. Instead, they seem to genuinely enjoy each other's company and despite previous tension between Miranda and Elinor, coexist happily once more in a threesome. Later, emboldened by the Chateau d'Yquem – and with Miranda and Desmond dancing to an ABBA record in the *petit salon* – I broach the subject with Elinor as she helps me to clear up in the kitchen.

'You know, you make quite a trio,' I say.

'What do you mean?' says Elinor, and I realise straight away that I have said the wrong thing. She stops piling up plates and looks directly at me.

'I just think it's great that you and Desmond and Miranda hang out together and are such good friends.'

'Why? What have you heard?'

'Nothing. I just think it's lovely the way you and Desmond look out for Miranda, and that you all get along so well together.'

Elinor is silent and it is obvious that she does not want to discuss it.

After lunch, the four of us sit by the fire in the *petit salon* to watch the Queen's speech and later we have tea with mince pies and some of the delicious clementine cake that Elinor has made. There is a potentially embarrassing moment early in the evening, when Miranda tipsily suggests that we all remove our clothes, but Desmond simply laughs the idea off. With admirable cool, Elinor simply replies: 'Not now, darling. I'm quite happy with mine on, thank you.'

'Spoilsports! You know you want to,' says Miranda.

'You know, you have done a fantastic job here,' says Desmond, moving the conversation on (for which I, for one, am very grateful). 'I don't just mean Christmas Day – which has been excellent – but the way in which you've done up this place. You really should be proud of yourself.'

I think back to a year ago, when the room we are now sitting in was bare, with untreated floorboards and stacked high with cardboard boxes and building materials. Maison Coquelicot has come a long way since then. With the log fire crackling and fairy lights glittering, it is the ideal setting for Christmas Day. We laugh, chat and – with the exception of Elinor, who is the designated driver – drink quite a lot of alcohol. It is close to midnight when they leave. After waving the three of them off, laughing and happy, into the frosty, navy-coloured night, I stretch out on the sofa and watch the tangerine flames of the log fire. It has been a really lovely Christmas Day.

Chapter 20

New Year's Eve

THE WEEK BETWEEN Christmas and New Year is quiet, spent mostly at home writing an article on the return of the clutch bag. I have no plans for New Year's Eve and am not bothered – I am more than happy to spend it home alone with my wood-burner – but a few days before, Mathilde calls to invite me to a New Year's Eve dinner at her house. Desmond, Elinor and Miranda, she tells me, are also invited. I readily agree, imagining that *réveillon* with my French friends will be civilised and low-key. And it is – until shortly after midnight.

Dessert has been cleared, champagne opened to toast the New Year and I am chatting to Sebastian about the renovation of his boat, when suddenly it all kicks off at the other end of the table. 'I hate you!' Miranda is shouting at Desmond. 'I really do.' She slams her glass down hard on the table, causing it to smash and Mathilde to run for a cloth.

Miranda is a fatal combination of drunk and angry. I do not know what she is angry about but Desmond appears to be bearing the brunt of it.

'You're a spineless tosser,' she is shouting.

The rest of us sit in shocked silence, apart from Elinor who looks quite serene as Miranda verbally assaults her husband. Mathilde and Sebastian look at a loss as to what to do. Mathilde tries to make a joke of it, saying, 'Eh come on, Miranda, Desmond he is not so bad.' But Miranda is having none of it. 'You don't know the half of it,' she shouts. 'You really don't.'

'I think it's time we got you home,' says Desmond, trying to laugh it off.

'Don't you dare talk to me like I'm a child,' says Miranda. 'DON'T YOU DARE. Or I'll tell these people everything. And you won't bloody well like that, I'm sure.'

'Come on, darling,' says Elinor. 'I'm tired and I think it's time we all went home.'

Eventually Miranda, wobbling on her heels, is escorted to the door by Elinor and Desmond, who makes a hurried apology, and they are gone.

'*Oh la la,*' says Mathilde. 'New Year's Eve. It seems to drive some people crazy.'

'That and drink,' says Sebastian.

'I wonder what caused the argument?' I say.

'Miranda, she was saying something about broken promises,' says Mathilde. 'Desmond said she had to wait a little longer and then she went crazy.'

'Oh, it's probably something to do with mending her wood-burner,' I say. 'He's been promising to do that for ages.'

Mathilde shrugs, Sebastian pours another glass of champagne and that is the end of the matter.

End of year dramas seem to follow me around, to the extent that two years ago, I implemented a 'No Going Out on New Year's Eve' rule, for which I foolishly made an exception tonight. I still cringe when I think of my swansong New Year's Eve in London, the events of which are the reason why Dave and I are no longer friends.

As I say goodbye to Sebastian and Mathilde, I imagine Miranda will wake up tomorrow morning full of remorse and regret. Naively, I had thought that Dave would too; but I waited in vain for an apology. Instead, he behaved like the wounded party, and has not spoken to me since.

Jon phones the next morning to say he will pick me up at 1.00 p.m. to go to Sarah Merryweather's annual party. I have never met Sarah but apparently her gathering is *the* place to be (among ex-pat Brits at least) on New Year's Day. 'So how was your New Year's Eve?' he asks.

'Not bad. I went to Mathilde and Sebastian's for dinner.'

'You didn't drop in at the Libertys' party then?'

'No. Did you?'

'Yes, I went after I dropped Jennie off at the airport. But I didn't stay long. I thought you might be there but you weren't.'

Jon arrives half an hour early, clutching a card that says 'Bonne Année 2007'. On it he has written: *'To Karen, I hope that 2007 is the start of a great friendship.'* He is obviously trying to reinforce the 'friendship only' message.

'Thanks' I say, putting the card on the mantelpiece. 'Yes, I'm looking forward to having at least one friend out here who isn't eligible for an old age pension.' Hopefully, this will reassure him that I have got the message loud and clear. 'Shall we go?'

'Well, there's something I wanted to tell you first,' he says.

'Oh?'

'Darla told Jennie that you and I were having an affair.'

'She did *what*?'

'We bumped into her at a party and she said that you and I had slept together at her house – the night of the dinner dance in Anzac. I think she meant it as a joke, but it caused a lot of trouble. I had to really persuade Jennie that we slept in the same room but on separate sofa beds.'

'That's really outrageous of Darla,' I say. 'I hope Jennie believed you?'

'I think so,' he says uncertainly.

I start to laugh. 'That's really hilarious,' I say.

'I know,' he says with a shrug.

We drive in silence through the countryside, which is radiant in the crisp, winter sunshine, the trees and hedgerows veiled in lacy white frost. Jon is not very talkative. I tell him about the little drama yesterday evening but I get the impression that his mind is elsewhere. 'What time does the party start?' I ask.

'Two o'clock.'

'Two o'clock?' I repeat, astonished. 'But we're going to be over an hour early. Something you should know about me is that I don't like to be early for *anything*.'

He turns from the steering wheel and looks at me intently. 'That's OK,' he says. 'I thought we could drive around a bit, since it's such a nice day.'

And so we drive around, past fields and through little hamlets for almost an hour. At one point Jon says, 'Oh, look. A pig farm.'

He stops the car and we get out so that he can admire the pigs and take some photographs of the piglets, which I have to admit are very cute. He tells me some interesting facts about pigs. 'Did you know, for example, that they keep the inside of their houses spotlessly clean?' he says.

'Er no,' I say.

As he mentioned before, he is planning to buy some rare breeds of spotted pigs, including a type called Oxford Sandy and Blacks. He shows me another picture in his digital camera. They are very cute with black spots and sandy coloured skin but, shamefully, my first thought is what a fabulous pair of shoes you could make from their spotty hides. They remind me of a pair of Christian Louboutin shoes that I gave to the *dépôt-vente*. I realise I have a long way to go before I think like a country girl. We get back in the car and drive around some more. On New Year's Day France is even more deserted than usual. We haven't passed any other cars for about half an hour. Jon considerately slows the car right down to a crawl as we pass a woman on horseback.

'Didn't we pass through this village about ten minutes ago?' I say.

'Yes. I think we did. I must have gone round in a circle.'

This is strange. One of the things I have learnt about Jon is that his sense of direction is infallible. It's as if he has an inbuilt GPS chip in his brain.

'I know,' he says suddenly. 'Let's go to Monkey Valley. I've got an annual pass.'

'Monkey Valley?'

Has he gone mad? Monkey Valley is the most popular of the local tourist attractions, and highly rated by people who have visited it, but I am dressed for a party, not for roughing it with monkeys, no matter how amusing their behaviour.

'Yeah, if you want to,' I say. Fortunately, when we arrive, the gates of Monkey Valley are locked – and will remain so until April. 'That's a shame,' I lie.

When we finally arrive at Sarah Merryweather's party, there are already half a dozen people there. As she opens the door of the old farmhouse, we are immediately in a large, cosy, terracotta-coloured kitchen, filled with the smell of Indian food cooking, which is instantly exciting. (Decent Indian food is impossible to get in the French countryside and therefore an enormous treat whenever it pops up.) Sarah Merryweather is friendly and asks how I know Jon – a question that I can answer honestly and without guilt. 'We are friends,' I say. 'We met in the Liberty Bookshop ages ago. And since Jennie, his girlfriend, had to go back early for work, he brought me to your party instead.'

After getting me a drink, Jon melts away into the crowd that the party has quickly become and does not talk to me after that. I am beginning to wonder if he even really wants me as a friend. Perhaps, in the light of the Darla incident, he doesn't want people to talk and he is trying to keep his distance. But I am perfectly happy as I mingle with the guests at the party. It is a mix of local French and English and like a New Year's Day audit of the people I have met over the past twelve months: several people from the Entente Cordiale conversation group at the Liberty Bookshop, including Florence Coppinger, who talks a lot and exclusively in English; a lovely lesbian couple from Yorkshire who I met when they were trying to find a home for an abandoned bull terrier; and a chap called Jo The Hoe (so-called because he seems to do just about everyone's garden). In addition to the full-timers, there are the part-timers – those who arrive for Christmas, Easter and summer holidays, temporarily widening the social circle of those of us who have decamped to France permanently – as well as a good turnout from among Sarah's French neighbours. The only people missing are Desmond, Elinor and Miranda.

Unfortunately, I am cornered by Florence Coppinger. 'Hello, dear,' she says, all crisp consonants and crystal enunciation. 'How nice to see you.' She enquires briefly about my New Year's Eve before proceeding to complain bitterly about hers, which was spent at a 'Murder Mystery' evening with the Civray Singles group. 'I was given the role of a dowager aunt,' she says, and I bite my lip to stop a smile (talk about typecasting). 'I was told to dress the part but it was frightfully badly organised. Such a waste of money.'

I look wildly around the room, hoping for rescue. Once Florence Coppinger has locked you into a monologue, you're looking at up to an hour of nodding commiseration at her latest woes. I spot Jon talking to an attractive woman in her twenties. She is throwing her head back and laughing at whatever he is saying, and I wish I was standing there too. Instead, Florence is telling me that she isn't looking forward to the coming year very much as she still hasn't met a man and she has to have an operation on her varicose veins.

Jon manages to avoid me for most of the three hours that we are at the party. Every time I look across the room he is the centre of some little group, chatting, pushing his hair back from his face and looking completely happy. Only when Darla and Geoffrey arrive does he come over and join me. 'Would you like another drink?' he asks.

'I'll get it,' I say, and when I return he is in deep conversation with Geoffrey. I wonder what they are talking about given that Geoffrey normally doesn't speak.

'So,' I say to Darla. 'What's this about me having an affair with Jon Wakeman? What on earth did you tell Jennie that for?'

'Oh, yeah,' she says in her slow drawl. 'I told her that you both slept together at my house. I kinda meant it as a joke but she didn't see it that way.'

'I'm not surprised.'

'I know. I know. Hey, hands up! I was drunk. I've already been hauled over the coals for this. I guess I was trying to disguise the fact that I'm after him myself. Anyway, I eventually convinced her that Miranda was the threat. Not you.'

'Oh, that's very nice of you! So she thinks Miranda and Jon are having an affair?'

'Yeah. I told her that Miranda was after him. You should be pleased. It takes the heat off you.'

'But Jon and I are not having an affair.'

'Betcha ya'd like to though,' she says with a mischievous grin. 'I know I would.'

'Where is Miranda anyway?'

'I don't know,' says Darla.

Jon comes over. 'Maybe it's time to get going?' he says.

It is raining as we drive home and, even though it's only 5.00 p.m., already dark. 'So are you missing Jennie?' I ask, emboldened by three glasses of red wine and the velvet embrace of darkness as we drive down the narrow deserted lanes back to Villiers.

'I love her a lot,' he says and I am surprised at how deflated I am by this news. There is a long pause and then he adds. 'But to be honest, we're more like brother and sister.' This is certainly an unexpected revelation. Even more unexpectedly, he turns and winks at me. 'There,' he says. 'At least you now know the truth.' On the car radio the Rolling Stones' 'Sympathy for the Devil', one of my all-time favourite songs, is playing.

'Would you like to come in for a drink?' I ask, when he pulls up in the narrow street outside my house. 'Why not?' he says. Inside, I close the shutters, draw the red silk curtains and switch on the red lamps on the side tables. I also light a few candles on the mantelpiece. While I open a bottle of wine, he gets the wood-burner going. Whereas I have to resort to lighting charred sticks of kindling over and over until they take, he soon has flames dancing off the logs. It's such a shame that he only wants to be friends. Here we are, sitting by a roaring log fire in a candlelit room, on New Year's Day, the pink light casting a flattering glow on our faces, having just got back from an excellent party. I hand him a glass of wine and sit down next to him.

'Thanks for taking me to Sarah's party,' I say. 'I really enjoyed it.' Then, thinking I've got nothing to lose, I ask the question that I didn't dare ask in the car. 'What did you mean about your relationship with Jennie being more like brother and sister?'

'Well, for a start, we don't live together. She is in the UK and I am here.'

'Well, only temporarily. Did you speak to her about that over Christmas?'

'Yes,' he says. 'But look, let's not talk about all that now.'

Instead, we talk about Miranda's no-show. 'It's a little strange,' I say. 'I thought she was really looking forward to it. Miranda never misses a party if she can help it.'

'I hope she's OK. I worry about her,' says Jon.

'I suppose I'd better go home,' he says after we have been chatting for a while.

'Oh, that's a shame,' I say. There is a meaningful pause. And then suddenly, I don't care if he has a girlfriend or not, there is something I have to know. Encouraged by the revelation about his relationship with Jennie, I put my wine glass down and move towards him. I am expecting him to put his hand up to stop me, pull away, deliver the 'I'm flattered, but...' speech. Then at least I will know. He doesn't pull away. He moves towards me and kisses me with a passion that takes me by surprise. I have my answer.

'I have wanted to do that for ages,' he says eventually.

'You have?'

'*So* badly.'

My heart jumps off a high wire at this news, performs several backward somersaults and a triple cartwheel.

'Really?'

'That night that we spent at Darla's? Do you want to know the real reason why I couldn't sleep?'

'You said I was snoring.'

'All night I lay there, thinking how much I'd like to be in the same bed as you.'

'I was thinking the same thing.'

'But you didn't seem at all interested. You got into bed fully clothed, remember? And zipped yourself inside a sleeping bag. I thought to myself, Wow, this is a girl who is taking no chances. And anyway, I already had a girlfriend.'

'You still do.'

'In theory. The thing is, I think I love you.'

It all seems very surreal. Since moving to France I've certainly had my fair share of unexpected declarations of love, mostly from unstable or cheating people, but this one makes my heart leap. 'But how can you love me? You've only known me properly for such a short time,' I say, struggling not to sound too euphoric.

'It doesn't matter how long I've known you,' he says. 'I love you. The night of that party in Anzac, I was watching you dance with Desmond all night and I was really, really jealous. I wanted you for myself.'

'But you spent the whole night talking to Miranda.'

'And I was pissed off that I wasn't talking to you.'

'And you didn't seem that keen to dance with me.'

'It looked like you were having more fun with Desmond. I even asked Miranda if there was anything going on between the two of you.'

'And what did she say?'

'She said no, you were just good friends and that Desmond was enormously fond of you. But I was still jealous. And that day when we bumped into him at the Christmas market and you flung your arms around him, I was so pissed off.'

'But I thought you only wanted to be friends with me. That's what you said and I took you at your word.'

'I know, and I immediately regretted it and thought what a bloody pillock I'd been to say that. And then as I walked around the Christmas market with you, all I could think of was how much I wanted to hold your hand. The very first time I saw you in the Liberty Bookshop, I wanted you.'

This was certainly news to me. The first time I met him in the Liberty Bookshop, he had treated me like I had something contagious.

'But you weren't even very friendly,' I say, incredulous.

'Because I assumed you were taken.'

'But didn't it occur to you that I was always in the Liberty Bookshop or Café du Commerce alone?'

'Yeah, but you just didn't look available. And then Gérard in the wine shop mentioned you had a husband *and* a boyfriend – a French one – so I didn't know what to think. But when you walked into that bar in Bléssy on your own that night, I just thought, Wow!'

'But even today at the party, you hardly spoke to me. It was like you were trying to avoid me.'

'But you were always talking to someone. I realised how I felt about you over Christmas and I just didn't think you felt the same way.' He shifts uneasily in his seat. 'Plus I haven't sorted out things with Jennie yet. I have to treat her fairly.'

Ah yes, Jennie. Suddenly, I feel very guilty. I just kissed someone else's boyfriend.

'On New Year's Eve, I dropped her at Bordeaux airport and all I could think about was getting back to you. I drove as fast as I could, hoping to make it to the Libertys' party as I thought you were going to be there. And when you weren't I was so disappointed. Then driving to your house this morning, I saw two magpies in a field. And it seemed like an omen.'

'What kind of omen?'

'Well, you know what they say about magpies?'

I shake my head. 'No I don't.'

He laughs and pulls me closer. 'Sometimes, you are *so* blonde.'

'So what do they say about magpies?'

'One for sorrow, two for joy.'

'Well, I've got a confession to make too. A lot of the drama about not being able to cope with the turkey was just a ploy to see you on Christmas morning.'

'I think this is the best Christmas and New Year's Day of my life,' he says.

I am thinking exactly the same thing.

'But there's one other thing that I really have to know,' I say.

'Ask me anything you want.'

'Why on earth do you have an annual pass to Monkey Valley?'

'I like Monkey Valley,' he says, with a grin. 'No, seriously, I thought the pass might be useful for guests at the B&B.'

I want Jon to leave now in case he changes his mind or tells me that this is all a wind-up. Plus I need time to take it all in. 'Look, this is all so unexpected,' I say. 'You still have a girlfriend and I need time to think this through.'

'I understand,' he says. We decide that he will come over for dinner tomorrow evening. I kiss him goodbye and after he's gone I turn the lights off and lie in the dark, the better to watch the flames of the fire leap and curl around the logs.

Chapter 21

Gone

MIRANDA, WHO USUALLY sounds subdued in the mornings (usually as a result of the bottle of white wine she has imbibed the night before), is in astonishingly good spirits when I call early the next day to tell her about Jon. 'I'm thrilled skinny for you, darling, I really am,' she says. 'He is such a lovely guy.'

I also tell her the unfortunate news that his girlfriend thinks that Miranda is chasing him. 'Don't worry, darling,' she says. 'I'm used to gossip. But what's he going to do about his girlfriend?'

'He's going to go back to the UK and tell her in person that it's over. But he wants to leave it for a week or so as he thinks it's a little cruel to do it so close to the New Year.'

'Oh dear,' says Miranda.

The first week of the year consists of a series of unforgettable evenings. Jon and I staying in by the crackling log fire. Jon and I going out: to the bar in St Secondin, to the market in Poitiers (where we go ice-skating on the slushy, fairy-lit rink that has been hastily erected in front of the town hall) and walking in the forest, which glistens with a post-Christmas icing of white frost. He calls me 'his darling minx' and he takes me to dinner in the Routier at Vivonne, where we eat steak and chips surrounded by French and Portuguese truck drivers (it might not sound very romantic but it is the best steak and chips for miles around) and he takes me to play pool in a nearby bar.

Lying on the sofa by the fire, we jokingly plan our wedding, which we decide will be a simple, hippy-style affair; I see myself barefoot in the field behind his house with flowers in my hair. We will have lashings of pink Laurent Perrier and *steak frites*. 'Minx, you are just so absolutely adorable,' he tells me over and over. 'I love your big cheeks and smiling eyes.'

I am happy but suspicious, as I cannot stop thinking that all of this is just too good to be true. There is also the problem of what to do about Jennie. Jon tells me that they had many conversations over Christmas debating whether or not to end the relationship – so it's unlikely to come as a shock to her – but we both agree that it is kinder to her if he makes a clean break as soon as possible. And so, in the second week of January he returns to the UK to tell Jennie that their relationship is over.

And he doesn't come back. I hear nothing from him for a week and then I get the phone call that changes everything: 'I am so sorry, Karen,' he says. 'I won't be coming back to France. I have decided to stay in the UK indefinitely. I don't know when I will be back.'

'Right,' I say. 'So no wedding in a field in November then. No flowers in my hair. No *steak frites* or pink Laurent Perrier.'

'I'm afraid not,' he says. 'In fact, it looks like I'm going to have to sell the house in France.'

'Can you at least tell me what's made you change your mind?' I ask.

'It's probably best if I don't,' he says. 'I am really, really sorry. I would never have wanted to hurt you. But I think it's best if you don't wait for me.'

Surprisingly, I am very calm. It is like I have been expecting this. All along it felt a little surreal, like it was too good to be true. And it's not like I haven't been here before. I stay in bed for two days, trying to figure out what made him change his mind so abruptly – the obvious answer is that he has decided to make a go of it with Jennie – but I can't make any sense of it. I call Miranda, my fairy godmother, who I know will have something to say that will cheer me up, but she is not at home. I leave half a dozen messages over three days but she does not call back so I call Darla and Geoffrey, who live in the same village, to see if they know where she is. 'Haven't you heard the news?'

'What news?'

'She's run away with Desmond to the Côte d'Azur.'

'What?'

'They've been having an affair.'

'An affair?'

'You didn't know? I thought it was an open secret?' says Darla.

'Oh my god!'

I did of course have my suspicions but they were so open about everything, I figured that they were just good friends. But then I think of all the times that Desmond and Miranda showed up on my doorstep unannounced, laughing and giggling together. I think of them dancing together in my sitting room on Christmas Day; Desmond's protectiveness towards her; and all the joint expeditions to Lidl. And I think of Miranda's behaviour on New Year's Eve. How could I *not* have noticed? It would also explain Desmond's dislike of Jon, whom he must have feared as competition for Miranda's affections – particularly when Jon showed up at Miranda's house the morning after the Anzac dinner. Desmond, after all, would have been behind those closed shutters when he called.

'How's Elinor taking it?' I ask, struggling to process the implications of this information.

'I don't know,' says Darla. 'No one has seen her.'

Shocked, I get in my car and immediately drive over to the hamlet where Elinor lives, to check that she is OK. There is another car, with French registration plates, parked outside the house. The dog goes ballistic behind the big iron gates and then Elinor appears wearing a slinky purple skirt and black lace top, several ropes of coloured beads around her neck. A cloud of Guerlain perfume – I recognise it as Shalimar, the perfume worn by Miranda – hangs heavily in the air around her and her long blonde hair falls with abandon around her shoulders. She does not look or smell like a woman whose husband has just left her. Nor does she look particularly pleased to see me.

'Come in, come in,' she says. 'I've got someone here at the moment for lunch. It's someone you know.'

In the kitchen, Victor the estate agent is seated at the kitchen table looking rather pleased with himself. He looks sheepish when he sees me, but when Elinor sits down next to him, he puts his arm around her.

Suddenly, nothing seems to make sense anymore.

'I'm so sorry to hear about Desmond,' I say.

'Are you?' she says. 'I'm not. I couldn't wait for him to go. Our marriage has been over for a long time.'

'I had no idea.'

'You must have noticed that he is infatuated with Miranda – and vice versa,' says Elinor. 'Well, they're bloody well welcome to each other.'

'Well… I'm glad you're OK about it,' I say.

I do not stay long as it is obvious from their body language that Elinor and Victor have plans for after lunch. 'So what's going on with Victor?' I ask, as Elinor walks me to the gate.

'Oh we had a little fling ages ago.'

'How long ago?' I ask, struggling to make sense of it all. Suddenly, I see Elinor's outrage the night that Victor wanted to meet me in front of the church in Beauchamp in a new light. She was angry and outraged on her own behalf, not mine. No wonder she was so keen to tell Victor that I had an SAS boyfriend.

'Let's just say our affair pre-dated your arrival here and now we've just sort of rekindled it.'

'But why didn't you and Desmond split up sooner if you were both in love with other people?' I ask. 'Why did you put up with him having an affair with Miranda for so long?'

Elinor pauses as if wondering whether to reveal all and what she tells me next stops me in my tracks. 'Well, it was a little more complicated than that. The thing is, we were also having an affair.'

'Who?'

'Miranda and I. It was me who introduced Miranda to Desmond, after she started coming to one of my yoga classes. The three of us had a lot of fun together, as you know, and I didn't mind Miranda and Desmond spending a lot of time together as it made it easier for us to conduct our affair. But I didn't count on them falling in love.'

This is a lot to take in: Miranda and Elinor having a passionate lesbian love affair under Desmond's nose. This is not the sort of thing that is supposed to go on in rural France – at least not among ex-pat Brits. They're supposed to be too busy worrying about their *fosses septiques*, chasing elusive artisans and drinking lots of cheap red wine.

'I had my suspicions and they were confirmed on Miranda's birthday last year, when I found a note that Miranda had sent him,' continues Elinor. You might remember I was quite upset, since you were there.'

I do indeed remember how Elinor disappeared for a long time that evening and came back with very red eyes, before telling Miranda that she ought to be ashamed of herself.

'This is… quite surprising,' I say.

'Yes, well. A lot of people had picked up on the fact that Desmond and Miranda were having an affair. But what no one realised was that I was deeply in love with Miranda.' She pauses. 'I hoped she would change her mind, drop Desmond and come back to me. I even thought we could live together as three – and we did for a short time.'

Suddenly, I am struck by a strong desire to laugh. The idea of Desmond, Miranda and Elinor living in a *ménage a trois* right under my nose is just too much.

'But gradually, as she and Desmond spent more and more time together, it became obvious that she wanted to be with him,' Elinor continues. 'And then she started putting pressure on Desmond to leave me. He would have been quite happy to maintain the status quo – she's a lousy cook, as you know – and had been procrastinating for quite a while but eventually, and after that little showdown on New Year's Eve, she got her way. *Et voilà*. Desmond has packed his bags and they've both gone to live near St Tropez.'

I think back to all the times that I spent with Miranda, Desmond and Elinor, unaware of the simmering passions. I think back to the dinner party at Miranda's, where Victor was also present and try to see everything again in the light of this new knowledge.

'And so eventually, I accepted that Miranda wasn't going to come back to me – and that's when Victor and I hooked up again,' Elinor continues. As she opens the gate to let me out, she adds in a conspiratorial whisper, 'He's a very good lover. Corsicans always are.'

I drive back home in the January sunshine thinking how nothing is as it seems. Suddenly, everyone has gone mad. Or, in Jon's case, just gone. I just don't know what to make of it all.

A few days later, Dave arrives in the village. It's uncanny how his visits always seem to coincide with the low points in my life. I spot him using the Internet in the Liberty Bookshop but mostly manage to avoid him. Then one morning I am having coffee and chatting with Dylan when, out of the blue, he says, 'I think you should try and build bridges with Dave.'

'What?'

'You two got on so well. Everyone could see it.'

'Yes, but…'

'Forget what he did or what he said. Life's too long. I think we all need to spread the love a bit more. It's all about karma at the end of the day.'

'I'm all for spreading the love,' I say. 'But he hates me. You've seen how he reacts whenever he sees me.'

'So prove that you're bigger than him,' says Dylan. 'Just do it. What have you got to lose?'

At first I think Dylan has been hitting the cannabis again (although I know he gave up years ago). But something must have struck a chord, because one day towards the end of January, on a whim, I decide that I would like to resolve matters between us and be friends again. I wonder if Dave knows about Elinor and Desmond. I think how nice it would be to sit by the fire and discuss it with him, to try and make sense of it all. I would even be prepared to drink his disgusting sweet white wine. Despite everything, I miss Dave's company and his friendship. In the light of what happened most people, I know, would not bother, but I have a short memory and, try as I might, I have never been very good at bearing grudges.

And so I buy a bottle of Sauternes from Gérard in La Cave Poitevine and head around to Dave's house early one evening. It is cold, the sky is the colour of steel and the smell of wood smoke and damp permeates the air, reminding me of the winter that Dave and I spent so much time here, just sitting and chatting in front of the fire. And it strikes me how much I've missed those deep, insightful conversations. How much I've missed him. I press the doorbell and wait, feeling very nervous. I have no idea how he will react. Even though it is late afternoon and the light is fading, the shutters are still open but he takes a long time to come to the door. When he finally appears, he looks neither pleased nor surprised to see me. But he's lost weight and looks more attractive than I remember.

'Hi Dave,' I say, brandishing the bottle of wine with a smile. 'How are you?'

'Fine thanks.'

'I just came to say that I miss being friends with you and… and… I wish we could at least be on speaking terms again…'

He looks startled and then I realise immediately from his bristling body language and withering expression that I am wasting my time.

'Look, I was hoping you would at least have a drink with me,' I say. 'For old times…'

'Who is it, babe?' A woman wearing a tight-fitting top and jeans that lace up at the crotch appears behind him and puts a proprietorial hand on his shoulder.

'Oh you're busy,' I say.

He turns pink again but he doesn't deny it. 'Well, good luck,' I say, thrusting the bottle of wine at him. 'Maybe another time.'

I walk away quickly, happy that Dave has finally found someone to love. All around me, it seems, people are embarking on new love affairs. I hear on the grapevine that even Florence Coppinger, seventy if she's day, has started a passionate affair with Jean-Claude, the elderly widower from the Entente Cordiale conversation group, and is telling people that she is having the best sex she's ever had.

So much has changed it seems, for so many people, in just in the space of a few weeks. Alone in front of my log fire in the evenings, I think back to how much I have achieved in the past year or so: my French house, which was unloved and falling apart when I found it, is now completely restored. And as I have rebuilt the house, I have also rebuilt my life. I have learned that I can move to a place where I know no one and create a new life for myself. It is very empowering to know that.

Chapter 22

The Bridge to the Île de Ré

IT IS RAINING as I throw my bag in the car and prepare to leave the spa. After four days of seaweed wraps and alternating hot and cold seawater hose-downs, I am several kilos lighter, and my skin is glowing as if powered from within by a nuclear reactor. I really lucked out on this work assignment – a spring detox break in a thalassotherapy spa. (It being France, the 'detox' still included half a bottle of wine with dinner.) I wasn't exactly thrilled when the commissioning editor told me that the spa I was to write about was on the Île de Ré, but the moment had come to make peace with my past. Ever since I moved to France, I've known that I would have to cross that bridge at some point. And four days ago, I finally did it.

This morning, after a final seawater hose-down, I even went for a walk around Ars, a little village on the farther most tip of the island that I had not visited before – and, according to the tourist sign, one of the prettiest villages in France (in spite of its unfortunate name). As I wandered around, and in and out of shops selling wicker plant holders, oyster-shaped soaps and stripy T-shirts, there was a real sense of anticipation, of new beginnings in the air. Although the famous *rose trémières* are not yet in bloom, the island is gearing up and beautifying itself in time for the official start of the tourist season. I passed artisans in white overalls painting the shutters of a small hotel in pale green, and a window cleaner hard at work on an icing-white cottage covered in wisteria. In one of the narrow streets, an enormous stone tub filled with flowers was being lowered onto the pavement by a fork-lift truck. As I strolled around, breathing in the clean sea air and the scent of seaweed (though that could just have been my skin) I felt a strong sense of living absolutely in the present.

And now it's time to leave the island behind. Even though it is April and raining, the cyclists are out in force as I head towards the bridge in the late afternoon. They pedal along in little shoals, visions of relaxed well-being, their complexions glowing with the fresh sea air. Most of them are French – I can tell by the way they look and their style of dress, for it is a particularly chic type of tourist that the island attracts. A recent article in *Madame Figaro* even provided a dress code for anyone thinking of visiting the island: Chanel bags and high heels, it declared, were 'out'; straw baskets and espadrilles 'in'. The tourists that I pass look like they have rigorously adhered to the prescribed uniform: pedal pushers (preferably navy gingham), a tiny cotton top and ballet flats for women; khaki shorts, sandals and a red or navy fleece for men. Today, in the rain, a waterproof jacket – navy, preferably – has been added to the mix.

Maybe it's the effect of all that seaweed and ozone, but as I approach that slender metal structure suspended over the

Atlantic, the Rolling Stones blaring on the car stereo, I feel liberated, truly at peace for the first time in years. Eric is behind me now, somewhere in La Flotte, probably up to his ears in pizza dough. As I cross the shimmering Atlantic and leave the Île de Ré behind, I know I won't be going back. This, I guess, is what they call closure. I feel a surge of happiness as I reach the other side of the bridge, the lights of La Flotte strung out like a necklace behind me.

Singing aloud, I speed away from the island that is part of my past, away from La Rochelle and towards Villiers and home. The sun appears in the sky somewhere past La Rochelle and, in the pale sunlight of late afternoon, I feel again the sense of spring in the air, of better things lurking just around the corner. Unfortunately, what is lurking around the corner for me is a flat tyre. I am just 15 kilometres away from Villiers when my car begins to make a loud rattling noise. It feels as if it is bumping rather than rolling along, before slowing down to almost a halt. Brilliant! I have broken down on a deserted country road, with only a dilapidated stone barn in the distance.

I get out of the car and see that the tyre on the front wheel is torn to shreds, and the wheel is down to the metal rim. I lean against the bonnet and take in the early evening scene before me, as I wonder which of my friends to call. I am surrounded by a vast expanse of countryside – a collage of different colours and textures. Winters's brown furrowed fields are green or gold with vegetation again, while the smell of woodsmoke and decaying leaves has been replaced by a crisp, green scent that is unmistakably *le parfum* of spring. The pale yellow grass in the verge at the side of the road is dotted with wild poppies and bluebells. And above it all, there is a huge pale pink sun in the sky.

As I pause to appreciate the stunning scenery – and realise again how lucky I am to live here – I hear a noise in the distance and eventually a car with an English registration plate pulls up in front of me. A man in his late thirties gets out, casually dressed in khaki T-shirt and jeans. He has longish blond hair and a face that has seen a lot of sun, with crinkled but kind eyes. He looks friendly, strong, laid-back, and he smiles as he walks towards me. 'It looks like you need some help,' he says. 'Tell me where your spare wheel is and I'll change it for you.'

I watch as toned, evenly tanned arms pull the wheel from underneath the boot of my car, golden hairs visible in the last burst of late afternoon sun. Above us there is a pink and blue tie-dye effect sky. If you are going to break down, I think to myself, you couldn't wish for a more beautiful setting or better time of day. As my rescuer crouches down to switch the tyre, he talks to me, interested to know more about what I am doing in France.

'So do you live here?' he asks.

'Yes, in a village about twenty kilometres away. Villiers.'

'Then we are almost neighbours,' he says. 'I have just bought a house in St Hilaire.'

'Yes, I know it,' I say, suddenly thanking the lord for the perfect timing of my flat tyre. 'It's about ten kilometres away from me. A very pretty village.'

'I only just moved here,' he says as he releases the old wheel. 'Two weeks ago.'

In the time that it takes him to sort out my car, I discover that his name is Andy Lawton, that he has just left the army, where he served for several years in Afghanistan, and that he has recently split up from his girlfriend. He has decided to make a new start, renovating a barn in France. He has told his friends that he is going for a year, just to see if he likes it. I do not have to probe for any of this information. He readily volunteers it. At the same time, he extracts key information from me, including the fact that I live out here alone.

Twenty minutes later, I thank him for his help and we say goodbye, before continuing on our way, both of us heading in the same direction. I am still driving along a country road alone, but it's no longer dark. The sky is an incandescent pink and pulsating with promise. And as I turn into the square in Villiers, my heart beats just a little faster at the thought of my new neighbour, who is heading home with my telephone number – so casually asked for – in his pocket.

Have you enjoyed this book? If so, why not write a review on your favourite website?

Thanks very much for buying this Summersdale book.

www.summersdale.com